Bureaucracy Against Democracy and Socialism

Bureaucracy Against Democracy and Socialism

EDITED BY Ronald M. Glassman,
William H. Swatos, Jr., and
Paul L. Rosen

Contributions in Sociology, Number 65

Greenwood Press
NEW YORK • WESTPORT, CONNECTICUT • LONDON

Library of Congress Cataloging-in-Publication Data

Bureaucracy against democracy and socialism.

(Contributions in sociology, ISSN 0084-9278 ; no. 65)
Bibliography: p.
Includes index.
1. Bureaucracy. 2. Democracy. 3. Socialism.
I. Glassman, Ronald M. II. Swatos, William H.
III. Rosen, Paul L. IV. Series.
JF1351.B87   1987   350′.001   87-227
ISBN 0-313-25454-0 (lib. bdg. : alk. paper)

British Library Cataloguing in Publication Data is available.

Library of Congress Catalog Card Number: 87-227
ISBN: 0-313-25454-0
ISSN: 0084-9278

First published in 1987
Greenwood Press, Inc.
88 Post Road West, Westport, Connecticut 06881

Printed in the United States of America

The paper used in this book complies with the
Permanent Paper Standard issued by the National
Information Standards Organization (Z39.48-1984).

10 9 8 7 6 5 4 3 2 1

Copyright Acknowledgments

We gratefully acknowledge the following sources for granting permission to reprint selections
from previously published material:

Chapter 2, by Robert Jackall, is reprinted from *State, Culture, and Society*, vol. 1, no. 1, A.
Vidich and S. Lyman (eds.) By permission of Associated Faculty Press, Inc. Copyright © 1984
by Associated Faculty Press, Inc.

Chapter 5, by Kathi V. Friedman, is adapted from *Legitimation of Social Rights and the Western
Welfare State: A Weberian Perspective* by Kathi V. Friedman. Copyright © 1981 by the
University of North Carolina Press. Reprinted with permission.

Chapter 7, by Ernest Kilker, is adapted from *State, Culture, and Society*, vol. 1, no. 1, A. Vidich
and S. Lyman (eds.) By permission of Associated Faculty Press, Inc. Copyright © 1984 by
Associated Faculty Press, Inc.

Chapter 10, by Ira Glasser, is adapted from *Doing Good: The Limits of Benevolence* by Willard
Gaylin, Ira Glasser, Steven Marcus, and David Rothman. Copyright © 1978 by Willard Gaylin,
Ira Glasser, Steven Marcus, and David Rothman. Reprinted by permission of Pantheon Books,
a division of Random House, Inc.

Chapter 11, by Ralph Nader, Mark Green, and Joel Seligman is adapted from *Taming the Giant
Corporation* by Ralph Nader, Mark Green, and Joel Seligman, by permission of the authors and
W. W. Norton & Company, Inc. Copyright © 1976 by Ralph Nader.

Chapter 12, by Robert A. Dahl, is reprinted from *After the Revolution* by Robert A. Dahl.
Copyright © 1971 by Yale University Press. Reprinted by permission.

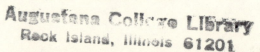

For our parents

"I think this kid ought to get lost."

Gomez said, "We can lose him."

"Some sort of bureaucratic tangle," Biff said. "You know, kid, once you get entangled with the cops, any damned fool thing's liable to happen."

"Sure," said Gomez. "We'll put him in the van for the funny farm this morning. It will be a good ten days before anyone straightens out that bureaucratic tangle."

"What will that get you?" Fletch asked. "A few days. You think I'd shut up about it?"

"Can't blame us for a bureaucratic tangle," Biff said. "I'm not even in this building this morning. You're not here either, are you, Gomez?"

"Naw. I'm never in this early."

Fletch Won
Gregory McDonald

Contents

5. Social Rights in the Welfare State: The Contrast
   between Adjudication and Administration in the United
   States
   Kathi V. Friedman   65

6. The Patient at Peril: Hospital Bureaucracy and Medical
   Records
   Paul L. Rosen   75

7. The Moral Ethos of Bureaucracy
   Robert Jackall   89

8. Bureaucracy and Civil Liberties: The FBI Story
   Kenneth O'Reilly   109

9. Bureaucracy and Rationalization in the Soviet Police
   William M. Jones   121

Part III: Solutions in Service to Democracy

10. Power versus Liberty in the Welfare State: A Bill of
    Rights for Social Service Beneficiaries
    Ira Glasser   135

11. "Constitutionalizing" Corporations: An Employee Bill
    of Rights
    Ralph Nader, Mark Green, and Joel Seligman   147

12. Industrial Democracy in the Era of the Corporate
    Leviathan
    Robert A. Dahl   155

13. Why Democracies Need a Legislative Ombudsman
    Donald C. Rowat   169

14. Quality Circles: Implications for American Management
    Lisa K. Armour   179

    Epilogue
    Bureaucracy and Its Discontents
    William H. Swatos, Jr.   187

    Notes   199

Introduction

Ronald M. Glassman, William H. Swatos, Jr.,
and Paul L. Rosen

Unlike Karl Marx and his followers, who offered a quasi-millennial escha-
tology of hope in the midst of modernity's agonies, Max Weber may be
envisioned as a latter day Jeremiah—a prophet of doom concerning the
development of modern society. As with the prophets of old, however, his
message was meant as a warning, not as a fated, irreversible prediction.
Weber's pessimistic analysis of modern society was written with the hope of
stimulating future generations of social scientists, politicians, and statesmen
to create and develop responsible proposals and programs that could establish possible solutions to the problems that were emerging. Though he railed
against utopianism of any kind, Weber remained passionately committed to
political action that could produce practical results based on the actual social
conditions of modernity.

What was the basis for Weber's pessimism toward the future of modern
society? The major problem Weber wished to bring to our attention was
bureaucracy. Earlier thinkers, such as Marx and, before him, the Enlightenment intellectuals—Montesquieu, Rousseau, or Saint-Simon—believed
that the excesses of patrimonial bureaucracy, as part of the *ancien régime*,
would disappear with the king, the royal court, and the nobility.[1] In England,
the first major European nation to free itself from the monopolistic kingly
state and feudal nobility, bureaucracy did decline. England became the first
country to emerge a powerful industrial nation-state in the wake of these
happenings—followed closely by its anti-monarchical, anti-bureaucratic off-
spring, the United States. On the basis of these events in Anglo-America, a
century of thinkers directed their attention elsewhere, believing that bureaucracy was a relic of the past.

First Tocqueville in France, then most centrally Weber in Germany, witnessed the conversion of patrimonial bureaucracy into modern rational

bureaucracy. Weber observed the linking of the expertise and rational administrative capabilities of bureaucracy with industrial development, and far from inhibiting Germany's industrial development, it hastened it. This insight led Weber to a set of predictions for modern society quite opposite to those of the Enlightenment thinkers and Marx. Juxtaposed to their optimistic visions of modernity's development, which no longer enthrall most thinkers in the contemporary West, Weber's pessimistic predictions weigh heavily upon us in today's world.

What exactly was Weber's nightmare vision of modernity, and is there any way out of it?

While the Enlightenment thinkers and Marx based their visions of the future upon the analogy of the ancient Greek *polis*, Weber based his upon the oriental empires. He stated his position thus:

History shows that wherever bureaucracy gained the upper hand, as in China, Egypt and, to a lesser extent, in the later Roman empire and Byzantium, it did not disappear again unless in the course of the total collapse of the supporting culture. In contrast to these older forms, modern bureaucracy has one characteristic which makes its "escape-proof" nature much more definite: rational specialization and training. . . . Wherever the modern specialized official comes to predominate, his power proves practically indestructible since the whole organization of even the most elementary want satisfaction has been tailored to his mode of operation. . . . Together with the inanimate machine it is busy fabricating the shell of bondage which men will perhaps be forced to inhabit some day, as powerless as the fellahs of ancient Egypt. . . . An "organic" social stratification, similar to the Oriental-Egyptian type, would then arise, but in contrast to the latter it would be as austerely rational as a machine. *Who would want to deny that such a potentiality lies in the womb of the future?*[2]

BUREAUCRACY AS ANTI-DEMOCRATIC

Although acknowledging bureaucracy's formal rationality and relative organizational stability, Weber warned in his typification of modern bureaucracy and its agents of their inherent authoritarian nature. Bureaucracies exhibit a hierarchical structure of authority, a chain of command not unlike that of a modern military organization. Hierarchical authority is antagonistic to the processes of collegial authority (a council of equals) and the individualism that are central to democratic institutions. The bureaucratic hierarchy is controlled by an elite of top managers who make decisions with the technical advice, but without the consent of those below them in the hierarchy.

Furthermore, bureaucratic rules and regulations, which govern all official actions in giant modern organizations, are not laws. They are not debatable or subject to amendment. They do not guarantee the rights of those who work within bureaucracies, nor do they limit the power of bureaucratic leaders. These rules, as well as decisions made by the elite, are not subject to open discussions or to constitutional interpretation. Bureaucratic authority, with its rules and regulations, is rational, but its rationality is totally different from that rationality emanating from legal authority.

What Weber saw as an ideal typification of bureaucratic organizational structure was a new form of despotic domination. This form of domination is subtle in that it controls decision-making and negates civil liberties without a secret police or conquering army. The hallmarks of democratic government—citizens' participation in decision making and leadership choice, the limitation of the power and tenure of leaders, and lawful procedures for rule making and rule enforcement—are replaced by an administrative megamachine controlled from the top down and insensitive to individual needs.[3]

One might counter: "But we have legislatures, law courts, and recall procedures. Why should bureaucracy overwhelm these institutions?" Weber believed that the specialized experts organized into smoothly functioning units by bureaucratic managers would provide these elite managers with a decision-making ability technically superior to parliaments and courts. He foresaw the dilemma contemporary congresses would face when presented with problems beyond their collective expertise. There is a continuing trend toward the abdication of decision making by the elected representatives of the people and toward the increasing importance of non-elected decision makers.

As the modern state emerges, non-elected presidential (or prime-ministerial) staffs are growing and they are increasingly running the government in coordination with the heads of giant corporations and government bureaus. C. Wright Mills was correct when he asserted in *The Power Elite* that Congress was being pushed down to a secondary level of power. Indeed, the function of congressional representatives is increasingly to act as quasi-ombudsmen who cut through federal bureaucratic red-tape to serve constituent-client interests. Rather than being a lawmaker, the legislator is a rule-circumventor. Reelection may well depend on what rules are circumvented and for whom. Weber understood this exactly when he wrote:

[A]s long as a parliament can support the complaints of the citizens against the administration only by rejecting appropriations and other legislation or by introducing unenforcable [sic] motions, it is excluded from positive participation in the *direction* of political affairs. Then it can only engage in "negative politics," that means, it will confront the administrative chiefs as if it were a hostile power; as such it will be given only the indispensable minimum of information and will be considered a mere drag-chain, an assembly of impotent fault-finders and know-it-alls. In turn, the bureaucracy will then easily appear to parliament and its voters as a caste of careerists and henchmen who subject the people to their annoying and largely superfluous activities.[4]

This was a Weberian prediction: at the time he wrote it, he also noted that the United States had thus far avoided the worst tendencies of bureaucratic states.[5]

BUREAUCRACY AS ANTI-SOCIALIST

For many years socialism stood out as an alternative to capitalist democracy. With the oligarchic elements removed from society, socialists believed that true democracy and dramatically increased equality should emerge. Weber, however, doubted that this could be the result; rather, he stated flatly that socialism would demand even more bureaucratization than capitalism. He further claimed that this bureaucracy would be fully fused with the politico-military might of the state, hence increasing the tendency toward despotic control:

State bureaucracy would rule *alone* if private capitalism were eliminated. The private and public bureaucracies, which now work next to, and potentially against, each other and hence check one another to a degree, would be merged into a single hierarchy. This would be similar to the situation in ancient Egypt, but it would occur in a much more rational—and hence unbreakable—form.[6]

Furthermore, in a bureaucratic economy, workers' control is a utopian dream that will collapse before the reality of control by managerial officials.

What would be the practical result? The destruction of the steel frame of modern industrial work? No! The abolition of private capitalism would simply mean that also the *top management* of the nationalized or socialized enterprises would become bureaucratic. [T]here is even less freedom, since every power struggle with a state bureaucracy is hopeless and since there is no appeal to an agency which as a matter of principle would be interested in limiting the employer's power, such as there is in the case of a private enterprise. *That* would be the whole difference.[7]

Thus, "this would be socialism in about the same manner in which the ancient Egyptian 'New Kingdom' was socialist."[8]

Nor would socialism necessarily cater better to the economic needs of the people. Instead, the needs of the bureaucratic organization and its managerial elite would become the goals of such a socialist economy—just as the profit needs of capitalists are the goals of a capitalist economy.

The economic organization of the future would have to be established . . . in the manner of a huge, state-controlled and compulsory consumer cooperative. . . . Again, it cannot be imagined how the "democratic" interests—those of the mass of the consumers—can be protected in any way other than through a parliament. . . . [9]

Though clearly favoring capitalism over what he argued would become stultifying bureaucratic socialism, Weber was not an apologist for capitalism. He did not excuse the selfishness of the rich, nor did he believe that capitalism served the needs of the workers. It simply was clear to him that if an economic planning bureaucracy were fused with the military and police power of the state, the emergence of a despotic system of government would increase in likelihood. This is precisely what he predicted for the Soviet Union shortly after the triumph of the Bolsheviks—a transformation of the dictatorship of the proletariat into a "dictatorship of the bureaucrats."[10]

Contemporary social democrats have been seeking ways to combine a socialized economy with some form of political democracy. Weber's warning stands as a beacon to the social democrats, just as it stands as a beacon to capitalist democrats, to steer clear of the dangers of authoritarian bureaucracy:

Given the basic fact of the irresistible advance of bureaucratization. . . .
1. How can one possibly save *any remnants* of "individualist" freedom in any sense? After all, it is a gross self-deception to believe that without the achievements of the age of the Rights of Man any one of us, including the most conservative, can go on living his life. . . .
2. In view of the growing indispensability of the state bureaucracy and its corresponding increase in power, how can there be any guarantee that any powers will remain which can check and effectively control the tremendous influence of this stratum? How will democracy even in this limited sense be *at all possible?*[11]

DAS VERSTEHEN MAX WEBERS

If Weber is a modern Jeremiah, then his pessimism is "heroic pessimism."[12] Heroic, because it exhorts us to confront the real problems of bureaucracy—to understand it and to prevent it from overwhelming us. This practical heroism should lead us to a "responsible optimism," toward an "ethic of responsibility," as Weber called it,[13] in which practical proposals for the maintenance of democracy, the control of bureaucracy, and the expansion of equality are created, considered, adopted, and adapted. Though Weber warned against utopianism—Marxian or otherwise—he encouraged responsible social and political action. He also argued that, though science could never determine ethical outcomes, a rational-scientific approach could help develop workable solutions to social problems.[14] Certainly Weber wished us to act to avoid the fate he prophesied for modernity:

No one knows who will live in this cage in the future or whether at the end of this tremendous development entirely new prophets will arise, or there will be a great rebirth of old ideas and ideals, or, if neither, mechanized petrification, embellished with a sort of convulsive self-importance.[15]

Will we renew the search for a promised land of freedom or accept the certainties of the fleshpots of ancient Egypt? Is there more to life than whether the trains run on time?

It is the intent of this volume to assess the current state of bureaucratic administration and then to consider possible solutions to the bureaucratic *problemstellung*. This book is unique, not in that it proposes "solutions" to bureaucracy—that has certainly been done before—but in that it takes the Weberian analysis seriously in order to assess possible futures for complex society in our time. We fully agree with Charles Perrow, for example, in his observation that most critiques of bureaucracy understand neither the model nor Weber's intent.[16] We find it shocking that current texts still claim that Weber was detailing a proposal for how formal organizations *ought* to work, that Weber actually thought bureaucracy was a good thing. Not only are such texts unfounded, but they also present solutions that are highly suspect.[17] After all, one must know what a problem is before one can solve it. Our concern, then, is not merely to "rehabilitate" Weber—which he hardly needs[18]—but more significantly to put contemporary organizational problem solving back on a responsible course. Let no reader go away from this volume ill informed on this at least: *Weber was anti-bureaucratic*, though he respected the contributions rationality had made to human existence. What Weber clearly recognized, but what later interpreters have often missed, is that formal rationality does not necessarily lead to substantive rationality, and indeed it may even work against it.[19] Thus in his articulation of the characteristics of bureaucracy, Weber notes their contradictoriness and inhuman qualities.[20]

Much American organizational theory has mistakenly identified Weber with the "scientific management" advocated by Frederick W. Taylor ("Taylorism").[21] There is an irony in this: the two were contemporaries whose work developed independently. Taylor advocated the very thing Weber criticized. That both should see the real possibilities for this style of management, that one should seek to implement them while the other agonized over them, and then that the two should be undifferentiated in their programs, is mind-boggling but frequently true. Taylorism is the proof that Weber knew what he was talking about, and most management theories to this day owe far more to the mentality of Taylor than to that of Weber. It is for this reason that we have drawn rather heavily in this discussion from Weber's political essays, "Parliament and Government in a Reconstructed Germany," now appended to *Economy and Society* in the English translation. These polemical writings are of great importance to understanding Weber's thinking on bureaucracy and its practical consequences in our time. We strongly urge readers who are unfamiliar with this material to give it their attention for both its continued timeliness and theoretical power.

Our work begins with a series of essays that seek to define the problems that continue to confront modern political, economic, and social organization and to throw these into relief by comparing Weberian analysis to that of

Marx and the Marxists, as Wolfgang Schluchter does. The continuing "romance" of socialism as an alternative to all of the problems of modern Western capitalism was rejected by Weber in its origins and cannot in itself be sustained theoretically today. The problem, simply put, is not socialism versus capitalism but bureaucracy versus democracy. If real progress is to be made in solving the dilemmas of modernity at either the political-economic or sociocultural levels, this distinction must be clearly understood. Neither capitalism nor socialism offers any hope if bureaucratic administration is near the core of the plan. Control of bureaucracy must be a global goal, one that transcends differences in national economic systems. Both socialism and capitalism in their dominant contemporary forms are so tied to bureaucratic administration that neither is ever going to be attractive as an alternative. A major stumbling block to positive international relations and world peace today is the self-serving quality of bureaucratic administration once in place. Managers do not want to lose their control over the system; yet that is fundamentally what system change is all about.

The second group of essays focuses on concrete examples of bureaucratic hegemony in the modern world. Kathi V. Friedman describes the growing power of the welfare state as compared to the goals of social welfare. She shows that as the gratuitous nature of the welfare state extends into more areas of life, social rights are undermined. Paul L. Rosen and Robert Jackall show how in the hospital—a "service" industry—and the business corporation, individual rights and personal freedoms are declining precipitously under the impact of bureaucratic hierarchies of power and organizational rules, regulations, and power struggles. Both indicate that the bureaucratic worldview creates a moral posture in which system maintenance becomes the only virtue. Kenneth O'Reilly and William M. Jones focus, respectively, on aspects of law enforcement in the United States and the Soviet Union, describing the complex interplay between law and its enforcement agents in both democratic and socialist contexts. Both essays indicate the gulf between the bureaucratic function of maintaining order and the democratic process of upholding the law. These five essays, then, urge that both democratic and socialist traditions are under assault from public and private bureaucracies.

What are some solutions to the growing problem of bureaucratic authoritarianism? Many have been proposed over the years. Some still consider socialism to be the answer. New plans for human betterment are constantly being advanced. The essays collected in Part III work from the assumption that the democratic tradition is a strong one and that our greatest hope lies in strengthening it. The first two essays, for example, deal with the extension of legal authority over giant bureaucratic organizations. Ira Glasser and Ralph Nader, Mark Green, and Joel Seligman suggest new "Bills of Rights" for social service agency beneficiaries and for corporate employees. Both essays articulate specific sets of constitutional laws that would protect individual rights. The third essay, by Robert A. Dahl, argues strongly for the extension of democracy into the economic sphere. Dahl claims that the dramatic change in the size and power of the modern corporation makes *laissez faire* obsolete as an appendage of liberal democratic theory. Donald C. Rowat, in the fourth essay, puts forth that even with constitutional rights guaranteed, a wholly new legal institution has been necessitated by the expansion of modern bureaucracy. This development results in the emergence of the "ombudsman." Inaugurated in Scandinavia, this office, or set of officials, acts as a "peoples' advocate" in the maze of bureaucratic officialdom. The ombudsman investigates and publicizes cases of bureaucratic incompetence, harrassment, and neglect on behalf of the citizenry. In the final essay, Lisa K. Armour looks at quality circles (QCs) as an aid to improved productivity and worker satisfaction and American management ideology as an impediment to their effectiveness.

In the epilogue, William H. Swatos, Jr., raises questions about the root causes of the failure of bureaucracies to embody the substance of rationality. He cautions, however, that solutions to the bureaucratic conundrum must be treated with care themselves. Without sufficient attention to the interaction processes that are the causes of bureaucratic failure, mere structural alternation will not attain the high promises that lie in either democratic or socialist visions. Whether we can or cannot break out of the bureaucratic "iron cage"—and what the cost of escape might be—remains to be seen. As scholars and as citizens, however, we can, as part of our calling, encourage programs and principles directed to the maintenance of democracy and freedom within the limits and conditions of modernity.

PART I

The Problem

_____

_____

1

From Government over Persons to the Administration of Things: Marx and Engels on Bureaucracy

Wolfgang Schluchter
Translated by Judith V. Marcus

Marx and Engels looked upon Saint-Simon as a utopian socialist whose ideas were by and large historically justified. His major accomplishment was that he was one of the first to perceive the connections between economy and politics and to formulate the problem of the "abolition of the state." This legacy is preserved (*aufgehoben*) in one of the central doctrines of the Marxist theory of the state. As Engels formulated it, the takeover by the proletariat of the state machinery, and the subsequent elimination of the conditions that had made the state necessary in the first place, will be followed by the gradually decreasing need for an autonomous state: "The government of persons is replaced by the administration of things and by the management of production. The state is not 'abolished.' It dies out."[1]

The formula concerning the conversion of political rule over persons into an administration of things refers to the institutional framework within which humanity, emancipated from all its natural limitations, can become its own master; thus Marx and Engels regard as one of its main prerequisites the organization of the productive forces at a high level through the systematic application of science and technology.[2] Unlike Saint-Simon, however, they do not envision domination by experts who guarantee instrumental rationalism, but rather the overcoming of the enslavement of human beings by the division of labor and its consequences.[3] Marx and Engels' ultimate aim, then, was to work toward the abolition of all the conditions in which "social relations of individuals appear as an autonomous power over individuals,"[4] and to dissolve all conditions in which human relations become reified and the "objectivity" of technical imperatives is but a cover-up for the domination of one human being over another.[5]

Marx and Engels extend Saint-Simon's formula by including the proposition that the state will wither away. On the one hand, the formula now means that forms of state—indeed, the state as such—are a product of the structures of different economic formations.[6] The forms of the state express the inherent contradictions of the economic structures and change with them. On the other hand, the formula represents the hope that an emancipated humanity will regulate its exchange with nature and shape its own destiny in a way that makes superfluous not only the state but all forms of domination. The idea that the state, similar to religion, is but the embodiment of those conditions under which man can objectify his essence "by subordinating his products and his own activity to the domination of an alien entity and by attributing to them the character of an alien power" also renders the Marxist theory of the state a study about the causes of bureaucratic domination.[7] In fact, from the beginning, and especially in Marx's case, the discussion of the state's role in bourgeois society was linked up with an analysis of the role of bureaucracy. The intimate connection is surely not always present or explicit in the writings on the state. Therefore, it is necessary to reconstruct Marx and Engels' ideas on the character of bureaucratic domination by analyzing the most important texts that deal with the problem of the state.

MARX'S CRITIQUE OF HEGEL

Marx's own ideas took shape in the course of his critique of Hegelian philosophy. This is also true with regard to the role of the political state in general and that of bureaucracy in particular. Marx's first significant statement on bureaucracy can be found in his *Critique of Hegel's "Philosophy of Right"*.[8] In the third part of his work, Hegel depicted the relations between family, civil society, and the state. He characterized the state as, on the one hand, representing an "external necessity" and a higher authority *vis-à-vis* the "spheres of civil law, welfare, family and civil society," and on the other, constituting their inherent purpose.[9] Hegel did not leave it at that, but went on to define the state as constitutional monarchy, describing the theory of its legitimation and its functional relationships in a realistic—almost sociological—manner, albeit in spiritualized disguise. Because the state recognizes the inherent right (*Eigenrecht*) of the particular interests unfolding in civil society, they in turn refer back to the state as the guarantor of their existence. The state's interest, manifesting the general interest, simultaneously regulates civil society and is determined by it.

This regulative function presupposes the emergence of a state organism in which "each of the three moments of the concept has its explicitly actual and separate formation" in the shape of the power of the crown, the legislature, and the executive.[10] Under the latter heading Hegel provides one of the first descriptions of the modern state bureaucracy. The executive power lies in the hands of the "executive civil servants and the higher advisory bodies, which are colleagually organized."[11] It takes care of the "execution and application of the monarch's decisions" and in general "the continued execution or maintenance of past decisions, existing laws, regulations, organizations for the securing of common ends, and so forth."[12] As the lawful executive power, bureaucracy faces civil society, a "battlefield where everyone's interest meets everyone else's."[13] It reconciles the private interests with the higher criteria and orders of the state. Bureaucracy is able to do this because it enjoys a relative independence from civil society and its members.

Hegel stipulates the institutional and attitudinal prerequisites of an officialdom that is loyal to the state, committed to the law, and service-oriented. Its characteristics are: hierarchical organization, formalized jurisdiction, selection and promotion from above, compensation received from the state, acquired competence, the achievement of a professional ethos that brings forth a "dispassionate, upright and polite demeanor," and a notion of the civil service as "a value in and for itself."[14] The relative independence applies both upward and downward. The executive power, which represents one component of sovereignty, must not become the means of carrying out arbitrary and despotic decisions. It represents a middle position toward which the different interests converge. The universal class (*Stand*), the class of civil servants, constitutes a middle class, a class in which the social ethic concerned with the interests of all can develop. For Hegel, then, bureaucracy has the function of preventing the particularization of the state's will and making apparent the fact that the regulative function of the state is an expression of universal interest.

By no means did Hegel underrate the danger of this bureaucracy becoming fully autonomous. Sociologically speaking, he thought this could happen if some group appropriated the institutional opportunities for itself and the ethic of service turned into an ethic of domination. Hegel was concerned lest members of the government and the civil servants should acquire "the isolated position of an aristocracy" and would be able to use their skill and education "as means to an arbitrary tyranny."[15] To prevent the bureaucracy's full autonomy, Hegel proposed, first, its subordination under the power of the crown, and second, the self-organization of civil society into communities and corporations. The understanding that the state represents not only an "external necessity" and a "higher authority" but is also an "immanent aim" of civil society brings with it the recognition of those organized particular interests containing "the rooting of the particular in the universal" and in which "the sphere of civil society passes over into the state."[16] However, this recognition of popular representation from below does not lead to denial of the primacy of the political state in general or of the executive in particular. Just the opposite is true. Hegel always considered popular elections to be an infeasible means of expressing the "universal will." In his eyes, to subject the state to the vagaries of popular elections must ultimately lead to its surrender to a "particular will," with the result that the state offices "turn into private property, the sovereignty of the state is enfeebled and lost, and finally the state disintegrates within and is overthrown from without."[17]

Marx recognized the all too realistic character of Hegel's analysis and made the sarcastic remark that what Hegel had to say about "executive authority" does not deserve to be called philosophical analysis: it could stand word for word in Prussian common law.[18] Marx regarded it as nothing more than a description of actual conditions which, in fact, lagged behind those of the neighboring countries.[19] He characterizes the Hegelian position bluntly: "*Voilà tout*! Hegel gives us an empirical description of the bureaucracy, partly as it is in actual fact and partly as it is on its own estimation. And with this the difficult chapter on the executive is done."[20]

Marx endeavors to rewrite this "difficult chapter" by taking seriously Hegel's analysis as an empirical description. In his eyes, Hegel's fear that bureaucracy could make itself independent, transforming the state's "general interest" into particular interests, and that the state could lose its legitimated regulative function is beside the point. For Marx, bureaucracy is but the most conspicuous expression for conditions in which particular interest imagines itself to be general interest. It does not matter in the least whether or not bureaucracy is "controlled" by the corporations of civil society or by the crown and the legislature. Bureaucracy is the state as corporation—that is, as the perfect corporation. It is only "the 'formalism' of a content that lies outside of it." Bureaucracy is the state that has actually turned itself into civil society, the "state as formalism."[21]

At first glance, then, Marx considers bureaucracy merely as indicating the general character of a political state that is based on civil society. This is one consideration, but there is another side to it. Bureaucracy as "executive authority" imparts a special quality to this formal state in that "state formalism" becomes its own material content. The bureaucrats are the "Jesuits" and "theologians of a state that turns its form into content and therefore must also pass off content for form. The bureaucrats administer, so to speak, the value of formality. In this way bureaucracy creates a "distinctive and separate" interest. It forces real objectives to appear as formal objectives. Bureaucracy attains an autonomous existence in complete isolation from civil society and real life. It becomes a "particular, closed society" within the state. Bureaucracy gains autonomy by creating certain institutional and attitudinal prerequisites. It establishes a hierarchy of knowledge based not on functional authority but on the authority of office. This hierarchy is based on the fictitious notion that the higher the rank, the deeper the grasp of the universal. It encourages attitudes that favor submission and require that action be based on "fixed principles, views and traditions" and that the world be degraded to the point of a "mere object" to be manipulated. Where Hegel's apprehension about the possible debasement of bureaucracy was tempered by his belief that any such development could be inhibited, Marx found bureaucracy to be inherently debased. Whenever the executive is embodied by the bureaucracy, "the identity of state interest and particular private purpose is established in such a manner that the state interest becomes a particular private purpose as against other private purposes."[22]

For Marx, then, autonomy and privatization of the state are identical processes. As his critique of Hegel shows, he was aware of several dimensions.

For one thing, the existence of the political state has always been the expression of an autonomous existence of state interest and its privatization. When "civil society has fully given birth to the political state,"[23] when the difference between an egoistic and an ethical individual appears in the contrast between the "bourgeois" and the "citizen,"[24] and when "man's species-life" is "opposed to his material life,"[25] the "state appears spiritualized as a higher essence,"[26] but is in reality nothing more than a material cover for universal egoism.

Furthermore, Marx considers a specific form of state to express a specific kind of autonomous state interest and privatization. When political life is reduced to its simple components and the nation's general concern is not "ideally independent of those particular elements of civil life," that is, when public affairs do not become "the general affair of each individual, and the political function . . . the general function," then executive authority will become spiritualized as a "higher essence."[27] But in reality it is nothing more than the cover for bureaucracy's status interests.

Thus, at a very early stage Marx seems to have distinguished between the general character of political domination and the particular character of bureaucratic domination. He defines the political state of civil society as the state of generalized egoism from which the bourgeoisie alone reaps an advantage because of private ownership of the means of production. At the same time, he interprets Hegel's constitutional monarchy as the political expression of social conditions from which profit not only the dominant particular interests of civil society but especially the holders of executive power, whose professional monopoly makes them the main beneficiaries of privatized state interests.

THE NATURE OF BUREAUCRACY

There are, then, two kinds of autonomous and privatized state interest. The first is the result of the differentiation of politics as a system of its own; the second emerges from the specialization, indeed the professionalization, of state functions. Both kinds seem related to one another, but at first the exact nature of this connection remains ambivalent.

If we understand bureaucratic domination to mean that matters of state are "transformed into objectives of the department, and department objectives into state objectives,"[28] because one professional status group has the objective chance to turn the world into an object of technical manipulation, then this could very well be the result of the fact that the state either is still politically incomplete or that the political state has become "radicalized," that is, has achieved its "perfect form." If one subscribes to the dictum of the *Communist Manifesto*, that constitutional differences can be largely disregarded in identifying the executive of the modern state as but a committee managing the "common affairs of the whole bourgeoisie,"[29] then it becomes superfluous to discuss further the differences between the two forms.

But in his critique of Bruno Bauer's treatise on the Jewish question, Marx expounded the difference between a Christian and a democratic state. It "makes a great difference whether the complete state, because of the defect inherent in the general nature of the state, counts religion among its presuppositions, or whether the incomplete state declares religion to be its foundation because of the defect inherent in its particular existence as a defective state."[30] What is said here about religion could very well be applied to bureaucracy. This raises the question of whether Marx considered bureaucratic domination to be a mere variant of bourgeois class domination or a mode of domination *sui generis*, either at certain stages of political development before the completed political emancipation or thereafter.

Bonapartism

Especially pertinent is Marx's analysis of the class struggles in France, from the February Revolution of 1848 to Louis Bonaparte's *coup d'état* in December 1851, summarized in the famous essay *The Eighteenth Brumaire of Louis Bonaparte*. Marx has two questions in mind. On one hand, he wanted to discover why the existence of a politically well-developed class antagonism between the bourgeoisie and the proletariat would lead to the supersession of the parliamentary and unitary republic—a constitutional form quite compatible with the bourgeoisie's political interests—by a militarist-bureaucratic authoritarianism. On the other hand, he sought to find out whether the bureaucratic independence of the state machinery under Bonaparte signaled a possible regression or the political fulfillment of the state most adequate to civil society. The answer to this question is crucial in our context. It alone can clarify whether it is permissible from a Marxist standpoint to assume that a developed capitalism and a developed class struggle may coexist with a political form of domination that can compel the class interests of both the bourgeoisie and the proletariat to subordinate themselves to a "third power."

Marx's analysis of the course of French history from 1848 to 1851 is first of all a historical analysis. But he wants to present neither a so-called "objective history" nor depict history as a stage for "great men." Further, he offers a materialist interpretation that ultimately falls back on economic constellations but also takes into account institutional arrangements, independent patterns of legitimation, and attitudes stamped by tradition.

Comparing historical "heroes" to actors on the stage, Marx views them as character-masks behind which lurk economic-political constellations from which they take their cues. Just as actors on the stage cannot exist without scripts, historical actors need a text provided by economic-political history: "Men make their own history, but they do not make it as they please; they do not make it under circumstances chosen by themselves, but under circumstances directly encountered, given and transmitted from the past."[31] These are the circumstances that helped Louis Bonaparte attain power, at first legally, then illegally. Thus, Marx is unwilling to write a history of "heroes"; rather, he sets out to demonstrate "how the class struggle in France created circumstances and relationships that made it possible for a grotesque mediocrity to play a hero's part."[32]

For our purposes the historical details are of little interest. It suffices to call attention to the most important phases that preceded Bonaparte's *coup d'état*. Marx distinguishes three: first, the February period, the overthrow of Louis Philippe, making way for the establishment of the Republic; second, the period of the constitution of the bourgeois republic, a governing alliance of all groups that had taken part in the revolution, especially of the diverse factions of the bourgeoisie; and finally, the period of the national legislative assembly, during which the propertied bourgeoisie, united in the "Party of Order," at first prevailed after the suppression of the proletariat and the enfeeblement of the republican bourgeois intellectuals, before it lost power increasingly to Louis Bonaparte, who was then the legally elected head of the executive.[33] This third phase, ending in the *coup d'état*, is of special interest. Marx had to explain how the bourgeoisie could be robbed of its direct political power in spite of the objective weakness of the proletarian forces.[34] The manner in which he explained this phenomenon influenced his judgment about the nature of the domination that emerged with Bonapartism and the new empire.

Marx provides two sets of explanations that cannot be easily reconciled. First, the party representing the bourgeoisie at large, the Party of Order, is not homogeneous ideologically or economically. Its many factions represent diverse property interests, modes of thought and attitudes. There is, for example, that republican remnant without influence, that "clique of Republican bourgeois, writers, lawyers, officers and officials" who hold onto the memories of the old republic since they make a living from service rather than property.[35] Second, there are the aristocrats of finance, who have become bourgeois to some degree but remain largely identical to the old landed aristocracy. Their economic base continues to be the large landed property holders. This class is essentially committed to the legitimate monarchy and holds onto its memories as the dominant class under the Bourbons. Third, there is the faction of industrial capital, working toward complete control of the town over the country and entertaining Orleanist illusions—from that period during which it had been the dominant class. In

Marx's view, then, the Party of Order is but a coalition of contradictory interests and illusions. It is incapable of putting forth a positive political program. As soon as it no longer needs to repulse outside demands and must push for its own demands, its structural weakness becomes all too evident. At a certain stage of development of the productive forces, the "old contrast between town and country, the rivalry between capital and landed property," comes to a head.[36]

These considerations constitute the basis for the first explanation of the dissolution of direct bourgeois power. Marx points to an ongoing war fought by the Party of Order on two fronts. In view of its structural weakness, the Party cannot wage an aggressive, but only a defensive, war. After all, the Party of Order is wedged between the citizenry and the executive power. Its parliamentary power is eroded by the centralized bureaucratic structure of the executive as well as by universal suffrage.

There is a vicious circle. As a parliamentary power, the bourgeoisie must try to limit the "ubiquity" and "omniscience" of bureaucracy by simplifying "the administration of the state," reducing "the army of officials as far as possible," and finally, by letting "civil society and public opinion create organizations of their own, independent of the governmental power." As a social force, however, it is in need of an ever-expanding state machine in which "it finds posts for its surplus population and makes up in the form of state salaries for what it cannot pocket in the form of profit, interest, rent and honorariums."[37] As a parliamentary force, the bourgeoisie must defend republican creations such as universal suffrage. After all, its political power is exclusively based on such creations. But in the interest of its social power, it must fight against the same universal suffrage, since the proletariat may turn it into a means for the disenfranchisement of the bourgeoisie.[38] In order to make the executive power serve its interests, the Party of Order must strengthen parliament; but in order to keep out the opposition as far as possible, it must weaken the bases of parliamentarism and, consequently, parliament itself. There is no easy way out of this dilemma. The struggle must end either in stronger executive power or in the strengthening of the oppositional forces. Thus, a situation is created in which the bourgeois are overwhelmed by a feeling of weakness "that causes them to recoil from the pure conditions of their own class rule and to yearn for the former, more incomplete, more undeveloped and precisely on that account less dangerous forms of this rule."[39]

In this way Marx is able to explain not only the legitimist sympathies of certain social groups within the bourgeoisie and that of their political representatives but, most of all, the readiness of the bourgeois class to break with its politicians and turn to Bonaparte. Through clever political maneuvering, Bonaparte manages to use for his own ends a conflict he was instrumental in initiating between parliament and the executive power. He makes the Party of Order appear as the party of anarchy, and himself, the guardian of order. Consequently, the aristocracy of finance and the industrial bourgeoisie turn

away from their political representatives. The finance aristocracy sees the struggle between parliament and president as a disturbance of order; the industrial bourgeoisie views it as a disturbance of private business.[40] Slowly but surely, Bonaparte is able to win the confidence of the "extra-parliamentary masses of the bourgeoisie."[41] By the end of 1851, the Party of Order is no longer the political representative of the social interests of landed property and capital. With little effort, Bonaparte now pushes this empty shell aside.

Such an explanatory model suggests that Bonapartism is a form of state in which a relatively independent executive serves the social interests of the bourgeoisie. Although the bourgeoisie can no longer exercise direct political power, it is sufficiently protected from itself as well as the proletariat. Instead of directly ruling in a parliamentary republic, the bourgeoisie can exercise indirect rule under Bonapartist dictatorship. Thus, both forms of state have the same political content: privatization of the state in favor of landed property and capital.

Marx offers, however, another explanation that does not necessarily lead to the same conclusion. The executive authority, which according to the *Communist Manifesto* manages only the affairs of the ruling class, has in France developed in an autonomous fashion since the time of the absolute monarchy. All revolutions, regardless of the groups for which they were attempted, ended inevitably in the strengthening of the executive. Absolute monarchy transformed the privileges of the landowners and towns into attributes of state power. The First Revolution reenforced this tendency toward centralization. Napoleon I perfected it. In time, the qualitative change in state authority was followed by a quantitative one. As the division of labor in society increased, the state administration expanded: "Every common interest was straightaway severed from society, counterposed to it as a higher, general interest, snatched from the activity of society's members themselves and made an object of government activity." The enormous and "appalling parasitic body which enmeshes the body of French society like a net and chokes all of its pores," curtails somewhat the ruling will.[42] Yet the more the bureaucracy's interests are taken into consideration, the more obedient this huge state machinery will be.

This interpretation serves as a basis for the second explanation of the dissolution of the direct rule of the bourgeoisie. Marx shows how the military-bureaucratic state machine increasingly strives to proclaim "its own regime as the highest" and how it discovers along the way that an authoritarian state serves its interests best. Just as the self-governing military has the tendency to make permanent the "periodic state of siege," so *the self-governing bureaucracy prefers not to serve society but to be served by society instead.*[43] Marx emphasized time and again the parasitic nature of bureaucracy, which he considered *an organized attempt to misuse the state,* "to turn it into a *chasing after higher posts,* the *making of a career.*"[44]

Bonaparte plays up to the gross materialism lurking behind the spiritual-

ism of bureaucracy. Early in the game, his attitude reveals that once he has ascended to absolute power, he intends to corrupt public administration. At first, he undertakes an extensive attempt at bribery, long before the *coup d'état*. He then demonstrates his mastery over the administration by establishing his own "private army." According to Marx, Bonaparte contributed only one original idea and action to his final seizure of power: the organization of the Parisian *Lumpenproletariat*. It is in the truest sense of the word a "benevolent society," seeking to benefit itself "at the expense of the labouring nation."[45] This society of "disorder, prostitution and theft" is the private complement to the public administration;[46] together they represent two sides of the same coin. By transforming the private army into a public one and vice versa, society's subordination to the state as well as the state's privatization has been accomplished. Bonaparte is the ideal ruler for a state machine that now stands in solid opposition to civil society. He leads the spiritualism of the bureaucracy to its final materialistic consequences. Thus Marx can argue: while under the absolute monarchy and under Napoleon I, bureaucracy was merely the means of preparing the rule of the bourgeoisie and eventually helped install it in spite of its own interests, under Louis Bonaparte bureaucracy has become an end in itself, and the state seems "to have made itself completely independent."[47]

For Marx, this is merely a matter of appearance. Such a conclusion would ultimately contradict his materialistic theory according to which even independent state power must finally be seen as the result of certain socioeconomic constellations. These could be summed up easily and identified with the first explanatory model he advanced, but he prefers another alternative and resorts to the famous thesis according to which even Bonaparte's power over the self-interest of the ruling clique and its following is "class-related" (*klassengebunden*) because it represents "the most numerous class of French society. . . . the small-holding peasants."[48] Notwithstanding the fact that small-holding property is a symbol of landed property given to free peasants by the bourgeois revolution, and thus has helped to establish a certain degree of solidarity between town and country, subsequent capitalistic developments undermined this "solidarity." The small-holdings were freed from feudal bonds but became beholden to bourgeois capital because of growing mortgage debts. Feeling cheated by the politics of the parliamentary republic and incapable of national organization because of their localism, the peasants look upon Bonaparte, a member of a "dynasty" that once granted their "freedom," as the true representative of their interests. More specifically, it is the conservative peasants who actively support his policies, which are ostensibly directed against the bourgeoisie. For Bonaparte they provide a basis of mobilization against the bourgeoisie and constitute a class whose condition cries out for an authoritarian regime. The small-holding peasants, after all,

cannot represent themselves, they must be represented. Their representatives must at the same time appear as their master, as an authority over them, as an unlimited

governmental power that protects them against the other classes and sends them rain and sunshine from above. The political influence of the small-holding peasants, therefore, finds its final expression in the executive power subordinating society to itself.[49]

This explanatory scheme puts Bonaparte's *coup d'état* in a different light. In this view, its success was possible not so much because of the self-destruction of the political representatives of the bourgeoisie and the political reorientation of its two large factions, but because of an anti-bourgeois coalition. The state machinery, the organized *Lumpenproletariat*, and the small-holding peasants have a common interest in the state's independence from the bourgeoisie. The loyalty of the small-holding peasants to Bonaparte is, to be sure, based on illusions that will soon "burst like soap bubbles" after coming into contact with economic reality. Once in power, however, Bonaparte will be able to retain at least the self-interest of the state machine in the maintenance of his regime. He must find ways and means to create, "alongside the actual classes of society, . . . an artificial caste, for which the maintenance of his regime becomes a bread-and-butter question." Nevertheless, in the end he is forced also to "work out in pure form the opposition between the state power and society."[50]

In such an explanatory scheme, Bonapartism is naturally perceived as that state form in which a relatively independent state subordinates class interests to itself and degrades society to the point of being a mere function of the state. This subordination does not exclude economic progress and can even acknowledge the most important class interests. Marx calls attention specifically to some of the welfare features of Bonapartism and opines that Bonaparte would like to "appear as the patriarchal benefactor of all classes."[51]

Although Marx was convinced of the ultimate futility of Bonaparte's effort and prophesied that his regime would end in "actual anarchy," "profane" the entire state machine, and eventually destroy the Napoleonic myth,[52] which served as a kind of integrative ideology, his explanatory scheme has room for another interpretation of the character of bureaucratic domination: Bonapartism represents a specific form of bureaucratic domination that, due to the omnipotence of the state machinery, is based not so much on a class equilibrium as on a latent conflict between class interests. Thus, the classes are guarded against themselves as against each other by the state—finance aristocracy against industrial capital, the small-holding peasants against the bourgeoisie, the bourgeoisie against the proletariat, and finally, the petty bourgeoisie against the proletariat. It is a form of domination favoring the political status quo, yet it does not freeze the forces of production. On the contrary, the state provides centralized guidance to an expansive, starkly imperialistic, economic development. It also distributes the growing social wealth "evenhandedly," based on criteria provided by the political status quo. Bonapartism, then, is a form of domination *sui generis*. It has effected, to use Max Weber's terms, a peculiar combination of political and rational capitalism.[53] Because of its socioeconomic content, it can no longer be looked upon as the exclusive administration of bourgeois class interests.

Whether the *coup d'état* is thought to be the outcome of the political reorientation of the bourgeoisie or the result of an anti-bourgeois coalition, the explanatory scheme is socioeconomic. Marx weaves both explanations into one fabric. Mainly for this reason, his account of the collapse of direct bourgeois rule in the Second Republic is quite sophisticated and largely free from dogmatic distortions. Nevertheless, the two explanatory schemes allow us to draw different conclusions about the content of Bonapartism, even though there is no fundamental contradiction.

This ambivalence makes *The Eighteenth Brumaire* a fascinating reference point for any analysis of bureaucratic domination. It permits the assumption that in a Marxist perspective bureaucratic domination results not only from the exploitation of class conflict that stagnates at a low level of differentiation (and therefore is an undeveloped political form), and further, that bureaucratic domination results not only from the exploitation of class conflict that stagnates at the highest level of differentiation, in favor of the bourgeois class (and therefore has reached its ultimate political form), but we can also assume that bureaucratic domination results from the subordination of all classes to the imperatives of the state machinery for the sake of the development of a welfare state. This would be a new political phenomenon. Such an assumption would certainly have some serious ramifications for the premises of the Marxist theory of the state. It would mean that Marx anticipated a situation in which the state would retain its ability to direct society in spite of the unfolding capitalist contradictions. It would also mean that domination is not identical with capitalism.

Marx himself, however, knocks the bottom out of any such assumption. He seeks to resolve the ambivalence arising from his structural analysis of French political developments from 1848 to 1851 and to reconcile it with the premises of the theory of the state formulated in exemplary fashion in the *Communist Manifesto*. In *The Eighteenth Brumaire* itself, Marx characterizes Bonapartism as "the shamelessly simple domination of the sabre and the cowl," which does not impart "new content" to society and ends in a parody.[54] This appears possible only in transitional periods. Bonapartism cannot stand in the way of the coming life-and-death struggle between the bourgeoisie and the working class—and may even hasten it.[55]

About twenty years later, after the fall of the Second Empire, in the wake of the Franco-German War and the proclamation of a new Republic, Marx considered Bonaparte's nationalistic and integrative government as "the only form of government possible at a time when the bourgeoisie had already lost, and the working class had not yet acquired, the faculty of ruling the nation."[56] Now he stated unequivocally that the Second Empire was the "last possible form" of bourgeois class domination. Albeit without political clout, the social and economic destructiveness of bourgeois class rule had reached its highest point.[57] The ambivalent conclusions that might have been drawn from the analysis of the *coup d'état* for the evaluation of Bonapartism's political content were homogenized by substituting one set of concepts for another "at a higher level." While Marx had spoken earlier of a contrast between direct and indirect political rule of the bourgeoisie, now he introduced the contrasting notions of anonymous and open political rule. Consequently Bonaparte's *coup d'état* disposed of only the camouflaged despotism of parliamentary rule—i.e., it put an end only to an "anonymous form of class rule."[58] Thus it made it possible to pinpoint exactly the historical contribution of this form of domination toward proletarian emancipation. Bonapartism simply laid bare the true character of the bourgeois class state, which was a full-grown state of repression, a "means for the enslavement of labor by capital."[59]

In this manner Marx provided a penetrating description of the bureaucratization that had affected French society and its political institutions since the days of the absolute monarchy. He saw in the military-bureaucratic form of domination the cumulative effect of bureaucratization. In the final analysis, however, bureaucratization did not signify the formation of a new political entity. At most, it shaped the form, but not the content, of political rule under capitalism. Just like the constitutional monarchy or the parliamentary republic, Bonapartism appeared as only one of several possible political forms through which the bourgeoisie succeeded in privatizing state interests. Nevertheless, the experience of the Bonapartist regime, the longevity of which he clearly underestimated,[60] compelled Marx in the end to revise one assertion. He abandoned the notion of the unitary republic as the ultimate form of bourgeois-capitalist society. This role was now assigned to the Second Empire. It appeared not as just one of the possible forms of bourgeois-capitalist society, but as "its most prostitute, most accomplished, and indeed ultimate political form. It is *the* State power of modern class rule, at least on the Continent."[61] Formerly defined as a transition, Bonapartism becomes the ultimate form, and the Republic, formerly construed as the ultimate form, becomes a typical transitional period.[62]

Engels on German Bureaucracy

In his study on the status quo in Germany, which, together with his "Outlines of a Critique of Political Economy," belongs to his early original contributions, Engels adumbrated the reasons for bureaucratic domination in "pre-revolutionary" Germany.[63] In England and France the revolutions of 1688 and 1789 laid the foundation for the destruction of the old political order and helped bourgeois property, town life, and the competitive forces to undermine landed property, the rural way of life, and structures of privilege. In Germany, however, the countryside still dominated the towns, and agriculture, handicrafts, and trade dominated industry.

To this state of affairs corresponds the distribution of political power. The landed nobility shares power with the petty bourgeois, who are the representatives of "local and sluggish competition," which operates with "little capital."[64] Neither the landed nobility nor the stagnating petty bourgeoisie is capable of a cosmopolitan outlook. The petty bourgeoisie especially contents itself politically with control over municipal or regional administration. It is not by accident that the classical creation of the petty bourgeoisie was the free imperial city instead of the nation state—not to mention the French representative state. A balance of power and a local or, at best, regional orientation prevent direct political rule by the landed nobility or the petty bourgeoisie. Rule is transferred to the bureaucracy. Its composition is influenced by both classes, especially the nobility. But the bureaucracy manages to gain a relatively high degree of autonomy when it comes to the big political issues, such as foreign policy. According to Engels, not even the newly emerging bourgeoisie can change this state of affairs decisively. Industrial capitalists have in fact become the leading class in Germany, but their claims lack any legal foundation. Consequently, they have been denied any direct political rule.

Still, Engels argues that only the bourgeoisie can do away with the backward German conditions by overthrowing the "compromise established between nobility and petty bourgeoisie in the bureaucratic monarchy." In a country in which the nobility is "too much in decline," the petty bourgeoisie and the peasants are "too weak," and the workers are "still far from sufficiently mature," only the bourgeoisie is capable of overcoming a regime "represented by the bureaucracy [which] is the political summing-up of the general impotence and contemptibility, of the dull boredom and the sordidness of German society." Because of its economic interests, the bourgeoisie, with the factory owners as its decisive sector, is the only class that has a national orientation and can be organized on a national scale. The bourgeoisie is compelled to centralize political power and to gain control over an already centralized bureaucracy, for this traditional system sets limits to its expansive dynamics at every turn. As soon as this is accomplished, "the independence of the bureaucracy ceases to exist; indeed, from this moment the tormentors of the bourgeoisie turn into their humble slaves."[65]

Engels thus holds that bureaucratic rule results from a kind of equilibrium between the two classes and from their political orientation, which is local, not cosmopolitan or even national. In a situation in which the economically rooted power distribution among the various social groups does not permit any group to exercise direct or indirect rule, a "social caste of officers and civil servants" steps into the vacuum, seemingly standing "beyond and above society" and lending the state the "appearance of independence from society."[66]

Closer examination of Engels' analysis of the German situation reveals that the development of an autonomous state can also be attributed to the lack of a representative state in which independent, only loosely connected "provinces, with separate interests, laws, governments and systems of taxation became lumped together into one nation, with one government, one code of laws, one national class-interest, one frontier and one custom-tariff."[67] Consequently, bureaucratic domination should not be viewed solely as a result of the balance of power among diverse economic-political interests, not only as a result of widespread localism, but also as a result of an incomplete political state. Its inadequacy merely reflects the limited development of capitalism itself.

The Paris Commune

Facing up to the historical significance of bureaucratization, Marx and Engels changed the tactics that they proposed to the working class. Given the structure of the modern military-bureaucratic state, they no longer considered it feasible for the working class merely to "lay hold of the ready-made state machinery and wield it for its own purposes."[68] In his now famous letter to Kugelmann, Marx observed that it no longer made sense "to transfer the bureaucratic-military machine from one hand to another"; rather, the task will be "to smash it." This was "essential for every genuine revolution by the people on the Continent."[69] In fact, Marx had anticipated this position already in the last chapter of *The Eighteenth Brumaire*, but the events of the 1871 Paris Commune served to strengthen his conviction. He came to consider the Commune "the direct antithesis to the Empire," the specific political form of social emancipation.[70] It was the first step toward creating a new historical situation in which the state would become superfluous. It radically changes the final political form of bourgeois society as represented by Bonapartism. What constitutes the Commune's political content is labor's domination over capital in order to uproot the foundation upon which class rule rests. As an antithesis to Bonapartism, the embodiment of fully developed bureaucracy, the Commune necessarily possessed an anti-bureaucratic form. With Marx, we can study the organizational measures taken by the Commune and understand why he perceived the first step toward the dismantling of bourgeois rule to be bureaucratic domination—and thus the first move toward replacing government over persons with the administration of things.

According to Marx, the Paris Commune had taken three exemplary anti-bureaucratic measures. The first was to replace the standing army with the armed people. Ultimately, the state had maintained its monopoly of physical force only through the standing army, and therefore the expropriation of the state had a double meaning: to help dissolve the solidarity of interest between the armed forces and the independent state bureaucracy and to reverse the bureaucratic trend emanating from the army.[71] Historically, standing armies and bureaucracies are closely related. A standing army is the opposite of the type represented by the self-equipped feudal army. A standing army not only presupposes a money economy but also a taxation system that requires an administration to help the state secure needed funds in order to centralize and monopolize the military "means of production." But the bureaucracy also fulfills another function, that of offering fallback positions to retired military men. In this manner the military and political form of domination are entwined.[72] Therefore, for Marx, arming the people is an anti-bureaucratic move.

The Commune's second important measure affected the bureaucracy directly: it eliminated the separation of powers as a specific form of the division of labor and established instead a working body that was "executive and legislative at the same time." Although chosen through the electoral process, this was not, in Marx's opinion, a parliamentary but a "working body," and it constituted the decision-making center of the new political form. Both the police and the administrators were now public servants, subordinated to the Commune. They were not meant to become a new instrument of domination that would serve the interests of the elected representatives. Two measures were taken to forestall their independence. They were elected officials subject to recall, and their salaries were reduced to "workmen's wages." Not only the police and the administrative agencies but also the judges and other judicial functionaries were to be subject to these regulations. Their purpose was to supersede the principle of the "hierarchic investiture" with that of "universal suffrage."[73]

The Commune had no time to carry through its third measure: to extend the principle of self-government to the producers across the land and to reduce the central government to a coordinator of those functions indispensible to "the unity of the nation." Yet Marx did not view the Commune as an anti-centralist organization: "The very existence of the Commune involved, as a matter of course, local municipal self-government, but no longer as a check upon the, now superseded, State power."[74] To be sure, the Commune is centralist, but it is not hierarchically centralist. It represents democratic centralism. It is a government, but not a representative-parasitic one. Rather, it is a direct and, as such, a "cheap government" because it destroys "the two great sources of expenditure—the standing army and State functionarism."[75] One might say that the Commune is the first "true Republic." Only now are the old democratic ideals realized, and as a result, efficiency is increased.

Marx held that these organizational measures were not ends in themselves. They were not the cause as much as the effect of the political content of the revolution against the state. After all, the revolution is grounded in the exploitation of labor. Accordingly, its aim is the emancipation of labor so that "every man becomes a working man, and productive labor ceases to be a class attribute."[76] But the Commune is not yet that community of free men or of associated producers[77] or that "commune" (*Gemeinwesen*)[78] in which humanity fulfills itself in accordance with the historical development of the species, and in which rational regulation and communal control of the "realm of necessity" provide the basis for the flourishing of the "realm of freedom."[79] The Commune is merely a "thoroughly expansive political form" that helps to bring humanity one step closer to this stage.[80]

In a two-step model Marx depicted the road to be traveled during the transformative period that lies between capitalist and communist society. The first phase will set free the elements of the new society that are "still stamped with the birthmarks of the old society from whose womb it emerges."[81] To be sure, it will eliminate capital accumulation for its own sake as the driving force of economic development. It will thwart the "theft of alien labor time,"[82] and labor will cease to be a "class attribute."[83] Nevertheless, there will remain the "economy of time"[84] as well as the tacit recognition of "unequal individual endowment and thus productive capacity as natural privileges"[85]—that is, individual inequality based on unequal qualification and performance. Only in the second phase can this reduction of man to worker be eradicated. Only then will the enslaving subordination of the individual to the division of labor vanish. In addition, direct labor and labor time will lose their historical significance as sources of wealth.

On another occasion, Marx offered a similar developmental perspective:

Real wealth manifests itself rather—and large-scale industry reveals this—in the monstrous disproportion between the labour time applied and its product, as well as in the qualitative imbalance between labour, reduced to a pure abstraction, and the power of the production process it superintends. Labour no longer appears so much to be included within the production process; rather, the human being comes to relate more as a watchman and regulator to the production process itself. (What holds for machinery holds likewise for the combination of human activities and the development of human intercourse.) No longer does the worker insert a modified natural thing [*Naturgegenstand*] as a middle link between the object [*Objekt*] and himself; rather, he inserts the process of nature, transformed into an industrial process, as a means between himself and inorganic nature, mastering it. He steps to the side of the production process, instead of being its chief actor.[86]

The revolutionary process of the forces of production that began under capitalism and was further developed in the period of the dictatorship of the proletariat culminates in a self-regulatory production-process: Human beings need to engage only in creative, directive, and controlling activities. Thus, work can even become "life's prime want."[87]

Such a socioeconomic interpretation of the developmental stages following capitalism relativizes the Commune's final stature. Still, the Commune initiated organizational measures judged by Marx and Engels to be the necessary components of every new society for some time to come. These measures were aimed at the elimination of the artificial differentiations present in the capitalism system. It is not by accident that Engels, in particular, pleaded time and again that the old democratic system of "mark organization" be restored under new conditions, or that Marx celebrated the simplicity of the Commune as the sign of its greatness. Both felt that the principle of self-government was actualized in the Commune in that public functions were reduced to "real functions of working men," and the functions themselves were freed from the spheres of professionalism and specialization. Marx regarded the Commune's great achievement to be the fact that it did away with the secretiveness surrounding administrative and political leadership activities as if they were transcendental functions to be entrusted only to members of an educated caste—state parasites, highly paid sycophants, and sinecurists—who try to coopt the best-educated of the masses and place them at the lowest level of the hierarchy in order to use them against their own.[88]

MARXISM'S DEMOCRATIC PROPOSAL

On the level of the productive forces, the "emancipation of labor" becomes possible only with "the transformation of the production process from the simple labor process into a scientific process," and further, when scientific knowledge and its application cease to be attributes of "capital accumulation for its own sake"—when "the conditions of the process of social life itself have come under the control of the general intellect and been transformed in accordance with it."[89] On the institutional level, the level of the organization of public affairs, the "emancipation of labor" already seems to be possible—neither the representation of common interests nor their administration requires specialized knowledge.

This line of thought, so closely related to the concept of self-government, has its basis in Marx's persistent idea of the parasitic character of bureaucracy. He views bureaucracy as the outgrowth of the ongoing differentiation of the social system. In turn, this differentiation is but the result of a capitalist social structure that is organized against the interests of the human species. Only the abolition of the social structure itself can bring forth simplified relations. The first to go will be the public functions that made themselves independent of society. Marx stated unequivocally that self-government is always "cheaper" than a highly specialized bureaucracy. In his "Critique of the Gotha Program," which recounts the economic state of affairs of the phase following the Proletarian Revolution, Marx remarked on the general costs of administration outside the production sphere: "This part will, from the outset, be very considerably restricted in comparison with present-day society and it diminishes in proportion as the new society develops."[90] While conceding that the outlays for "communal purposes" (official poor relief, for example) will have to keep rising, Marx held that self-government is not only the more efficient but also the less costly form of administration. Direct democracy, then, as a political form is not only more humane, just, and free, but at the same time, it is also simpler and therefore cheaper and more effective.

Lenin further elaborated these ideas. His reconstruction of Marx and Engels' theory of the state from a 1917 perspective vindicates Marx's statement about the expansion of bureaucratization. What was true for France in Marx's time has become a universal trend for Lenin. Bureaucratization has transformed capitalism into state capitalism and further enhanced the "development, perfecting and strengthening of the bureaucratic and military apparatus."[91] Lenin accepts, however, the validity of the Marxian proposition that bureaucratization is not irreversible. Bureaucratization does not follow, as the functionalists want us to believe, from the "complexity of social life," and "differentiation of functions, and so forth."[92] It is, Lenin asserts, the result of the class character of bourgeois society. With its elimination, these very functions can be simplified, a goal for which capitalist production helped to prepare, but cannot realize. Lenin links any such simplification to the process of de-professionalization of both politics and administration and states:

Capitalist culture has created large-scale production, factories, railways, the postal service, telephones, etc., and on this basis the great majority of functions of the old "state power" have become so simplified and can be reduced to such simple operations of registration, filing and checking that they will be quite within the reach of every literate person, and it will be possible to perform them for "workingmen's wages," which circumstance can (and must) strip those functions of every shadow of privilege, of every appearance of "official grandeur."[93]

Marxist thought thus confronts bureaucratic domination with an organizational model of "primitive democracy" that owes its existence to the achievements of capitalist culture. Lenin admitted as much. For him, it is obvious that the "transformation from capitalism to Socialism is *impossible* without 'return' to 'primitive democracy.' "[94] Accordingly, he pleads for the abolition of the separation of powers and parliamentarianism that goes with it, for the elimination of every form of organized antagonistic pluralism, and finally—at least as long as certain special functions remain—for selection and control in the form of election and recall. These mechanisms are supposed to inhibit any move toward administrative independence and should be strengthened by the rotation principle. They are, however, built into a centralized structure that alone can insure the nation's unity. Thus a pyramid of representative bodies must be created according to regional and functional criteria. In the Marxist view this leads not to a closing, but rather to an opening of social relations. After all, the simplification of functions, de-specialization, and liberation from enslavement through the division of labor guarantee both subjective and objective participation by all. To be sure, these preconditions can be improved only in the course of a developmental process. They presuppose a growing "general intellect" and an increasing control over nature. To that extent, the historical perspective is a built-in component of the Marxist organizational model. Whatever the outcome of the development, Lenin is certain of one matter: all traditional administrative functions can immediately be assumed by the working class. Together with Marx, he holds that at least in this respect, direct democracy is attainable without delay.

Thus Marxism offers a program and organizational model that is diametrically opposed to every form of bureaucratic domination. This domination includes all conditions in which human beings fall prey to the technical imperatives of their own creations after the bourgeoisie has revolutionized the forces of production. This program and organizational model can be critically opposed to any attempt to install a merely instrumentally rational social order, for they proclaim as their foundation the "free social individual."[95] Hierarchy and association, specialized knowledge and all-around development of human potentiality, achievement and need, hierarchical investiture and universal suffrage, efficiency and participation are some of the antithetical elements of the two models. If taken out of their specific intellectual contexts, they exhibit extremely different notions of social order with which the industrial age has responded to one of its central problems: the common and simultaneous historical origins of industrial and democratic revolutions.[96]

2

Max Weber and the Possibilities for Socialism

Ernest Kilker

Socialist groups were among those who presented themselves as the precursors of Germany's future in Weber's day. According to Weber, however, such movements would inevitably fail because they fundamentally misunderstood the nature of "absolute evil" in the current order. Since they assumed that capitalism as an economic system was the real enemy, they failed to recognize, in Weber's view, the more important foe that was already in their midst and in the process of transforming their own parties: bureaucracy. Weber saw a strong historical probability that state bureaucracy would rule alone if private capitalism was eliminated. Socialism would betray its democratic ideals while producing a stagnant economy in the process. It would destroy the possibility of a "rational" freedom in which the individual could "choose his own gods" in the process of forming an autonomous personality. Instead, one would be forced to accept the new socialist catechism, and cultural life would "ossify." The end result, Weber argued, would resemble the total bureaucratic domination achieved in antiquity in Ancient Egypt and Rome.

In Weber's view, socialism had an even stronger elective affinity to bureaucratic control than capitalism. He argued that bureaucracy is "the *means* of transforming social action into rationally organized action."[1] It is the power instrument *par excellence* for the one who controls the apparatus. Its full development can be seen in the modern state in the form of the bureaucratic agency, in modern capitalism in corporate bureaucracy, and in the modern university in departmental specialization. The advance of bureaucratic forms is a result of their technical superiority over any other form of organization.[2] The whole bureaucratic process was as inevitable as the dominance of precision machinery in the mass production of goods, and it stems from the same source.[3] Capitalism itself now depends upon such arrangements. It requires calculable rules that operate without regard to persons—"business is business." In politics the appointed official derives his authority from above, not below. The elected official, Weber argued, is more likely to serve a political following, while the appointed official (i.e., the bureaucrat) is more likely to be able to meet the demands of the day and objectively and impersonally carry out his assigned tasks.

Bureaucracy aids the internal pacification and economic expansion of a nation's life. It expands to meet the administrative needs of a large standing army demanded for power politics. It expands to meet the opportunity that a quantitative increase in wealth potentially affords for qualitatively refashioning external life for the welfare of the masses. It expands in order to meet the general desire for order and protection.

Bureaucracy is at once both at the service of and in tension with democratic principles. By eliminating the arbitrariness of kadi-justice—the charismatic, "It is written, but I say unto you"—bureaucracy theoretically rises above playing favorites and the administration of law with regard to a person's class or status. However, this formally rational leveling process works against the political prospect of using the law in an instrumental way to level substantively and redistribute the national income. It resists control from below and guards its administrative secrets, its monopoly of technically utilizable knowledge, with a vengeance. It welcomes a poorly informed public and attempts to emasculate, through lack of information, its representative bodies.[4]

Weber argued that the material fate of the masses, including that of private capitalism, depends upon the correct functioning of bureaucracies. Any thought of their elimination is an ideological illusion. Weber removed bureaucracy's halo, however, which led many scholars of the older generation—especially students of public administration such as Gustav Schmoller—to believe that it could act as a politically neutral force—the repository of disinterested political wisdom. Yet it was not a neutral force. It served instead to protect the interests of those groups already in power. It preserved current values but was incapable of administratively producing any new cultural meanings. Its basis of technical superiority was also the very foundation of the "mechanical petrifaction" of society. It had an inherent tendency to transcend its instrumental function and become an independent regressive force distorting the goals and character of a nation.

Bureaucrats as a status stratum had an insidious effect on the values of a society. The determination of national goals and values should be the function of intellectuals and politicians, not bureaucrats. This, then, is the Weberian irony in the concurrent assertion that bureaucracy is the absolute prerequisite for the material welfare of the masses. Once in place, there has never been a historical example of its dissolution without the historical destruction of the host culture with it. Regimes may come and go, but the bureaucratic apparatus—the machine of government and commerce—remains. A change in master hardly affects the powers of domination. Revolution, in Weber's view, becomes more and more an impossibility, its form increasingly that of a *coup d'état*.[5] In the end, it is not revolution but the bureaucratic apparatus that remains "in the saddle."

Socialism is no exception here. It simply increases the functions of bureaucracy, eliminates the innovations of the entrepreneur, and dictates the worker's wages and employment. In short, it could only *increase* the extent and intensity of rule by bureaucratic, instrumental reason. The United States, too, was bound to succumb to its charms as a result of World War I.[6] The result, according to Weber, would be the Europeanization of America in terms of the inexorable march of universal bureaucratization: "Everywhere we find the same thing," the separation of the worker from the means of production as a part of a more general process—bureaucratization.[7] The worker's plight would thus be no better if industry were in the hands of a minister of state rather than an entrepreneur. The same quality of discipline and factory organization would be required. The lot of the miner is not affected by who officially owns the pit.[8]

Any differences would be, indeed for the most part, to the disadvantage of workers. Strikes against the state to improve the situation of workers would be impossible. If an adumbrated form of "socialism" in the form of state and private corporate planning and cooperation were to become the norm, the result would be only "socialism for the entrepreneurs." Corporations, because of their technical expertise, would inevitably dominate such a partnership. This turn of events should doubly benefit corporate interests, since it would have the additional effect of diverting working class hatred toward the state.

According to Weber, the definitive feature of socialism is a collective economy administered by officials. In his view, the ultimate socialist vision of the end of the "domination of man over man" and the reign of "an association of individuals" is an illusion. We are never told what such an association would look like. In fact, the class structure is not evolving in the direction of leveling class distinctions, but in creating new ones.[9] Not the proletariat but the trained worker, the specialist, and the administrator are destined to be predominant in the future. The result will be the dictatorship, not of the worker, but of the official. What if the employer could be eliminated? Who would take command of the new economy? Workers themselves lack the required knowledge to run their own workplaces. The only answer would be (as it was in Russia) to leave the industrialists at the head and restore capitalist incentives for the sake of output.[10]

The socialist slogan, "the separation of the worker from the tools of his trade," betrays the deeper and inescapable process of "universal bureaucratization."[11] What does the slogan really mean? The worker is separated from the material resources with which he produces and forced into "wage slavery." This is in contrast with the Middle Ages, when the worker owned the tools with which he produced objects which he sold on the market.[12] Weber stresses that this separation can also be seen in the university, where the scientist is separated from the means of research. Further, the mass of the workers at the university, especially the assistants, are an intellectual proletariat whose lack of rights and small income create a status not fundamentally different from that of the trained worker.

The same situation recurs in the military. The knight was the owner of his own horse and armor, self-equipped. The modern army came into being when the soldier ceased to own his tools of warfare.[13] So, too, the modern official is separated from the "tools" of administration. The "technical requirements" of modern technology will cause such a separation to pertain under any regime, socialist or otherwise.[14]

The characteristic discipline of subordination to the needs of the bureaucratic "machine" coincides directly with mechanical production within the factory: "enslavement to the machine" and the factory system. According to Weber, it is factory work discipline that ultimately produced modern socialism,[15] but this is not perceived in the socialist solution.

In his essay on "Socialism" Weber considers the claims and prospects of utopian socialism, especially as they are laid out in that "prophetic document," the *Communist Manifesto*.[16] He is concerned with the practical significance of the *Manifesto* as well as its theoretical merit. He also clarifies the reasons why the emphasis in his own sociological work is not on the "laws of motion" of capitalist development, but rather on the "laws of bureaucratic development" which envelop those of capitalism. He attacks the *Manifesto*, "in its way a work of scholarship of the highest order," on the basis of both its empirical claims and its prophetic ("scientific") predictions—the end of capitalism and of "man's dominion over man."

Weber argues, by contrast, that Marx's revolutionary collapse thesis is no longer accepted by most socialists. Power has not, in fact, devolved upon the worker, but rather upon the administrative official—"it is the dictatorship of the official and not that of the worker, which for the present at any rate is on the advance."[17] The emerging "administrative class" does not identify with the proletariat, but with aristocratic traditions and pretensions.[18]

The universal historical reasons for Weber's attitude toward the process of bureaucratization and his suspicions about the prospects of socialism are not, however, merely an attempt to dialogue once again with the ghost of Marx. Rather, they are intimately related to his research into the social development of ancient Egypt and Rome and the associations he finds there.

The historical model of all later bureaucracies is the New Kingdom in Egypt.[19] The development of bureaucracy in Egypt was, in part, a technical and economic necessity because of the need for centralized regulation of the water supply for the whole country. It was further developed by an extensive building program and the needs of power politics. Officials, although formally free, in fact were slaves of Pharoah.[20] There was no freedom of movement, because a man's "idea" was where he paid taxes and was subject to personal liturgies. If he moved to another community, he could be sent back to his original idea at any time to fulfill public charges. Although dominated by a primarily natural economy, the New Kingdom required money to support salaried bureaucrats, a standing army, the state religion, and an active foreign policy. At the same time that it desperately needed money to meet state expenses, it also seemed intent on strangling the development of a fledgling market economy. State monopolies were numerous and included the most basic and important resources: oil and salt.[21] Oil was sold at fixed prices by government fiat after the court deducted enough for its own consumption. Important foodstuffs such as wheat were regulated by the state administration. Banking was also monopolized. Monopolies increased constantly and included heavy products and items of mass consumption: clothing, building materials, and so on.[22] The system of liturgies was intended to make someone financially responsible for the performance of each public service.[23]

Weber determined that the earliest bureaucratic stateadministration was in Egypt. This included a collective economy, a socialistic rationalization of the tax system, and unfree labor and military forces in the service of Pharoah. It was a "regime of favorites" where patrimonial bureaucratic officials were picked only from the supporters and clientele of the king.[24] Education was a completely clericalized affair with no counterweight to its closed system of concepts. The result was intellectual ossification.[25] Furthermore, its bureaucratic "house of bondage" disappeared only with the demise of the total culture.

Weber's study of Rome provided another deep backdrop for his current evaluation of the Western cultural situation.[26] As Weber's work on this civilizational complex has recently been given brilliant restatement by Robert Antonio, the details of this topic need not be expanded upon here.[27] The central claim is that bureaucracy stifled private enterprise and initiative in antiquity. But this relationship is not peculiar to antiquity—every bureaucracy tends to intervene in economic affairs with the same result. Rome and Egypt, then, form ideal-typical models for the potentially disastrous consequences of unimpeded bureaucratic domination, notwithstanding the utopian promises of modern socialism.

Weber's chilling foresight in this regard, however, should not blind us to the limitations of his method of historical hindsight. In associating socialism dogmatically with Egypt and Rome, he ignores the uniqueness of modern technological innovation and cultural values, including democracy.[28] Instead, he highlights the increase of the technical forces available for domination while dismissing those values and innovations available for liberation. Indeed, he insists the latter will inevitably turn into the former! Such an argument is tendentious on its face. Although open, at least methodologically, to the unrealized possibilities of the past, Weber was pessimistically closed to the possibility of constructing a truly alternative future. He was the victim of the same loose analogical reasoning for which he justly criticized his contemporaries. In fact, in attempting to prove the incompatibility between socialism and freedom, Weber labored to show that their coincidence and coexistence was an objective impossibility, from his own methodological perspective, a scientifically untenable position.[29]

Weber's notion of recurrence and development isscientifically valid only if it is used with methodological restraint. However, Weber uses it too often in a static and reductionist fashion, which emphasizes present similarities with the past rather than differences—recurrence at the expense of development. At the same time, his use of these concepts is imbued with ethical significance. It is exactly the struggle *against* the current (that is, humankind's bureaucratic destiny) which, for Weber, is decisive in the formation of a free-willed personality. It is characteristic of his anthropological pessimism that "freedom" and "individualism" are seen as being part of an "unrepeatable" unique sequence of historical events, while bureaucratic domination is viewed in cyclical terms as not only "repeatable" but practically inevitable. Such a position seems to employ the same kind of *a priori* "scholastic" logic that Weber decried in his methodological writings. Here, however, he had a practical, existential purpose:

This might happen *if* a technically superior administration *were to be the ultimate and sole value* in the ordering of their affairs, and that means: a rational bureaucratic administration with the corresponding welfare benefits, for this bureaucracy can accomplish much better than any other structure of domination. This shell of bondage, which our unsuspecting literati praise so much, might perhaps be reinforced by fettering every individual to his job (notice the beginnings in the system of fringe benefits), to his class (through the increasing rigidity of the property distribution), and maybe to his occupation (through liturgic methods of satisfying state requirements, and that means: through burdening occupational associations with state functions). It would be made all the more indestructible if in the social sphere a status order were then to be imposed upon the ruled, linked to the bureaucracy and in truth subordinate to it, as in the forced-labor states of the past. . . . Let us assume for the moment that this possibility were our "inescapable" fate: Who would then not smile about the fear of our literati that the political and social development might bring us *too much* "individualism" or "democracy." . . . ?[30]

Here, finally, is the clue to why Weber chose to view scientific probabilities, in this context, as future historical certainties and willingly assumed the role of a gloom-and-doom prophet, a modern-day Jeremiah, stressing the "fatefulness" of bureaucratic cultural processes. Throughout his life and work, Max Weber was passionately involved in the fate of human freedom and individuality in modern society. The real prospect of their disappearance helped inspire his own prodigious academic and political efforts. It also provided him with a practical political purpose and mission. In attempting to mobilize the energies of individual men and women in resistance to their collective fate, he refused to provide them with alternative revolutionary pictures. Instead, he implored them to read what was for him the obviously disastrous and anti-utopian "writing on the wall" and then make their own responsible choices for individual action.[31]

Fate, for Weber, was not an implacable cosmic process, nor was the spirit of rationalization, as Karl Löwith mistakenly argues, a primordial totality. Our modern "fate" is not a metaphysical certainty but an empirical probability imposing itself on us with seemingly cosmic force. The knowledge of the "fate" of our epoch comes too late for us to begin to change decisively its course. Our irrational "destiny" is the result of the paradox of unintended consequences, a web of elective affinities spun by the actions of real historical people. Their legacy inevitably prevents future generations from playing a free hand—the deck is stacked, the dice are loaded. The practical question thus becomes: "Given this overwhelming tendency toward bureaucratization, how is it still possible at all to preserve *some* remnant of *some* sense of 'individualistic' freedom of movement?"[32]

Why does Weber not simply accept his fate passively in the face of such an "overwhelming tendency"? Why does this awareness not result in passivity or moral antinomianism? To the contrary, for Weber it was the technical means of freeing himself to resist and oppose it creatively, individually. Like the Puritan, resistance did not insure salvation; rather, it was the technical means of getting rid of the fear of damnation. Resisting "inevitable" bureaucratization, swimming against the current, was a test and a struggle. This is the essence of politics. It is a proving ground for souls turned self-saving individuals. Proof of salvation, of successful resistance to inevitable "damnation," can come only by way of political success—by the victory of one's ultimate values in the face of overwhelming opposition: "And even those who are neither leaders nor heroes must arm themselves with that steadfastness of heart which can brave even the crumbling of all hopes. This is necessary right now, or else men will not be able to attain even that which is possible today."[33]

3

Max Weber and the Crisis of Liberal Democracy

Wolfgang J. Mommsen
Translated by Jose V. Casanova

Max Weber realized that the ideology of traditional liberalism had lost much of its persuasive power in an emerging industrial society characterized by growing bureaucracies and industrial combinations. The conviction of classical liberalism that the power of the state should be restricted as much as possible, in order to allow society to develop along "natural" lines, also seemed to him entirely inadequate to the politics of modernity.

The problem of how to adapt liberal principles to the conditions of emerging industrial society was, for Weber, of first-rate importance and just as much a political as a personal issue. Gradually, in light of his conviction that the only creative factor in society is the free initiative of the individual personality, he came to realize more and more keenly how serious the situation was.

WATCHMAN TELL US. . . .

Around the turn of the century Weber was inclined to view the future with gloom. Already in his own day—according to his pessimistic outlook—some of the elements were being created that would eventually help to bring about a stagnant bureaucratic society which in some ways was likely to be similar to the conditions of the late Roman Empire. He predicts that the bureaucratization of society, according to all available knowledge, will someday triumph over capitalism in our civilization, just as in ancient civilizations. In our civilization, too, the "anarchy of production" will be supplanted in due course by an economic and social system similar to that typical of the late Roman Empire, and even more so of the "New Kingdom" in Egypt or the sway of the Ptolemies.[1]

He couched his fears in forceful language, which is at times reminiscent of the Jewish prophets. He maintained that eventually rationalization and in-tellectualization—the two most effective revolutionary forces in contempo-rary world history—would no longer permit individual creativity and personal values to play any significant role in social relations. At best, sublime values would be allowed to survive in the retreat of complete pri-vacy, while the social system would be totally dominated by purely instru-mental (*zweckrationale*) social relationships and interactions.[2]

In Weber's essays on *The Protestant Ethic and the Spirit of Capitalism*, one can find the most powerful formulation of his fear that if left to run its course undisturbed, late capitalism would bring "a new age of bondage," not unlike that of late antiquity.[3] Modern capitalist industrial society, organized ac-cording to the principle of sheer formal rationality, could lead into a de-humanization of the world of work and further the displacement of the individual personality from social life.

Already in *The Protestant Ethic and the Spirit of Capitalism*, Weber had clearly pointed out that capitalism, which was entering its mature stage, no longer needed the specific individualistic driving force to which it owed its origins. It enforced its own will, rather, whether those affected by it liked it or not: "The Puritan *wanted* to work in a calling; we are *forced* to do so."[4] According to Weber, the advanced capitalist system was exhibiting increas-ingly mechanical, ultimately "inescapable powers over man such as have never before been seen in history,"[5] enforcing in the process forms of the conduct of life which were no longer in accord with the classic liberal ideals of individual freedom. At best, it was only in the private sphere that one could still preserve the value-creating spontaneity of the individual.

Hence, the vital question of the age was: How, under the rule of bur-eaucratic capitalism, are such things as the rights of man, individual liberties, the freedom of the press, and so forth, possible?[6]

Weber's gloomy, at times even apocalyptic, prognoses were based on a precise analysis of the basic model of capitalist economic and social organi-zations. He was extremely pessimistic:

When the rationalization of the means of satisfaction of all political as well as all social needs will be completed, disciplinization as a universal phenomenon will make irresistible headway in every sphere of human life. Consequently all individually oriented forms of social action and even charisma will have less importance.[7]

Weber was not, however, willing simply to resign himself to this. He resorted in a heroic pessimism to a series of fairly radical measures designed to keep the open society of his day open, as long as there was any point in doing so. It is here that Max Weber reveals himself as a liberal in despair. For the moment there were no prophets around, and it was futile to do nothing while waiting for them to appear. Rather, one should do everything possible to keep society as dynamic as possible.

Thus, Weber was convinced that economic development itself was leading to an ever-increasing restriction of freedom, and therefore, one had to struggle to enforce liberal principles in late capitalism "against the current of material constellations."[8] He was deeply concerned that the rapidly developing monopoly capitalistic structures were making the classical liberal model of society obsolete and that the trend towards the formation of ever more powerful bureaucratic machines would accelerate immensely. In 1905, on the occasion of the trade-union debates in the *Verein für Sozialpolitik*, he took the position that it was no longer possible to proceed from the assumption that, given the emergence of "giant concerns," the trade unions would still be powerful enough to assert themselves against the big corporate enterprises without the necessity of additional protective measures from the state and that they could still be effective in securing appropriate wages for the working classes. Yet he rejected most emphatically a mediatization of the trade unions through direct state intervention or through state-regulated arbitration. In any case, he wanted to avoid a curtailment of the competitive struggle between the working classes and the employers' associations. He deemed it necessary, rather, to look for ways of improving indirectly, through appropriate methods, the starting conditions of the working classes in contingent labor struggles. In 1912 he tried to bring new life into the lame social politics of Germany by founding an association of active social politicians. The objective of such an association was to ease the relations between employers and employees and to pave new ways for the emancipation of the working classes within the existing system.

BUREAUCRATIC DOMINANCE

Weber did not share Marx's conviction that the contradictions of capitalist society would be eliminated by a proletarian revolution abolishing the private appropriation of the means of production. He did not think that socialism offered a solution to the pressing problems confronting humanity. He was firmly convinced—and I think that in this respect history has since been on his side—that it is not capitalism and the capitalist pattern of the distribution of property which is putting a humane order of things in jeopardy, but rather the growth of bureaucracies. In view of this, nationalization of the means of production did not alter things in the least. Far from emancipating the working classes from the status of alienation, it would make matters worse. All socialist policies were, in his opinion, bound to foster bureaucratization, and hence to reinforce the tendencies toward ossification of society.[9] Therefore, the alternative proposed by Marx—that is, the socialization of the means of production as a panacea to free the working classes from oppression—was for Weber only a surrogate and not a solution, since the socialization of the means of production would only further strengthen the already existing universal trend to bureaucratization. Apart from this, the modern industrial system simply could not do without the initiative of energetic, individualistic, enterprising personalities.

Weber was fully convinced that there was no sure way out of this situation. He saw no possibility whatsoever of eliminating, through some kind of revolutionary transformation of the social order, the fundamental conflicts which had manifested themselves.[10] He viewed the strategy proposed by Marx—namely, a socialist revolution through which the masses would liberate themselves from their "alienation"—as inapplicable in every respect. On the contrary, a socialist revolution that entailed the expropriation of the means of production and its control by a class of state functionaries—the only form of socialist economy that to Weber's mind presented any chance for survival—would only exacerbate the existing problems, since it would advance even further the universal tendency of the bureaucratization of all life relations, including those of the economic sphere.

SOCIALISM AS CAPITALISM WORSENED

Max Weber's criticism of socialist theories does not mean that he was satisfied with contemporary social conditions under capitalism. To be sure, he did not consider the situation of the workers to be as hopeless as Marx had claimed it was, and regardless of this, he viewed as highly problematic Marx's proposals concerning how the workers were to be helped. His principal argument has already been touched upon: a socialization of the means of production would in no case bring the class struggle to an end because it would change only the composition of the "positively privileged classes," which control the key positions in the economy, without improving significantly the lot of the workers as such. Worse still, the workers would henceforth be subjected to the all-powerful control of anonymous government bureaucracies, far more powerful than a multitude of private entrepreneurs, who, among other things, would have to figure upon government intervention in the case of serious class conflict:

While now the governmental-political and the private business bureaucracies (the cartels, banks and giant firms) stand alongside one another as separate entities, and one can therefore always hold the political power in check with the economic, then both bureaucracies would be a single body with united interests and be no longer controllable at all.[11]

The question arises of how Weber imagined the assertion of the sphere of individual personality under conditions such as those created by capitalism and its great ally, modern bureaucracy, or in other words, how the foreseen, long-term, dehumanizing tendencies of the modern industrial system might be counteracted.[12] At first glance, his answer is paradoxical. Starting from the conviction that there can be no simple solution to this problem and that a nationalization of the means of production would only worsen the situation, he inclined toward making the best of the capitalist system rather than eliminating it.[13] His view was that it was essential above all else to strengthen the dynamic elements within the capitalist system in every conceivable way. Therefore he defended a capitalist system of liberal character, one that guaranteed a maximum of free competition on the economic as well as the social level. Not a stagnating, but an expanding capitalist system with a high degree of social mobility was his ideal. Under such conditions, he thought, the greatest possible emancipation of the working classes would also be attainable.

From this perspective, Weber considered two things to be necessary: first, strengthening of the dynamic factors within the capitalist economy itself and not the furtherance of bureaucratization through socialist measures; second, the creation of a truly democratic system, in which all social groups would be given the opportunity of vigorously representing their social and economic interests within the limits of the legal system. Weber readily granted Robert Michels that this proposed solution left much to be desired. But he added that it would be, assuming its eventual attainment, "not such a small thing."[14]

In point of fact, this alternative position is not free of problems or contradictions. On one hand, Weber counted upon the dynamic effects of free competition in the economic as in the general societal realm, while on the other, he viewed the constant growth of cartels, trusts, and other monopolistic formations apprehensively as typical trail blazers of bureaucratization in the economic sphere. Weber never systematically discussed this aporia of his own alternative. In determining what his standpoint was, we are dependent on the use of comparatively peripheral statements. After 1906 Weber was in doubt as to whether the model he had stood for so firmly—in which conflicts of interest between the working classes and the entrepreneurs were freely fought out with the tools of the trade-union struggle—was not outdated in the face of the development of giant corporations and overpowering employer organizations. He energetically advocated reestablishment, through suitable legislative measures, of an equal footing between the working classes and their unions on the one hand, and the entrepreneurs on the other, in their continual struggle over wages and working conditions. In so doing, of course, the free, spontaneous action of the working classes was to be encumbered with the fewest fetters possible. Therefore, Weber would hear nothing of governmentally established, consolidated unions or arbitration bodies in which the government bureaucracy was involved. Weber's espousal of progressive social politics was on the same plane. This was not for the service of ethical or moral ends, but rather to improve generally the opening position of the working classes in their battle with the entrepreneurs in an epoch of growing entrepreneurial power.[15]

These observations permit generalization. The state should be in some measure a corrective to bureaucratization and petrification processes in the social realm.[16] This was not the least of the reasons for which Weber placed such a high value upon dynamic, future-oriented leadership as well as a proper system for the selection of political leaders. Weber looked primarily to the political realm for a solution to the structural problems first addressed by Marx, and not to any profound changes of the capitalist structure of the economic system as such. In this connection, his advocacy of plebiscitary leadership democracy with a charismatic element deserves notice.[17]

PLEBISCITARIAN DEMOCRACY

Weber was convinced that, given the social conditions that emerged in the advanced industrial societies of the West, the classical liberal ideas had largely lost their concrete power of expression or, at least, their unequivocal meaning. Thus, he believed that a revival of liberalism could not just fall back upon the classical liberal theory of human rights. It was necessary to interpret them anew in relation to the concrete social conditions of late capitalist industrial societies.

According to Weber, if democratization was to have a precise meaning at all, it could be only that of "a minimization of the power of the civil servants in favor of the most 'direct' rule of the 'demos' that was possible, and in practice that means the rule of its party leaders."[18] Thus, Weber wanted to reformulate the classical liberal demand for the self-determination of the people to mean the right of the people to choose their own leaders in a formally free way, together with institutional arrangements that guaranteed the resignation or replacement of the leaders whenever they had lost the trust of the masses.

Through the use of their personal charisma and—in the positive sense of the word—their demagogic capabilities, the leaders procured for themselves a following from among the people whom they needed in order to carry out their own personal goals. Throughout this process the people play a merely passive role. For Weber, at least in modern mass states, this personal plebiscitarian form of establishing political authority (and with it individually accountable domination) was simply inevitable.

Only a plebiscitarian democracy, one led by great charismatically qualified politicians who, in contrast to "the outmoded negative democracy which only demanded freedom from the state," could strive for effective rule and for the greatest use of the means of power at their disposal in internal as well as external relations. Only such a democracy would be, according to Weber, capable of implementing a dynamic policy in a society increasingly defined by bureaucratic structures.[19]

As a rule, the "plebiscitary democracy" still makes use of the traditional instruments—that is, parliament and a constitutional system—to ensure that political conflicts are kept within limits. At the same time, however, Weber emphasizes the charisma of the ruling, plebiscitarian great politician who is in a position to go beyond parliament and the administrative machine by appealing directly to the masses. The model of the constitutional state in its parliamentarian variant, which as a type belongs to that of legal domination, is here combined with the charismatic principle of domination by virtue of personal authority, which derives formally (but not substantively) from, and is legitimated by, the consensus of "the ruled."

In light of subsequent experience with fascism, one cannot but find objectionable a theory of democratic domination that accentuates rather emphatically the preeminence of the leading politician in contrast to the mass of citizens. Such a theory has not always been able to prove itself immune to a reinterpretation in an authoritarian, even fascist, direction—as shown, in fact, by the case of Robert Michels, who justified his support of Mussolini and Italian fascism by explicitly referring to Weber's theory of the charismatic politician.[20] Yet, at the same time, one should not overlook the fact that such a thing was certainly not intended by Weber. The strong emphasis upon the principle of democratic leadership in his writings and lectures of 1918–1919, to the neglect, comparatively speaking, of the opposite principle of legitimation of personal authority through plebiscitarian consensus formation, was brought about for the most part by specific circumstances. Presumably, under different historical conditions, Weber would have emphasized other aspects.

This concrete problem notwithstanding, the force of Weber's political thought manifests itself precisely in the fact that he was able to advance with extreme intellectual honesty to the very limits of the thinkable, political positions, theories, and tentative resolutions, in order to reveal their potential consequences in utmost clarity. Irrespective of the time-conditioned nature of many of the solutions he proposed, his position was marked above all by a principled openness *vis-à-vis* alternative solutions modeled in view of new political or social development. In his view, it was the task of science (to which he was committed personally) to provide the information that would make it possible to choose responsibly from among the greatest number of possible options, instead of submitting more or less without any will power to supposedly factual constraints or pursuing "professional politics without a calling,"[21] without long-term social perspectives.[22]

4

Conflicts between Legal and Bureaucratic Systems of Authority

Ronald M. Glassman

Max Weber argued that the conflicts between legal and bureaucratic authority would constitute the central sociopolitical problem of the twentieth century. Legal authority, he held, could eventually be overwhelmed by bureaucratic "necessity" in the modern technocratic state. The need for complex coordinative administration in both the political and economic spheres was and is so compelling that it may overcome all resistances to it. Since the *laissez-faire*, parliamentary form of government cannot in itself provide technocratic administration, the bureaucratic state may eventually take its place. There are several reasons why this should be considered problematic.[1]

THE SEPARATE HISTORIES AND DISTINCTLY DIFFERENT INSTITUTIONAL LINKAGES OF BUREAUCRATIC AND LEGAL AUTHORITY

When one is presented with a category such as legal-bureaucratic authority, one might logically presuppose that legal and bureaucratic forms of organization had a long history of interconnection. Yet, nothing could be farther from the truth. In actuality, the origins and histories of legal authority and bureaucratic organization are completely separate, even antithetical. Bureaucratic administrative organization arose among the agricultural sultanate empires, whereas legal authority arose among the commercial-piratical city-states of the mediterranean.

The Rise of Bureaucratic Authority

Bureaucratic administration arose, as Weber describes, in the ancient empires, in which large-scale political integration and complex economic productive and distributive systems demanded a great deal of coordination.[2] The first administrators of this structure were priests, who governed these early bureaucracies well, but shrouded their activities with mysticism, magic, ideology, and manufactured charisma.[3] They also accompanied their administration with large doses of terror and force, including human sacrifices and cannibalistic ceremonies (held in public view).[4] Succession lines to priestly offices were open to very few individuals, and the priests themselves eventually became an aristocratic leisure class as the wealth of the empires increased. Yet, more and more administrators were needed as the empires became larger, richer, and more diverse.

In the "old world," waves of conquest by less pious, more militarized, herding peoples came, increasing feudal power based upon military might and reducing the need for theocratic coercion. The administrator-priests were gradually replaced by the scholar-priests of the world religions, and as the need for ever more administrators continued, the military kings tended to draw upon other strata to fill the expanding administrative offices.

First, the brightest sons of the peasants, then the sons of the merchants, and finally the sons of the high bureaucrats themselves competed for administrative offices. Thus, a stratum of secular officials responsible for all administration emerged in the ancient empires.[5] Some priestly control, in the form of religious examinations, still remained. Even this eventually passed away, however, and the bureaucratic stratum in some empires developed religious ideologies and ethics of its own. Confucianism is the religion most purely influenced by the bureaucratic stratum.[6]

In China, the bureaucrats were called "Mandarins," in Egypt, "Nomarchs," in Arabia, "Wazirs," and "Nobility of the Cloth" in Toltec Mexico. Whatever their title, these officials came to control the means of production and administration in the ancient empires. They did not come to control the military power, nor the totality of the means of ideological production, which were controlled by the military and priestly aristocracies to which the bureaucrats were attached as functionaries.

In fact, as Weber has pointed out, bureaucratic authority never succeeded in becoming fully legitimated by itself.[7] It always remained linked to kingly or priestly power (or both). Though bureaucracy did not come to stand alone in terms of power or ideology, nevertheless bureaucratic administration did become pervasive, and in periods where kingly, feudal, or priestly powers waned, bureaucrats often came to control empires on their own (though acting through the weakened kingly state).

Bureaucratic administration, then, was linked in its origins to large-scale, centrally directed, despotic political systems. These not only managed the political processes relative to internal order, but also regulated the economic system. Bureaucratic administrators, backed by the traditional authority of divine kingship, the military power of the aristocracy, and the ideological legitimation of the world religions, acted as agents of the kingly court.

All political action beyond the village level was conducted according to the decrees of the kingly court and the rules of administrative procedure of the bureaucratic organization. Disputes were handled by the bureaucrats, either in accordance with local village norms, bureaucratic regulations, or sultanate decrees, depending upon which was the appropriate mode of adjudication in the system. However, in principle, kingly decrees superseded bureaucratic regulations, which in turn superseded village norms whenever these were in conflict.

The bureaucrats administered the economy by overseeing planting and harvesting, directing irrigation and fertilization, managing storehouses where excess crops were kept, collecting taxes (in services, produce, or money), and even by redistributing water, grain, and food from areas of plenty to areas of scarcity. Finally, they directed the massive corvée labor projects initiated by the sultans (or necessitated by economic, military, or political problems). All of this is well known but is being reiterated here in order to remind the reader that bureaucracy, in its origin, was linked to "oriental despotism."[8] Therefore, nothing in the way of legal rules or democratic procedures, collegial authority, or limited power was built into bureaucracy as it emerged in history. Rather, bureaucracy is characterized by a civilizational history of elite decision-making procedures, hierarchical power structures, and sets of rules and regulations which, though fully rational in administrative intent, are of a nondebatable character. All of these characteristics are anti-democratic and authoritarian.

The Rise of Legal Authority

Legal authority arose as a distinct form of legitimation only in the piratical-trading city-states of the mediterranean (of which Greek, Roman, and Phoenician cities made up the majority), and then centuries later, in the emerging commercialized nation-states of Western Europe, from the Renaissance to the present. In fact, the establishment of legal authority in Europe was an ongoing process never fully completed in most of Western Europe until after the Second World War, and has not been completed in Spain even now. The incompleteness of the inculcation of legal authority in Europe is a central problem of world politics today. First, however, we will look more closely at legal authority in its origin.

The critical factor in the breakdown of traditional authority in the ancient world was the rise of merchant-oriented city- states separated from the great agricultural empires and defended by fanatically trained, heavily armed citizens' armies and navies.[9] In agricultural empires, the merchants were originally servants of kings and priests. They were sent on dangerous missions of trade and protected by military escorts. As the fruits of trade came to be valued by the ancient empires, attacks upon tradesmen decreased. As trade increased, the merchants were allowed to keep more wealth for themselves. Their motivation increased, and they eventually developed ratio-nalized trade procedures. Barter gave way to money exchange, and money itself became a desired commodity—not only because of its convertibility into material goods, but also because of its convertibility into power. The merchants created codes of secular law having to do with trade procedures and business contracts. For the first time, law meant something beyond customary norms, kingly decrees, or religious codes.

The secular law of the merchants was significant in that it was supposed to be manipulated to change with changing situations. It was supposed to be rationally discussed and debated and judged on its utility. It was written down, furthermore, in a rational, rather than a mystical, manner.[10] Even where "constitutions" of "founding laws" were surrounded with mythology, ideology, and charismatized father-founders, the laws themselves could still be analyzed, amended, and altered through rational debate.

Armed with this new two-fold mechanism of political action—money and secular law—the merchants sought to extend their political power and economic wealth. They succeeded greatly in the latter, but as Weber has shown, they never succeeded in the ancient empires in increasing their power or status commensurate with their new-found wealth. Then, as Weber asserts in *The City*,[11] an anomalous event occurred in the eastern mediterranean. Independent trading centers were allowed to emerge by the competing empires.[12] From numbers of separated, tiny, independent coastal and island trading communities, Greeks, Phoenicians, and Romans came to dominate the lands of the region. In these settlements, traditional authority waned quickly.

Legal authority has its origin in these trading cities, then, in large measure due to the absence of traditional authority. Divine kingship either never existed (though elective war kingship had) or had disintegrated under the new socioeconomic conditions. World religion also never developed in these military-trading cities as in the empires. Instead, a secular, rational world view (culminating in Greek "science," mathematics, and philosophy) emerged to replace the naturalistic-magical totemic religion of the Greek pastoral period. No organized priesthood—either pagan or world-religious—was institutionalized in these city-states, even though temples and temple gods and goddesses continued to be worshipped. For those for whom the secular, rational world view was deficient as an explanatory ideology of the existential problems of morality, life, and death, cultic sects arose. But these sects never produced either a politically powerful priesthood or a unifying ideology.

No administrative bureaucracy arose in the city-states either, for economic activity was not of the kind that demanded centralized administration. Economic activity was either conducted through military conquest, which resulted in piracy-acquisition of goods and long-term tribute arrangements, or through private enterprise. Ancient trade-capitalism flourished as a market money economy developed. Capitalist farming procedures, in which crop production and distribution were linked to the market and to money profits, were also institutionalized.[13] Corvée labor projects were accomplished through money payments to the poorer classes of the populace, or through slave labor. The slaves were directed and overseen, however, not by a centrally controlled bureaucracy, but by volunteer, tenure-limited citizen-officials, who had the time and money for such activities and were backed by the military organization of the society.

As to this military organization, the mediterranean commercial city-states did not exhibit armies composed of heavily armed aristocrats and lightly armed, poorly trained peasants, but rather armies of heavily armed aristocrats and very well-armed middling citizens. Since the numbers of citizens of a city-state were far smaller than the numbers of peasants of an empire, these citizens had to be better trained and better armed, or the city states would have been wiped out by the adjacent empires. Therefore, the city-states were characterized by fanaticism in warfare training technique.[14]

One of the unintended results of the heavy armament and rigorous training of the citizens was the undermining of the aristocracy. With its military power reduced, relatively speaking, the status of the aristocracy was also reduced. "Hoplite," or citizen-soldiers did not bow down or avert their eyes or tremble before their aristocrats, nor was there a religious orientation which conferred divinity to "royal" clans. The increasing reliance on naval power was a further democratizing factor.[15] Eventually, the aristocracy—along with its political institutions—declined, and political institutions reflecting the power and ideology of the commercial-military citizens (but excluding slaves and women) emerged.

With the money economy expanding along with military conquests, class distinctions based on wealth emerged from among the citizens. Therefore, oligarchic as well as democratic councils and assemblies replaced kingly courts. Officials of limited power and tenure acted as administrators and were linked to the oligarchic and democratic councils. Collegial authority, or the shared authority of equals, exemplified these societies as opposed to the hierarchical authority of the divine kings and landed aristocracy of agricultural society—even though violent conflict between rich and poor citizens erupted. In fact, it was precisely because authority was viewed collegially, and the power and tenure of leaders was strictly limited, that class conflicts arose. That is, the lower and middle classes no longer recognized the traditional claim of the rich and powerful to high leadership and demanded instead: participation as equals in the leadership process, limits on the power and tenure of all leaders, and rational, debatable, amendable rules for political order (i.e., laws).

These laws were originally linked to the trade-capitalist merchant class, which had developed contract law and monetary exchange procedures to replace barter and piracy. Secular, civic law emerged with the commercial class even within agricultural empires, and this kind of law was extended to many spheres of secular civic regulation. World religious ethical codes superseded such laws in most cases of judicial action, however, and world-religious priesthoods predominated in judicial actions. No secular lawyers or judges emerged. Neither legislators nor lawyers nor secular juries existed in the agricultural empires. Priests, bureaucrats, aristocrats, and kings accomplished these functions. Thus, even in the secular sphere, bureaucratic rules and regulations predominated in the ancient empires, so that nothing like legal authority ever developed. The king was above the law—he was divine. World-religious ethical codes were sacred and nondebatable. Bureaucratic rules and regulations simply had to be followed (or the bureaucrat bribed to circumvent them).

In the commercial city-states, on the other hand, secular bodies of citizens—tenure-limited and power-limited—acted in these capacities.[16] Within the commercial-military city-states, the ideology of legal authority was developed to its utmost, along with the institutionalization of law (which replaced traditional rules of order). Ideologies arose to assert the authority of the laws above individuals, whether these were aristocrats, charismatic war heroes, wealthy, wise, or whatever. "Natural law" philosophy was engendered, in which the protection of a citizen's freedom—political, economic, and social—was claimed to be "natural" and "inalienable," and the denial of such rights, "perverse," unnatural, or degenerate, as Aristotle stated it.[17] These natural laws were claimed to supersede any religious, traditional, or other claims that would counteract them. *Constitutions*, or codes of law governing political conduct, emerged, replacing traditional authority with rational assessment of leadership, power, and citizens' rights. Even though these constitutions subsequently took on a hallowed, nearly sacred, and almost "traditional" quality, they remained amendable, debatable, and—in principle—alterable by ongoing rational procedures.

One can see, then, that legal authority, in its origin, was linked to democratic or semi-democratic political institutions, and that, in fact, legal authority itself produced the founding ideology through which "rational" processes of politics could be institutionalized.

The Emergence of Contemporary Legal and Bureaucratic Authority Structures

Bureaucracy, in its ancient form, continued to be linked to the sultanate empires that existed until modern times. Legal authority, on the other hand, declined with the collapse of Greco-Roman civilization and did not reemerge until the rise of the commercial city-states of the Renaissance. Roman law was preserved and studied by the Christian priesthood during the Middle Ages, and many vestiges of Roman law continued to exist as part of the feudal and kingly political systems of the medieval world. "Government by law," however, was hardly central to European feudal political relationships.[18]

As in the ancient world, legal authority was carried in the post-feudal world by a class of commercial, trade-capitalists and by free citizens of cities. These commercial and city classes engaged in revolutionary activity against the feudal classes and the kingship, and wherever they succeeded, after centuries of complicated struggles and shifting alliances, legal authority came to replace feudal-patrimonial traditional authority. Where this occurred, democratic political institutions along with legal authority were established.

These nation-states were also characterized by a *lack* of centralized, professionalized administrative bureaucracies. They relied instead upon tenure-limited, amateur officials for the accomplishment of administrative tasks. As in the early years of the ancient city-states, these citizens were often wealthy men with the time and money for such activities, so that oligarchic tendencies again exhibited themselves. As in the ancient world, economic production and distribution was left to the actions of private citizens. What is significant about the democratic or oligarchic or "mixed" constitutions is that amateur, citizen, tenure-limited administration was one of their hallmarks.[19] In fact, the rise of modern rational bureaucracy does not emerge from these democratic-legal nation-states, but from the patrimonial kingly states which preceded them (and which helped to destroy medieval feudalism).

Just as in the "oriental" world, the rise of the centralized kingly state in "occidental" post-feudal Europe brought with it the emergence of bureaucratic administration. The professional, secular bureaucracy grew through a linkage to the expanding kingly state, as it did in the ancient empires. In France and Spain, Germany and Austria, the bureaucracy grew hand-in-hand with the expansion of the power of the kingly state. It is no wonder that Weber, having observed the Prussian state, first described and analyzed bureaucratic organization and ideology, while British political scientists and economists make no mention of them as political institutions and French political and social scientists simply described them as part of the "*ancien régime*," which they believed would soon be destroyed. Because the history of the world was then dramatically altered by the industrial revolution, it seemed that the need for bureaucratic administration of the economy and polity was not necessary and that bureaucracy was truly an artifact of kingly-despotic regimes.

Yet—with Weberian irony—the remarkable success of capitalist industrialism and of the political institutions carried by the commercial, urban, and industrial classes eventually began to diminish and the administrative needs of the new large-scale, complex nation-states began to increase. Just as ancient, republican Rome had to develop some form of centralized administration in order to coordinate its vast empire, so England, Holland, and the United States—those nations most linked to legal authority and most free of bureaucratic administration—had to develop some form of centralized rationalized administration to coordinate their vast commercial-industrial "empires."

England eventually developed its exemplary civil service system, while the United States, the most commercial, most law-oriented of modern nations (with hardly a vestige of feudal-kingly tradition outside of the South), resisted (and continues to resist) even the civil service bureaucratization which England finally established. It is significant that the nations most linked to law and democracy are the nations in which bureaucracy was longest absent and most grudgingly institutionalized. In England, even after the establishment of the civil service, patrician oligarchic amateurs (members of the commercially oriented gentry class) continued to dominate the civil service, rather than professional bureaucrats. In the United States to this day, bureaucracy is feared and despised as antithetical to citizens' freedoms and legal-democratic political processes.[20] In Germany and France, in which the kingly state and the feudal-aristocratic classes and ideologies remained strong—as they did in Russia—bureaucratic administration was developed earlier and more fully.

CONFLICTS BETWEEN LEGAL AND BUREAUCRATIC AUTHORITY

It should now be clear that *legal-bureaucratic* authority, as it has emerged in the contemporary world, represents not a simple synthesis but a complex, conflicting set of institutional processes and ideologies. Whether legal-bureaucratic authority can survive as a type of authority at all is a question we should look at closely, as Weber urged (and warned).

Legal Rationality

Laws vs. Administrative Rules and Regulations. The political result of legal authority is to establish as central a set of rational processes of *legitimation.* Under a system of legal authority, government by law replaces familial and traditional procedures of government, clan justice, kadi-justice (religious courts),[21] the king's justice, and bureaucratic or administrative justice.[22]

The most significant aspect of secular civil law, even where constitutionalism is surrounded by ideology, is that it is open to change and subject to rational debate. Amending and abolishing procedures are institutionalized and encouraged. Furthermore, at least in principle, the breaking of a law by an individual also sets in motion a process of rational debate and evaluation for the determination of guilt, and should guilt be established, for the determination of punishment.

While it is clearly understood that no process of amending or abolishing-norms or world-religious codes existed in traditional societies and that kingly decrees were hardly open to rational debate, it is not as clearly understood in the modern world that bureaucratic rules of administrative procedure are different from laws. Such rules are not open to rational debate. They are created instead by elite cliques in relatively closed sessions. No institutionalized channels for their amendment or revocation exist, and their rationality is not that of the entire political entity, but only of the organization whose hierarchy they support.

This clash between legal procedures (laws) and bureaucratic procedures (regulations or "red tape") is central to the problem. It is extremely difficult to extend the rule of law to bureaucratic organizations because the wall of organizational rules often prevents individuals within bureaucracies from responding to laws at all. The very efficiency of the bureaucracy is related to its rational rules of procedure (regulations). "External" laws may be seen as an impediment to efficiency and a threat to the hierarchical authority structure; therefore, they are resisted.

Political Participation. Under legal authority, rational debate is institutionalized and encouraged as the proper process of decision making. Of course, whether this is a direct or representative process is significant. But even where this is a representative process in a "mass democracy," rational debate at the local level and numerous local and national elections do produce continuing discussion within the population at large, as well as among the representatives themselves.

Whether such debate is actually directed and limited by a corporate-controlled media that establishes the focus and boundaries of the debate, as C. Wright Mills asserts in *The Power Elite*,[23] is crucial—it is also truer than American liberal theorists have been willing to admit. Alternative media of expression do exist, but they have very "small voices." Nonetheless, in nations where legal rationality exists, the idea of debate as open to, or even incumbent upon, all citizens also exists. Where legal rationality does not exist, the controversy over whether debate is free or controlled never arises, for debate is repressed directly.

In the same vein, whether the representative process in mass democracies actually produces popular participation in political decisions has been much debated, not only currently, but at least since the days of Hume and Rousseau.[24] Whether mass representative democracy is truly participatory, or whether it is overinfluenced by the rich to produce a "veiled oligarchy," as Marx asserted, is obviously a critical issue for investigation.[25] In the present context, however, it is enough to note that where legal rationality exists, direct and representative participation are cherished as ideals to be maintained at all costs.

In its decision-making process, by contrast, bureaucratic rationality prohibits open debate as administratively inefficient and disruptive to the long-term planning of the bureaucratic organization. It is interesting to note in this regard that even Alexander Solzhenitsyn, who fought so hard for free speech and other basic rights in the Soviet Union, has criticized lawful-parliamentary procedure as being too chaotic and inefficient.[26] Apparently, life in a huge bureaucracy affects even those so oppressed by it as to risk their lives for civil liberties. That reactions like those of Solzhenitsyn are not atypical is, of course, one of our major concerns.

The Limitation of Power and Tenure of Leaders. Under a system of legal authority, limitations on the power and tenure of political leaders are institutionalized. The recall of leaders who are poorly evaluated, or who break the law, is also institutionalized, through electoral or court procedures. Furthermore, either "amateurs" or lawyers (at least semi-independent professionals) are preferred as office holders.

Conversely, few limitations are placed on bureaucratic administrators. Life tenure replaces limited tenure, and professionally trained specialists are logically preferred.

Rational Succession Procedures. Since tenure of office is limited in legal-democratic societies, the procedure for leadership succession occurs constantly and therefore has to be rationalized. Although powerful groups and classes have often sought to appropriate both access to office and the electoral process itself, thus far they have always failed to overcome the ideology of legal authority for an extended period of time.

Certainly, attempts to control this rational electoral procedure and influence the incumbents continues, not only by powerful groups, but also by any organized groups in society. Indeed, this is one of the bases for action organization in legal-democratic societies. Again, whether certain power-groups (e.g., the rich) succeed in overinfluencing the electoral process and the incumbents of office is an important question for debate between Marxists and liberals. It is not insignificant that bureaucrats can attempt to form pressure groups to assert their own ends within the electoral structure.

By contrast, however, electoral succession procedures are entirely missing from bureaucracies. Leadership and succession are determined through a combination of expertise and purely "Machiavellian" or uncontrolled power and manipulation techniques.

Access to Leadership Offices. Within a system of legal authority, access to all political leadership roles may be open to all citizens or legally limited to a specific class of citizens. Technically, legally closed leadership offices can be established. For instance, property and educational qualifications have existed and still may exist (e.g., county attorney). These, however, have never lasted as general restrictions over an extended period in a society that continues to claim a legal-rational base because the logic of legal rationality, with its open debate and election procedures, leads away from elitist, closed, hereditary politics—at least in principle if not always in fact, and at least procedurally, if not substantively.

In bureaucracies, access to leadership offices is quite different from that of legal authority, though they do exhibit the apparent similarity of providing open access to leadership roles. Open access in bureaucracies, however, is not linked to the natural-law ideology of equality before the law of all individuals or the duty of "amateur" citizens to participate in the decision-making processes of government and in the leadership offices of the state. In bureaucracies, it is specialization and technical expertise that theoretically leads to the system of open access to leadership offices. Nepotism and aristocracy are eliminated because familial and old class ties do not guarantee the kind of expertise demanded by bureaucracies for their proper administrative and technocratic functioning. Thus, though open-access leadership roles do exist, they do so within the logic of bureaucratic rationality, rather than legal rationality.

Furthermore, and perhaps even more important, the selection process in bureaucracies is directed by those at the top of the organization. Thus, the democratization of bureaucracies is rarely fully extended, since leadership cliques entrenched at the top direct and limit access to leadership positions. Although the elimination of nepotism is democratizing in its effect, this is accomplished not out of the legal-rational principle of open leadership succession, but because of the technical needs of specialization. A great gulf, then, separates the motives.

The Separation of the State from the Economy. Under a system of legal authority, economic action may be relatively free of state control. This may be a logical rather than historical connection within legal rationality, for the separation of economic from political activity provides an important limitation on political power.[27] Even if the Marxists are correct in arguing that rich capitalists use this separation to control the polity, because this control is indirect and must be veiled where actual oligarchy is illegal, both the influence of the middle and lower classes and the civil liberties of all are maintained.

The bureaucratization of the economy, alternatively, leads to administrative centralization and the linking of economy and polity. The power of political leaders can be greatly enhanced by this, since the power of the state—its military and policing power—is now joined to the power of the economy—the control of the necessities of life sustenance. Whether the legal limitation of power and tenure can be extended over a bureaucratized, centralized, state-directed economy is not yet known. Democratic-socialists believe that it is possible.[28] What is clear is that the basis for law in the economic sphere—contract law—may be superseded by bureaucratic rules and regulations in such systems. One of the historic underpinnings of legal authority is thus weakened.

Bureaucratic Rationality

Bureaucratic rationality is linked to and evoked by administrative and

large-scale organizational efficiency and stability over long periods of time
(in the ideal-typical case).

Specialized Experts vs. Amateur Officials and Lawyers. Whereas legal
rationality encourages amateurism and mass involvement, with the only
essential specialists being lawyers themselves, bureaucratic rationality demands the installation of specialized experts at every level of its organizational structure. Where lawyers are retained, the intent is frequently to use
their expertise in the law to frustrate the effects of the law.

Hierarchy vs. Collegiality. Most critically, a hierarchical form of authority, with power emanating from the top down and with strong authoritar-
ian-clique tendencies at the top, replaces the collegial-democratic,
limited-power, structure of legal authority.

The Power Elite vs. Citizens' Participation. Decision making is not a
process open to debate, persuasion, or even mass manipulation; rather, it is
shrouded in secrecy, emanating from the top—the elite—of the hierarchy.
Decisions are not debatable and are closed to the majority below. Suggestions may be solicited from the lower ranks and expected from the middle
levels of the hierarchy. Such input is in fact necessary if those at the top of the
hierarchy are to make efficient long-term decisions. This input, however, can
be accepted or rejected at the will of those at the top and can be used by those
at the top to regulate movement within the hierarchy. In the ideal-typical case
this is the exact opposite of citizens evaluating a candidate on the basis of his
or her proposals for action. The superficial similarity of these two types (i.e.,
the candidate may also draw upon the technical expertise of a staff) should
not obscure this fundamental difference in the locus of ultimate decision
making. This difference of locus still pertains even if the electorate is in-
tentionally misinformed by the candidate.

The Power Elite vs. the Limitation of Power. No institutionalized limitation of leadership powers exists in bureaucracy, nor can limits be forced
upon leaders by those below. No institutionalized channels of limitation or
recall exist either in hierarchical authority structures. Leaders are not accountable to, or removable by, those at lower levels, but are checked only by
others in the power clique at the top—power against power, maneuver
against maneuver, manipulation against manipulation.

Power Struggle vs. Rational Electoral Procedures. One of the great anom-
alies of bureaucratic "rationality" is that rational succession rules do not
exist for the top leadership positions in bureaucracies. Clearly, rational
criteria for promotion and hiring exist at all levels of bureaucratic organization except at the top. Of course, throughout the hierarchy, promotion is
often based on "politicking" which, though stripped of direct coercive power
in most cases, is nonetheless psychosocially ruthless, as Robert Jackall will
detail subsequently. By contrast, with the electoral judgment of the populace
placed between combatants for leadership positions in legal rationality (even
though people can be manipulated by demagogues and media), the simple
fact that leaders must take their struggle to the people and find grounds on

which to manipulate them lessens the immensity of total bureaucratic domination. As venal as the senators of Rome may have appeared in their day, the emperors after Augustus—who did not have to go to the people for affirmation—made them look like angels of grace.

Within bureaucracies, then, qualifications for high-level succession are based less on technical assets (specialization) and more on power plays. Only minimal specialized expertise is demanded of those at the top (thus the ease of circulation of elites). Beyond this, succession to high bureaucratic posts is determined purely by maneuvering. The lack of specialized qualifications for top levels of control in bureaucracies is a clearly irrational element in this structure of domination. It may, in fact, be the greatest flaw in bureaucratic organization. Certainly it is the hardest to alter. It is also a regression from the rational succession procedures of legal authority.

If the bureaucracy is linked to the political state and top leaders have the coercive power of the state at their disposal, then of course the Machiavellian maneuvering becomes not merely a power play where losers drop out, but a coercive struggle where losers are tortured and murdered along with their families and followers. Byzantine politics replaces the "executive suite" when bureaucracy and the state are synonymous. In neither case do legal-rational succession procedures operate.

Life Tenure vs. Limited Tenure. The whole Enlightenment and *polis* tradition is negated by bureaucratic life tenure. Accountability and limitation are removed, and a whole system of "little dictators" is created in lieu of democratic governing processes.

The Repression of Charisma vs. the Institutionalization of Electoral Charisma. Charismatic leadership is inhibited, rejected, and expelled under bureaucratic authority. Under legal authority charismatic leadership is not necessary. At the same time, its own institutionalized procedures allow for the expression of charisma in its safest and most controllable form—elections. Weber saw charismatic plebiscitarian democracy as a possible political salvation for the modern legal-bureaucratic state. Unfortunately, there are problems within this solution that Weber did not foresee.[29]

Again, bureaucratic rationality absolutely opposes charismatic leadership because charismatic leaders by their very definition tend to break people loose from the regulations, institutions, and ideologies of the organizational and societal structures within which they operate. This is too threatening for bureaucrats to handle. They prefer stability and longevity to dynamic and dramatic success; indeed, in bureaucracy success is often redefined in terms of mere persistence. The bureaucratic army prefers the Eisenhowers to the Pattons; the bureaucratic corporation prefers the MacNamaras to the Iacoccas. Within legal rationality, though no president is above the law, the populace and, in some cases, their representatives, cherish charismatic leaders—like Washington, Roosevelt, Disraeli, and Churchill—while denigrating mundane leaders—like Polk, Coolidge, Gaitskill, and Heath.

Organizational Rules vs. Laws. In bureaucracies, it is the organization itself that makes the rules. The people and their representatives make the laws under a system of legal authority. Of course, organized political interest groups linked to class, ethnic, reference, and other power strata intervene between individuals and their representatives in the law-making process. But laws remain open to public discussion. They can be changed, newly initiated, amended, and continually scrutinized. Bureaucratic rules, on the other hand are made in secrecy, are not subject to debate, and are not open to alteration (except by the power elite of the bureaucratic organization itself). Systems of appeal, or grievance procedures, do exist in some bureaucracies, but the judges and juries of such appeals, as Friedman explains, are members of the organizational hierarchy itself. A neutral, rational judgment, therefore, is difficult to achieve.

Certainly, bureaucratic regulations can be appealed before the legal rationality of the court systems, and in such cases the rationality of law clashes head on with the rationality of administration. However—and this highlights the conflict between these two types of rationality—where this has occurred, bureaucratic organizations have exhibited a remarkable disregard for the decisions of law courts when such decisions go against them and demand the alteration of their rules or procedures.[30] The rationality of law courts and the protection of citizens' rights are usually viewed by bureaucratic organizations as threats to their efficiency and stability. Whether such bureaucracies are public or private matters little in terms of their antagonism to legal authority. The multinational corporation presents a special case of this problem, inasmuch as it is sometimes difficult in this organization's extensive world to determine what court actually has legal jurisdiction over corporate regulations. Furthermore, within governmental structures themselves, the tendency of bureaucracies to resist electoral leadership and inhibit the executive task of carrying out enacted laws has been increasing over the years (as Kenneth O'Reilly indicates in Chapter 8).[31]

CONCLUSION

Although bureaucracy is procedurally and organizationally rational, it operates politically in a highly irrational manner. It discourages participation, lives on secrecy, prevents the limitation of power, inhibits checks on and recall of leaders, creates power hierarchies, and destroys individualism and collegiality. It produces not consent but acquiescence.[32] So today, as in ancient Rome, increasing formal rationality does not entail increasing substantive rationality; indeed, greater and greater irrationality may well be the result.[33]

The establishment of bureaucratic authority tends to undermine legal authority precisely because it inhibits the rational processes of legitimation made central by legal authority. Legal authority establishes rational procedures for consent-getting—i.e., participation, limitation, and law—and allows for the expression of charismatic leadership (constraining the irrational bond between the charismatic leader and the populace within the restrictions of constitutional law).

Bureaucratic authority leans on the irrational processes of consent-getting—such as institutional charisma, office charisma, and manufactured charisma, cooptation, and organizational rules and regulations. Bureaucracies sometimes lean on forms of coercion as well where other processes fail to produce acquiescent consent. Blackballing, blacklisting—even physical and psychological violence—may be resorted to by bureaucratic leaders against individuals who challenge the organization.

It is possible, given this latter analysis, that the ongoing bureaucratization of the economy, the polity, and the social service sphere could undermine legal authority entirely. It was Weber's hope that this would not occur, that a generation of scholars and statesmen would devote themselves to this problem and find solutions for it. In this spirit of analysis and application, the remainder of this book seeks to take up the challenge that Weber prophetically laid down.

PART II

Authoritarian Tendencies

5

Social Rights in the Welfare State: The Contrast between Adjudication and Administration in the United States

Kathi V. Friedman

Max Weber delineates two ideal-typical constructs to account for the protection of persons by persons and the protection of rights by law: administration and adjudication. These are alternative social structural modes through which political authority is enforced. The difference between them, according to Weber, is that *administration* is an arrangement in which only the political authority has rights; the ruled do not. *Adjudication*, however, is an arrangement in which the right of the political authority is limited, however rudimentarily, by the rights of subjects.

Weber recognized that the transition is gradual from the case in which a right exists to one in which "the legally secured interest of a party is but the 'reflex' of a 'regulation' and where the party does not possess a 'right' in the strict sense."[1] Weber here posits a correspondence between empirical reality and an analytic continuum for ranking the status of a benefit. At one end of the continuum is the *right*, created by legislation and amenable to adjudication in regular courts of law. At the other end is the *gratuity*, enjoyed by dint of the discretion of the one granting it. The benefit is gratuitous in the eyes of the benefactor: one dispenses the benefit not from legal obligation, but from personal motive. The benefit, in turn, is but a contingency from the standpoint of the beneficiary, who usually must "curry favor" or otherwise serve, please, or obey his patron. Because the benefit enjoyed stems purely from the discretion of the one bestowing it, there exists no right of appeal should the giver, for whatever reason, decide to discontinue providing the gratuity. The "administrative principle" and the "adjudicative principle," therefore, form two poles of a continuum, referring respectively to the chances of an individual to enjoy benefits either by discretion of the benefactor (i.e., gratuitously) or by law that guarantees the right to them (i.e., rightfully).

Following Weber, I accept the essentially antithetical character of ad-ministration in its relationship to adjudication. The latter involves the sub-jection of official conduct to a more general legal code. Laws that provide the prospect of appeal are thus the *sine qua non* of adjudication. Weber's ideal type of "administration," by contrast, refers to authoritative decision making unencumbered by a larger framework of legality. Here decisions are made on a case-to-case basis according to expediency or some other principle useful to the purposes of the organization or official. The absence of rules allowing for appeals to be made precludes the possibility that a claimant might become an "appellant." Instead, the individual is confronted with the very real possibility of arbitrary official decisions.

It is evident that modern rulership could not be carried out without vast apparatuses of administration, including administrative adjudication. This incontrovertible fact may be termed "the administrative imperative." If administration, including administrative adjudication is imperative, then a true dilemma exists from the standpoint of Western welfare regimes and their commitment to the tradition of individual rights. That dilemma lies squarely upon the fact that unless the applicant (who is also a "citizen" under the rule of law) has some independent authority to whom he can appeal in the event that his claim is turned down under administrative adjudication procedures, the agency has exercised all three functions of rule—legislative, executive, and judicial—over him. Analytically, this is the trademark of *premodern* rulership—i.e., administration as domination—and it under-mines the legitimacy of the redistributions made in the name of the welfare state. It compromises the notion of the supremacy of the law, the cornerstone of which is the individual's right of appeal to an independent judicial author-ity once an "enforcing" arm of the regime has restrained or otherwise exercised authority over him. The specters of "authoritarianism," "tyr-anny," "totalitarianism," "despotism," and the like are invariably raised.

Accordingly, my argument will be that Western regimes gain legitimacy when they make redistributions in the form of social rights, that is, within the framework of national citizenship, itself protected by the rule of law. By contrast, contemporary Western regimes do not gain legitimacy, and indeed, suffer "backlashes" as well as other criticisms, when they devolve largesse onto the citizenry in any manner that approximates patrimonial or premod-ern gratuitousness.

SOCIAL RIGHTS VS. WELFARE ENTITLEMENTS

When our society is agreed that a benefit is "rightful," such as a retirement supplement or pension, that benefit is institutionalized clearly and unequivo-cally. Part of the institutionalization of such a benefit is the right of ultimate appeal through the regular civil court system. The case is thus eligible for "adjudication."

When, by contrast, our society is ambivalently committed to the claim of recipients to certain types of benefits, those benefits are institutionalized more tenuously. The institutionalization of such benefits—food stamps, general relief, or low-income housing, for example—remains essentially within the administrative mode of governance. At the discretion of directives promulgated by the executive agency in charge, both the content of the benefit as well as eligibility criteria are more open to variation than in the case of "rightful" privileges. Appeal of agency staff decisions is made by potential beneficiaries through administrative channels within the agency only. The case is subject primarily to "administrative remedy" and not, under normal circumstances, to adjudication through the regular courts of law. Hence, the distinction is drawn between the adjudicative and the administrative modes of institutionalizing benefits in the welfare state.

In *Legitimation of Social Rights*, I referred to adjudicable benefits as "social rights," and to administratively conditioned benefits as "entitlements." This usage of "entitlements" differs from the standard use of the term to refer to a broad range of benefits under the welfare state, regardless of their mode of institutionalization .

One question immediately arises from this distinction: under what conditions does our society, acting through its welfare state legislation, create social rights to benefits, rather than the more tenuous entitlements to them? Social rights are created when the reason for which the recipient population would be receiving the benefit is deemed highly justified. For example, retirees were among the earliest "rightful" beneficiaries of the social rights of welfare states as they emerged throughout Western Europe and North America during the twentieth century.

We all hope to live long enough to retire. If we do, we want income security in exchange for the contribution we made to society during our working years. To strengthen the principle of income security for our society's aged citizens, Title II of the 1935 Social Security Act ushered in the welfare state in the United States by making Old Age and Survivors Insurance (i.e., retirement supplements) a right. Administrative determination of eligibility was—in contrast to the entitlement programs to be created in the future—virtually nil. Retirees needed only to have met certain nationally uniform standards of age and length of service in the work force during which they had paid into the Social Security system. Uniform standards were also applied in determining benefit levels. From the outset, claimants had clear rights to these benefits.

In the same vein, Title III of the 1935 Social Security Act institutionalized the right to unemployment compensation. Again, there is a high degree of legitimacy attached to the reason for which such a claim would be made: sudden and blameless job loss. The deservingness of a worker who is precipitously jettisoned from the labor force is beyond question.

When, however, the reason for claiming a benefit is not completely defensible in the collective view of society, the institutions guarding the claim are more tenuous. These claims are institutionalized as entitlements (as I am using the term). The United States' food stamp program is a case in point.

The 1964 Food Stamp Act was a first step toward entitling Americans to a minimum level of nutrition. Under the terms of the Act, the federal government set the benefit levels, but the state governments had authority to determine eligibility criteria for beneficiaries. Also, states had discretion to decide if they even wished to offer the food stamp program to their residents. Such discretion is characteristic only of entitlement programs, never of social rights, which are "universal." In any case, the 1977 Food Stamp Act and its ensuing amendments have gone much further than the 1964 legislation toward entitling Americans to a minimum standard of nutrition. Eligibility criteria are now nationally uniform, and if states offer the program in one locality, they must offer it throughout the state.

Several factors circumscribe the legitimacy of claims to entitlements, making these claims more tenuous than claims to social rights. First, there is still a tendency in the United States to "blame the victim" for his or her deprived circumstances. We resent the needs of the needy. Second, entitlement programs are not self-financing; rather, they are paid from general tax revenues. Third, in the case of food stamps, the program emerged as a new version of the Food (surplus commodity) Distribution Program initiated during the Depression. As such, considerations such as the United States Department of Agriculture's policies involving farm price supports and the costs of storing surplus food entered into the impetus for creating the food stamp program. These three factors—questionable deservingness of recipients, public financing of the program, and program motives unrelated to a rationale justifying citizens' claims to benefits—are not elements of which legitimate claims are made. Snakes and snails and puppy dog tails do not add up to adjudicable social rights.

Unquestionably, the method by which a program is financed is one of the most crucial indicators separating entitlements from rights. This is particularly true in the United States' welfare system. Benefits that are social rights are paid for entirely by beneficiaries and other actors (such as employers) in the private sector. Entitlements, by contrast, are always publicly financed, whether by federal, state, or local tax dollars.

Indeed, the rationale for making retirement supplements and unemployment insurance "rightful" under the terms of the United States Social Security Act was that the financing of them was actuarial and was carried out through the payroll tax on both employees and their employers. That is, moneys paid in covered benefits paid out, and no general public funds were involved. There was thus a straightforward rationale that citizens had legitimate social rights to benefits for which they had already paid through an earmarked tax on their earnings. Benefits were "earned."

By contrast, the financing of the food stamp program manifests its relationship to general revenues through appropriations bills passed each year by Congress. Program benefit levels are subject to variation according to the amount of money appropriated for that year. This is similarly true for all entitlement programs subject to annual appropriations of public moneys: the school lunch program, housing subsidies, student loans, weatherization assistance, and the like. And, of course, such programs may be completely eliminated or drastically curtailed simply by failure to appropriate funds for them, depending upon the economic or political climate that year.

In *Legitimation of Social Rights* I anticipated the type of furor that would arise, and the machinations that would have to transpire, should social rights be curtailed. We can compare the relative simplicity of using appropriations bills to cut entitlements as the Reagan administration has done, with the elaborate procedures that were used to raise the retirement age for Social Security recipients, cut their benefit levels, and finally, tax a portion of their Social Security income. Retirement supplements have such legitimacy as "social rights" owing to the solid rationale through which they were brought into existence—that even the most elaborate of procedures and the best of justifications for tampering with them have still left the impression that rights have been abrogated. Time and again President Reagan was assailed on this issue, largely by persons who supported his policies on entitlement benefits. These events illustrate particularly well the ultimate meaning of the distinction between entitlements to benefits and social rights to them.

In sum, statutes that create rights to benefits also must delegate authority to administrative agencies to carry out these statutes (e.g., the Social Security Administration). But these agencies have far less discretion in interpreting such statutes than do the agencies that implement legislation that authorizes entitlements. If remedies applied by agencies charged with distributing social rights are unsatisfactory to claimants, the road to appeal through regular courts of law is relatively open. In the case of remedies applied to the granting of entitlements, this is not the case.

Both administratively conditioned entitlements and adjudicable social rights are but two points on a continuum that runs from purely discretionary gratuities to legally secured social rights. In Western societies this may be traced historically from the charity of the medieval era (before the birth of the modern state) to the advanced institutions of the welfare state: entitlements and social rights. This movement may be treated in terms of Weber's concepts of the rationalization of law.

Civil, statute, and administrative law have all undergone rationalization from the medieval era to the present. Social rights fall within the purview of rationalized civil or statute law. Entitlements fall within the ambit of rationalized administrative law. The precursor of today's rationalized administrative law was the completely discretionary, word-of-mouth "reglementation" of patrimonial administrators. We have come a long way toward the rationalization of reglementations into modern entitlements.

Two aspects of the rationalization of contemporary administrative law are legalization and judicialization. As it pertains to the functioning of administrative agencies today, *legalization* refers to the degree to which an agency uses definite rules and standards when agency staff make a determination on a case. *Judicialization* refers to the degree to which determinations made by agency staff are open to appeal. Accordingly, entitlements are the modernized form of charity or gratuitousness, stripped of its discretionary and personalized character. From this standpoint, entitlements are a genuine institutional breakthrough compared to earlier forms of social assistance. Despite their tenuousness compared to social rights, entitlements need not be viewed with condescension. The impartial and impersonal nature of their availability to eligible claimants are two aspects of their rationalized character.

Nevertheless, one issue of constant debate concerning claims to the benefits of the welfare state revolves around whether entitlements should be elevated to the status of social rights. This is not the actual vocabulary in which the question is posed, of course, but it is the underlying issue. The question is: How "rightful" —i.e., how institutionally irreversible—should a benefit be? The key word here is *should*. It touches upon two points: a society's values relative to its poor and needy, and a society's financial capacity to underwrite the costs of the benefits.

This twofold issue may be considered at length in both philosophical and practical terms. At rock bottom, however, is the matter of costs. Since the scope to create benefits is theoretically limitless, by what criteria can such scope be closed? By what standards is it decided what the benefit levels should be, who is eligible for benefits, and according to what justifications?

First, costs can be held down by making eligibility criteria more stringent. Since the terms of entitlement programs guarantee that all eligible claimants must receive benefits if they apply for them, setting the eligibility criteria is the first gateway to cost control. The chief factors that have traditionally been accorded legitimacy in eligibility claims have been illness, age (whether too young or too old to work), disability, or inescapable responsibilities to others that have kept one from normal labor force participation.

Once the values of a society have been applied to legitimize which categories of people are eligible to participate in entitlement programs, a second device is used to hold costs down. This device is a "means test"—a standard against which a claimant's assets (means) are measured. If a claimant's income and possessions fall below a certain level, she or he is eligible for the entitlement. Social rights, by contrast, are "universal," not "means tested." That is, eligibility extends to all members of a specified category, irrespective of their assets. Even multimillionaires may collect Social Security benefits if they have paid into the system. The justification for this is inherent in the program.

FROM WELFARE STATE TO WELFARE SOCIETY

In concluding this brief discussion of the distinction between the adjudication of social rights and the administration of entitlements, I would like to make a few comments on the larger context within which this analysis might profitably be viewed: namely, the welfare state came into being first and foremost as an institutional response to the failure of the market to allocate income to individuals in society for their labor force participation. The welfare state is a set of social values that have been concretized in governmental institutions that assume responsibility for placing a floor below which citizens need not fall in terms of income security, nutrition, health, housing needs, and certain social services. The administration of this extensive "floor" has been partly responsible for the issues raised in this book: the imperatives of bureaucracy as they affect the principles of democracy and socialism. Many of the problems surrounding the inherently authoritarian character of administration could be eliminated by reducing the endless need for citizens to interact with bureaucracies to maintain a credible standard of living.

In this respect, there are at least two schools of thought on the meaning and value of the welfare state. On the one hand, the welfare state may be viewed as a desirable way to equalize both opportunities and income for individuals in society. From this standpoint, its vast administrative apparatus should be retained, but its functioning should be improved in order to bring about greater effectiveness in reaching social equality. Improvements should similarly revolve around reducing undue authoritarian administration over individuals claiming benefits.

On the other hand, it should be remembered that the welfare state historically came into being on a limited basis to alleviate the worst outcomes of economic dislocations within the labor force.[2] Expanding the welfare state and making it permanent has been tantamount to admitting that our economy cannot—and will never be able to—provide sufficient opportunity for individuals to sustain themselves adequately through participation in the labor force. If the need for a welfare state is closely allied to economic failure to promote and distribute wealth through the use of citizen talent, then the welfare state must necessarily advance along a collision course with decreased governmental tax revenues to sustain rising claims to benefits. Each percentage point rise in the unemployment rate costs approximately twenty-five billion dollars in lost tax revenues and added expenditures for income transfers and services. To offset this loss, there has been a reduction in entitlement programs, leaving people increasingly vulnerable as the economy worsens.

From this vantage point, the welfare state may be viewed as a self-limiting phenomenon whose high-water mark has been reached (and is starting to recede). At this writing fully 42 percent of the United States' budget goes to direct income transfers to individuals. Even so, the United States is considered a "welfare laggard" relative to other Western nations. The problem is that no "follow up" strategy was ever conceived or anticipated by policymakers in the United States or other Western nations; they simply expanded the welfare state, only to prune its growth coldly once it became financially unwieldy.

In a forthcoming volume—*Beyond the Welfare State:Institution-Building for the Twenty-first Century*—I will be treating the transition from the welfare state to the welfare society as a positive response to our current dilemma. The institutions of the welfare society will guarantee individuals the opportunity to develop and market their talents for compensation that provides a reasonable standard of living throughout the life cycle. Reinstitutionalizing society to permit individuals the chance to direct their own fortunes should substantially reduce the need for reliance upon administrative apparatuses, as these harken to shifting political winds and unanticipated economic realities.

Specifically, the reinstitutionalization of "work" will be the chief task of the twenty-first century. At issue will be the way individuals in American society are connected to one another through "the division of labor." As Emile Durkheim argued in 1890, it is the quality of the division of labor that conditions social integration.[3] Marx would not disagree with this analytic point. A vast welfare state is synonymous with unresolved problems within the division of labor. No society can consider itself socially integrated if millions of its members are excluded from the labor force and are increasingly reliant on stopgap programs to maintain themselves in an erratic economy.

The unemployment rate in the United States has ratcheted up from under 4 percent in the late 1960s to over 10 percent in 1983, and is at an "acceptable" 6.7 percent in 1986. Over the long term, we can reasonably expect this to get worse before it gets better. Moreover, it is widely known that official statistics on unemployment seriously underestimate the true extent of un- and under-employment in the United States today.

Unarguably, a redefinition of the issues is needed. Labor force policy has been strictly problem oriented. Just as our health policy has been oriented toward sickness rather than health, so too, our labor force policy has been defined in terms of the reduction of unemployment, not the development and vital exchange of talent among the citizenry. This administrative definition of the situation has created the fragmented and fire-fighting character of the United States' labor force policy. Comprehensiveness and foresight have been lacking. Program proliferation of the welfare state—such as Trade Adjustment Assistance, Federal Supplemental Compensation (i.e., extended unemployment benefits), and the like—bespeaks a definition of beneficiaries as merely an available labor pool, or as a herd of potential consumers whose purchasing power must be bolstered, not as creators or contributors. While these programs are to be commended for keeping Americans from descending into a state of complete expendability to the ongoing life and work of their society, they nevertheless show no insight into the profound changes surrounding "work."

Some of these changes are the United States' new positioning within the international division of labor, the increasing capacity to use robots and computers, and the enormous demographic changes (age, gender, racial and ethnic composition) that will continue to take place in the United States. These factors guarantee that a new definition of work and the conditions of its compensation are on the horizon, if not on the national agenda. The future of work must be structured with social vision.

We are now at a point in human history when "work" in the most pejorative sense of the term can be drastically reduced in advanced techno- logical societies. Over and over it has been observed that our shift from a mass industrial society to an information society will carry changes more profound than the nineteenth century shift from an agricultural to an indus- trial society. Technology is rapidly changing the nature of work, but nothing can change the meaning of work and the relationship of people to one another and to their society through it. People still need to be connected to each other through an exchange of what they do. What kind of society the United States becomes will depend on what talents people will exchange, the institutions within which this exchange will take place, and the results of this social exchange in terms of compensation, creativity, and contribution.

If we continue some of our past policies, we will "make work" for people whose jobs no longer exist or who have little skill, or we will retrain people for jobs shortly to disappear. We will do this for the standard reasons: to keep people off the streets and to put money in their pockets so that they can be consumers. If, on the other hand, we recognize that the unthinkable utopian dream is now a concrete, realizable possibility, we will structure the future so that people can discover their "strong suit," educate it, and market it to others for a fair price. In a word, we will base our economy on a thriving exchange of talent for money. Only the present organization of work, in- cluding old assumptions and entrenched habits, prevents our ability to en- vision a well-integrated division of labor—straight ahead as we look into the future.

In the end the ultimate social right is the right to be a contributing member of society. It is the right not to be excluded. This right cannot be created and administered by a welfare state. It cannot be created by a statute and ad- judicated in the regular courts of law. It is a right that goes beyond the problems of bureaucracy versus democracy and socialism. It is an issue that goes to the very heart of a society's values and its willingness to create new institutions to cherish new values. It is a matter of citizens being able to complete themselves through their relationships to one another and to their society. It is nothing less than this right to which tomorrow's citizens have a legitimate claim.[4]

6

The Patient at Peril: Hospital Bureaucracy and Medical Records

Paul L. Rosen

The hospital as a distinctive social institution can be traced historically to the fourth century BCE, a period denoted by the incipient decline of Athenian culture. Throughout its first thousand years of existence, the hospital remained at best an institution of dubious medical utility and questionable legitimacy. Indeed, the medieval hospital, known principally as a repository for social and political deviants, was animated as much by the mission of spiritual cure as it was by a concern for providing physical care. Even the gradual infiltration of the hospital by physicians, which began in the fourteenth century, did not alter appreciably its basic political image and function. Most Western governments certainly showed little or no interest in hospitals and medical care. In the nineteenth century, this was consistent with the politics of *laissez faire*. Health care was an individual matter, not a significant issue of public policy. With the subsequent triumph of liberalism and the cause of social engineering, however, the hospital emerged from historical obscurity to occupy a preeminent place among major service institutions, with unfathomable claims on the public purse. Accordingly, only of late has the hospital come to be perceived primarily as a social center for treatment and cure.[1]

The ascent of the hospital during the past century from an uncertain civic status to the incomparable prestige of a critical total social institution, without which no community is complete, occurred with remarkable speed. But this accelerated institutional development was not without problems. When social change runs rapidly ahead of legal change and control, *lacunae* develop in the civil order, which threaten the continuity of traditional values. Because the central forces shaping modern society—bureaucracy, scientism, and technology—simultaneously converge in the modern hospital, the political ramifications of its operation in this age of retreating individualism have become ominous. The hospital without doubt is a microcosm of the liberal democratic state, and in this sense it represents some of its most redeeming and, at the same time, reprehensible tendencies. It is precisely because the hospital, to use Philip Reiff's words, "is succeeding the church and parliament as the archetypal institution of Western culture,"[2] that it must be held accountable and required to serve the constitutional standards of democracy. That is, the hospital, no less than government itself, ought to be evaluated and judged, not only for its contribution to public health, but also for its compatibility with the central democratic values of autonomy and dignity for every individual.

BUREAUCRATIZED HEALTH

Bureaucracy, it has been widely noted, tends to take on a life of its own and seeks as its rational end goals no more extensive or higher than self-preservation. In the pursuit and service of its own prerequisites, bureaucracy is capable of reproducing its own culture and enveloping and transforming multiple facets of human experience. Indeed, as a new form of social experience bureaucracy has the capacity, as Ralph P. Hummel notes, to neutralize the volitional element of social action. In so doing, it may impinge on the individual in all the major categories conventionally used to classify and explain human behavior. These include the critical social, cultural, psychological, linguistic, and most important, political realms of experience.[3] When bureaucracy, moreover, as a system of administration and control becomes coterminous with the infrastructure of a total institution like a prison, military unit, or in this instance, a hospital, where all individual needs, both physical and psychological, are managed, the culture of bureaucratic rationality can become for the consumer, a culture of coercion.

With its internal ethos of rationality and logic, bureaucracy normally requires few external alliances or sources of support to operate with overwhelming influence. It possesses the capacity of stifling or easily brushing aside random challenges to its authority. Faceless clerks at the point of bureaucratic contact may appear to the hapless citizen to be representatives of an imperial order with an appropriately impassive mein. When, however, bureaucracy is reinforced and staffed by personnel with an external supply of legitimacy, it becomes a redoubtable force and concurrently a serious threat to the rule of law and the continuity of democratic values.

Three and a half decades ago in a classic article, political scientist Norton Long emphasized that bureaucracy not only implements policy, but also for the foreseeable future "is likely, day in and day out, to be our main source of policy initiative."[4] Attuned to the growing influence of bureaucracy, Long nevertheless failed to detect the intrinsic tension between bureaucratic culture and its priorities and the constitutional values central to a democratic order. Democracy in the form of interest group pluralism would, he believed, reshape and mitigate the bureaucratic regimen. Given the wide sway and diverse functions of varied governmental bureaucracies and with an open recruitment process, bureaucracy, Long suggested, could play an even more effective representative role than the traditional political organs of the democratic state. In this twist of Madisonian theory, bureaucracy would be only one of many political factions vying to realize self-serving ends. Bureaucracy, so the argument runs, would thereby contribute to a pluralistic equilibrium that no single faction could disturb or dominate. This myth of representative bureaucracy ignored, however, the larger cultural import of bureaucracy. An especially troublesome dimension of this general issue is the unique problem posed by the technical agendas of modern bureaucracies, which now frequently employ professional personnel with their own peculiar and distinct agendas and commitments.

In the case of the hospital, the power of its administration flowing from the intrinsic structural strength of bureaucracy, a form of social organization designed to transcend human frailty, is augmented considerably by the extraordinary prestige and status attributed to the physicians who compose its highly trained medical staff. There arises in the hospital, then—a total institution interfacing widely with individuals from all social strata, frequently under stress and with depleted powers—the unusual instance of the fusion of bureaucratic authority with an external paramount form of authority. Consequently, hospital bureaucracy operating with this reinforced hyper-authority can be likened in its potential for coercion to a modern counterpart of the Hobbesian Behemoth, a menacing creature whose "bones are as pipes of brass; his gristles are like bars of iron."[5]

Medical societies today reflect some of the exclusive founding zeal and single-minded purposefulness suggested by the original Latin usage of the term *societas*. As Hannah Arendt has explained, the word *societas* "originally had a clear, though limited, political meaning; it indicated an alliance between people for a specific purpose, as when men organize in order to rule others or to commit a crime."[6] The medical profession in consequence of its superb organizational skills and effective interest group pressure activities has set a heady pace among the labor force in entrenching and codifying privilege, in what is an ostensibly free and competitive labor market, as a basic right and condition of employment. Indeed, no other interest group has managed to battle and fend off state interference and meddling in its work place, while at the same time extracting and preserving monumental concessions and charter rights that significantly color the delivery of its services. The medical profession, as Eliot Freidson has observed, enjoys a veritable state-guaranteed monopoly to provide medical service and to define the social reality of health, as well as the terms of debate over health issues and questions. In Freidson's words, "the state has both made it illegal for other workers to compete with physicians and given physicians the right to direct the activities of related occupations. 'In a way unparalleled in any other industry, the physician controls and influences his field and all who venture near it.' "[7] Small wonder, then, that hospital bureaucracy, fortified as it is with professional privilege, can manufacture formidable obstacles for a patient who favors personal autonomy and dignity over hospital bureaucratic control prerequisites.

THE MEDICAL RECORD AS A "FILE"

Chief among these control mechanisms is the hospital medical record. As has been noted for all bureaucracies, "without permanent records, activities are difficult to inspect and analyze for the purposes of future correction and control."[8] For the hospital bureaucracy, however, the medical record possesses transcendent importance. The hospital's critical interest in the medical record is usually understated and tends to be masked. This is generally accomplished through the attribution of multiple functions to the basic record-keeping task. These functions are typically expressed in the verbiage of higher ends that are taken for granted and are popularly believed to be vital and essential to the public weal. Accordingly, the American Hospital Association stresses that:

The primary purpose of the medical record is to document the course of the patient's illness and treatment (medical care) during a particular period and during any subsequent periods as an inpatient or outpatient. . . . It is an important tool in medical practice. It serves as a basis for the planning and evaluation of individual patient care and for communication between the physician and other professionals contributing to the patient's care.[9]

Pointedly missing from the communication purview of the record is any suggestion that the patient might appropriately be a participatory party in that communication process and might conceivably have an intelligent interest in what remains in the final analysis his or her personal health record. Of secondary importance, the Association states, is the use of the record to meet the hospital's legal liabilities and as a source of clinical data for purposes of research.

The Ontario (Canada) Council of Health, an advisory body to the Minister of Health, reported similarly that the medical record is "a multi-purpose document" and "should be an orderly written documentation of the experience of the patient, containing sufficient information to identify him and justify his diagnosis and treatment. The medical record should serve the patient and the providers of health care, as well as purposes of education and research." In elaborating on the record and its multiple purposes, the

Council explained: first, the informational and communicative role of the record in patient care and its use as a data base for responding to authorized and official requests for information; second, its use for peer assessment and evaluation of hospital performance by several self-policing professional medical bodies; third, its use as a pedagogical instrument to teach students "how to compile an appropriate record" and as a device to enable instructors to evaluate the "thinking process" of students; fourth, its application to research, including constructing morbidity and mortality studies; and fifth, the record exists as documentary evidence to chart the patient's illness, facilitate the continuity of care, and notwithstanding all previous uses, to be of assistance in "protecting legal interests of the patient, the physician, the hospital and its staff."[10] Conspicuously absent from the report is any affirmation (or even suggestion) of an absolute right of access on behalf of the patient to his or her own record.

The general perception and celebration of the hospital medical record as an instrument facilitating qualitative patient care, scientific communication and research, and audit and peer review procedures is part of a larger mythologic view of medicine and of the doctor as kindly folk hero. In practice the medical record contains a much more extensive range of information, some of highly disputable scientific quality, than is warranted or required to perform stereotypically defined services. So well recognized in legal circles is this phenomenon that the term "medical record" has come to be regarded as "somewhat of a misnomer, since it, in fact, records far more information than just medical matters."[11] These extramedical data can include observations about an individual's private life on such sensitive issues as sexual orientation and hypothesized sexual behavior, drug and alcohol use, and family milieu and relationships.[12] Character assessments—some real, others imagined—may be gleaned by readers from varied and motley entries in the record. The interest and press of third parties to gain access to medical records—penetration of the record-taking place both within the law and often surreptitiously outside—attests clearly to the fact that the medical record can be a treasure trove of intimate details, having use and application for varied purposes far remote from the legitimate scope of medicine.

If that scope, for example, is defined by and consistent with the first principle of the Canadian Medical Association's code of ethics, "Consider first the well-being of the patient,"[13] then some professional usages of the hospital medical record appear in a most disturbing light. Historically, physicians have not, interestingly enough, as Freidson has reported, taken a particularly lively interest in the medical record, nor have they been enamored of it, because "the record was recognized as a profound threat to their autonomy." More recently, however, physicians have found the record to be an extremely useful bureaucratic instrument, particularly to cue colleagues into the identity of so-called "difficult" patients—those who do not enter the hospital as supplicants or who are not inclined to render hospital authority surplus homage and deference.

When a physician unwittingly referred a demanding patient, he sometimes used the chart to communicate his problem in order to be excused by the consultant for referring an ostensibly unnecessary case and to solicit support from the consultant in soothing the patient and discouraging his demands. Sometimes rather tactless remarks about the propriety of the referral were written in the record by angry consultants, and sometimes in seasons of the year when time permitted, witty remarks were written into the record about what were thought to be neurotic patients for the appreciation and sympathetic eyes of colleagues.[14]

Pejorative entries in the medical record, either in explicit form or woven into the context of the report, effectively serve to filter the flow and circulation of patients. These entries extend and enhance bureaucratic control over the consumers of health services—flagging, in effect, the files of patients the health providers estimate are likely to disrupt hospital routine or, worse, who are viewed as potential threats to professional imagery and mythology. Possible patient assault on professional vanity is not the only reason for utilizing the medical record to screen for such would-be offenders. Malpractice suits in the United States, and to a lesser extent in Canada, are perceived as a breach of the professional privilege of self-regulation and, more important, as an ever-growing and unacceptably high cost of doing business. So serious a financial drain has pervasive litigation become that the American Medical Association has declared "a new medical malpractice 'crisis'" to be in effect. To counter this threat to pecuniary morale, the bureaucratic record-keeping task has been extended in at least one jurisdiction: the Los Angeles County Medical Association has recently begun to operate a telephone hotline that physicians can call to ascertain which of their prospective patients is "deemed likely to sue."[15] Whether this determination is based on scientific criteria and constitutes an expert medical judgment remains to be seen.

THE MEDICAL RECORD AS CONTROL AND CONTROLLING

In view of questionable uses of medical records, it is not surprising that hospital bureaucracy remains reluctant to provide access to the record, least of all to patients. A common characteristic of bureaucracy, as Weber notes, is its drive to exercise control over vital information:

The bureaucratic structure goes hand in hand with the concentration of the material means of management in the hands of the master. This concentration occurs, for instance, in a well-known and typical fashion, in the development of big capitalist enterprises, which find their essential characteristics in this process. A corresponding process occurs in public organizations.[16]

Hospital bureaucracy prizes secrecy because it abets patient control and pacification and undergirds medical mythology. In general, secrecy is regarded as a normal prerequisite of bureaucratic administration. "Every bureaucracy," Weber writes, "seeks to increase the superiority of the professionally informed by keeping their knowledge and intentions secret. Bureaucratic administration always tends to be an administration of 'secret sessions': in so far as it can, it hides its knowledge and action from criticism."[17] Paradoxically, however, the secrecy surrounding hospital medical records is highly selective. While patients in most jurisdictions have at best limited and circumscribed access to their medical records, such is not the case for various third parties—some of whom, from the perspective and interests of the patient, have exceptionally dubious claims to virtue or good intentions.

While incremental progress has been made, American law in general has been slow to advance patient access rights. Even though the medical record, as Ellen Klugman observes, may be the single most important document for an individual, as it contains miscellaneous personal details with potentially ruinous consequences should it be misconstrued or misused, "many states continue to deny or restrict a patient's access to his medical records."[18] In Canada, with the exception of two provinces, the legal situation is comparable. A uniform absolute right of patient access to his or her own hospital medical record simply does not exist.[19] The province of Ontario is a case in point. Though the province maintains a progressive universal medical insurance plan with coverage from cradle to grave and an enviable system of public hospitals, Ontario remains less than progressive in the matter of patient access rights. As Mr. Justice Horace Krever, the author of a royal commission inquiry on health information, has concluded: "Current Ontario legislation does not recognize the right of a patient to access to his or her health information. No remedy exists to which the patient can resort if he or she is refused access."[20]

As previously indicated, bureaucratic secrecy prevailing against the individual as the primary subject of the medical record does not seem to apply to other interested third parties. These parties, many of whom have little or no concern with medicine and health, are proliferating and include diverse governmental agencies, insurance companies, police officials, private investigation firms, schools, employers, and credit agencies.[21] Some record disclosure authorized by law obviously serves legitimate purposes: the collection of data that relate to governmental health program benefits, occupational and accident prevention programs, surveys of communicable diseases and personal abuse, and so forth.[22] But many collections of data from medical records occur well beyond the pale of law. Violations of the integrity and confidentiality of medical records are carried out with routine abandon.

The Krever Commission, for example, has documented large-scale penetration of medical records by private investigators from sundry sources. The hospital, it determined, was no more a secure repository of sensitive personal data than other storage centers. Testimony was received of investigators who simply borrowed lab coats from the rack and proceeded to scrutinize records having a vital bearing on the court resolution of insurance claims. The Commission found that "no source of information was safe from these investigators."[23]

It thus appears that bureaucratic secrecy in the form of legal restraints impeding patient access to medical records affects basically only those with the most legitimate interest in the contents of the record and thus the very individuals most likely to be harmed by unauthorized and mischievous surveillance of the record. Bureaucratic secrecy, ironically, is a secondary concern and need not be vigorously enforced by the hospital with respect to third parties because they pose less of a direct threat to the interest and well-being of the hospital bureaucracy. In some respects, indeed, their very existence reinforces hospital bureaucracy.

Physicians have traditionally disputed patient access rights on paternalistic grounds. Medical records, it is argued, are intended for professional communication and are written in a technical language beyond the ken of a lay audience. Patients, therefore, instead of understanding the record are likely to misinterpret it. Moreover, patients conversant with their medical records, it is backhandedly argued, run the risk of being harmed by them. Misapprehension and anxiety compounded by record reading can adversely affect the healing process. The proper conduit, then, for relaying medical information to the patient is the physician (and other "health professionals") skilled in the nuances of the question of what a person needs and ought to know.[24]

Yet the arguments articulated and the opposition generated by the medical profession toward patient access rights may not accurately or necessarily reflect the issue of probable harm to patients. One study, for example, showed that only 28 percent of a physician sample was in favor of a patient having part or full access to the record. Three-quarters believed that patients would be harmed by such exposure. But of the larger group that found record reading to be harmful, many nevertheless had no opposition to their patients having access to their records. On the other hand, many who dismissed the harm factor were not in favor of patient access.[25] Another study conducted to test the effect of patients receiving their record during hospitalization actually found no instance where a patient was harmed by being offered the record. Conversely, this study suggested that the open record was "a safe and inexpensive aid to the rehabilitation process," consistent with the need of the patient "to negotiate his own health care in an increasingly complex and mobile society."[26]

While the question of patient harm from record exposure may be debatable, particularly in the context of some psychiatric care,[27] no doubt exists of the epidemic fear that medical records can be harmful to hospitals and physicians. This harm would be apparent if hospital records were routinely available to patients and also freely permitted to be used as evidentiary instruments in courts of law. On this point there is a consensus that the medical record could wreak incalculable harm to health providers. Such fear is not unfounded. Lawyers understand well and preach the evidentiary value of the medical record. They advise repeatedly that "hospital records can be a motherlode of supporting evidence to a lawyer involved in medical malpractice litigation."[28] Attorneys should leave no stone unturned and "should meticulously scrutinize medical records the way a detective inspects a crime scene: all the evidence they need to prove their case may be right there."[29] Physicians are warned consequently that medical records must be fastidiously maintained because they "form the primary line of defense."[30] Unless unimpeachable, comprehensive, and accurate records can be introduced in court on behalf of a physician, his legal position will be untenable. Without adequate explanation: "unavailable, incomplete, or damaged medical records create a legal inference that a physician acted in a deliberate dereliction of duty. Also, an absence of data in a patient's medical records creates an inference that satisfactory medical care was not provided."[31]

Once litigation becomes a major rationale for composing medical records, the priorities which are ideally stated for maintaining them are distorted further. Many technical and critical questions are involved in keeping medical records. The length of time records ought to be preserved is one such question. When it is suggested that the criteria for answering this question can be established with reference to the "statute of limitations" for malpractice suits in various jurisdictions instead of, for example, epidemiological requirements,[32] the patient's primary interest in the record is obfuscated and ignored. More and more, it appears that the medical record is becoming a record against patients, rather than for them.

The patient's interest in the record beyond the obvious subject of health has, for several reasons, become an issue of critical civil libertarian concern. Because medical records are now shared by a large number of users for purposes redundant to medicine, it is essential that individuals at least have the opportunity to be apprised of and check for the accuracy of medical record data.[33] Severe disabilities can be incurred when gratuitous, inferential, and pejorative assessments are lodged in a patient's medical record without his or her knowledge. One such typical incident is instructive:

Jason Kantor was injured in a mortorcycle accident, and the male friend accompanying him died. When Jason left the emergency room of a well-known hospital, he assumed his medical record would simply reflect treatment for the injuries he had sustained. Several months later, Jason anticipated applying for a job for which a security check was required. As part of that process, Jason would have to consent to releasing all medical records to his prospective employer. Unknown to Jason, an emergency room psychiatrist had misleadingly recorded Jason's overwrought concern with his friend's death by noting in Jason's medical chart that there was no evidence of sexual relations between the two men. Jason's attorney demanded that the misleading statement be eliminated from the medical record, but hospital policy proscribed any altering of medical record entries. The hospital finally agreed to draw a line through the entry.[34]

It goes without saying that the computer revolution has exacerbated the problem of unprincipled access to and use of medical records. The so-called "paperless medical record" has now gained wide currency, especially in the United States. While the health advantages of computerized records cannot be minimized, enthusiasts of such systems, though recognizing the potential for increased abuse, fail to comprehend that the computer dramatically escalates a problem already intrinsic to the medical profession.[35] The general family practitioner has become a relic of a bygone era, and a mobile population no longer has a one-to-one relationship with a single physician. The profession itself having grown more highly specialized increases the impersonality of the practice of medicine and creates a renewed and intensified dependence on records. The elements of confidence and trust, still confirmed in the abstract to be the lodestar of the medical profession, are bound to be swept away by the relentless momentum of bureaucratization.

The linkage of records among various health providers abets the collusive tendencies of a profession not known to favor the rigors of market competition. Linkage, whatever its benefits, thus compounds the difficulty of obtaining independent medical assessments. In addition, medical record linkage has a tendency to spill over into other fields. In Britain, for example, the installation of a social service department computer terminal in a hospital emergency department raises profoundly disquieting questions. In this instance, it became possible for medical staff to view the social service records of a patient, and alternatively, for social service staff to examine the medical records.[38] Patients provide personal information to health professionals on the basis of an assumption, shown to be demonstrably false, that the information will be safeguarded, remain confidential, and be used only for limited treatment purposes. But as the Krever Commission has found, information provided for health reasons, "will often ultimately find its way into a computer system for any variety of purposes."[39] This leads to the open-ended prospect that "unauthorized persons may read the information, link it to other information, share it with unauthorized third parties, use it to undermine a person's insurance status, exploit it for purposes of personal embarrassment, and so forth."[40]

In the United States the Reagan administration's drive to cut domestic spending, especially health-care costs, has not only fortified, but ironically, has greatly expanded the scope and intensity of the power of hospital bureaucracy over the practice of medicine. The result has been, given the convergence of federal health policy and rapidly developing computer technologies, that hospital medical records have become a more intrusive, all-encompassing, sensitive, and vulnerable source of personal data than ever before. As Brannigan and Dayhoff point out, the administration's prospective payment system, first put in place to reduce Medicare and Medicaid expenditures, subjects physicians to constricting pressure from hospital bureaucracies, to justify tests, diagnoses, and treatment procedures, lest hospitals incur the penalty of losing government reimbursements. This radical-conservative governmental health policy, not only interferes with the preserve of the physician's autonomous practice of medicine, but further jeopardizes the rights of hospital patients, by encouraging directly a frenetic escalation of the hospital record-keeping function. "The effect is to require that the medical community establish a system for determining what is an acceptable diagnosis, what indications lead to that diagnosis, and what range of therapies are allowed. Each step of the decision will be recorded, made part of the record, and subject to later challenge. The medical record must be capable of explaining and justifying the physician's action."[41]

In line with this goal, medical computer technicians nurtured by and organized in a new American College of Medical Informatics are pioneering new informational horizons for the once-stylized and theoretically restricted record-keeping task. As it is of great social significance, it is interesting to note that this preoccupation with records promotes the transformation of the locus of the medical decision-making process away from the individual practitioner to national centers or, perhaps, even to computers themselves. Not surprisingly then, "medical records, which formerly included limited information about the patient, now chart the patient's entire life."[42] This means, of course, that the opportunities and incentives for third-party invasion and exploitation of computer-stored records, for example, by authorized or unauthorized telephone access, are dramatically enhanced. A plethora of hard questions remain to be answered, as Brannigan and Dayhoff suggest: "What information is to be collected? How long will it be stored? Who will have access? What is the security of the system? Who is responsible in the institution for answering these questions?"[43]

Bureaucratic management and control of hospital medical records is rooted in the law. In virtually every jurisdiction medical records have the legal status of hospital property and are viewed as "the hospital's business record."[44] The amorphous nature of this business does not preclude confrontational transactions between the individual and the hospital bureaucracy, placing that person, it has been argued, at considerable risk, and allowing for future imposition by unknown parties of unforeseen and undefined penalties. Hospital bureaucracy, it has been demonstrated vividly by pathology reports, "found blowing around 12 Toronto blocks" is most often at its best in safeguarding medical records from patients, as opposed to other transgressors.[45] It is unlikely that hospital bureaucracy will gracefully and voluntarily relinquish its authoritarian control over medical records. For in the words of Mr. Justice Krever: "Knowledge is power. Knowledge about another person, knowledge, that is, that the other person does not have, is surely, power over that person."[46]

The multifarious uses of hospital records, as well as the questionable practice of sculpting them explicitly for litigation purposes,[47] or even the serious possibility of their deliberate destruction for the purpose of evading legal accountability, makes the right of patient access a critical civil libertarian concern. Recent amendments to the New York State Public Health Law and Mental Hygiene Act, which took effect the beginning of 1987, go some way in addressing these access concerns. Yet New York's newly promulgated statutory right of access is a qualified one, and it does not apply, for example, to the personal notes and observations maintained apart from the formal record. More importantly, the New York State right of access is subject to denial by the individual practitioner on the statutory grounds that the requested information "can reasonably be expected to cause substantial and identifiable harm to the subject or others which would outweigh the qualified person's right of access to the information."[48] Such denial will be based on the Acts' commodious framework of enumerated criteria, which allows ample leeway for the rationalization of vested interests. The acts do provide for appeal to a medical-access review committee. But it remains to be seen how successful such appeals will be, insofar as the members of the committee are appointed by the health commissioner from a list of nominees submitted by the state medical society, all of whom will be licensed physicians.[49]

Further judicial review is available, but the legal process is often a time-consuming and costly form of redress, for the denial of what ought to be considered in the first instance, a routine request for information. Finally, because the 41,000-member state medical society is on record in opposition to the legislation,[50] doubts will not quickly evaporate as to the objective and dispassionate administration of what is, in the final analysis, a peer-stacked and orientated access and review system.

The codification of access rights, such as the incremental progress made in New York, will not alone rectify the sundry problems discussed here of hospital bureaucracy and medical records. Improved patient access rights is but one path toward effective bureaucratic reform. Undoubtedly, however, until bureaucratic secrecy is checked by uniform, comprehensive, and workable patient access law, and improved restrictions and penalties for the unscrupulous use of medical records are put in place, the hospital patient will remain needlessly at peril.

7

The Moral Ethos of Bureaucracy

Robert Jackall

Business ethics is rapidly becoming big business. The last decade has seen the publication of a great number of books and articles on ethical issues in business,[1] the emergence of several centers and institutes either wholly or partly dedicated to the subject,[2] the proliferation of business ethics courses in college and business school curricula,[3] and, in some corporations, the development of seminars on ethics for executives. This ground swell of attention to ethical issues in business continues a historic tradition dating at least to the turn of this century, when the big corporation began its ascendency in our society.[4] The recent upsurge has been, of course, a boon to moral philosophers, a precariously positioned occupational group. With the titles of "ethicist" or even "ethician," they have applied their considerable mental acumen to analyzing the conundrums of the hurly-burly worlds of commerce and industry. In doing so they have extended the much longer tradition of moral casuistry in quite new directions.[5] Unfortunately, most of this analysis has been of hypothetical cases, or real-life cases abstracted from their intricate organizational contexts, or of the well-publicized corporate scandals in recent years. There has been little detailed analysis of the day-to-day structure and meaning of work in business or of how the conditions of that work shape moral consciousness.[6]

In particular, there has been among ethicists little appreciation of how bureaucracy, the dominant organizational form of our epoch, shapes the very rhythm and tempo of our society and indeed, to borrow Emil Lederer's phrase, its very sociopsychic constitution.[7] The thorough bureaucratization of our society in the last century, beginning with industry and commerce, extending later to government, and now reaching every nook and cranny of the occupational structure, has profoundly reshaped our class system, shredded and reknit whole communities in new patterns, and made individual life-chances largely dependent on bureaucratically constructed careers. It has also, as I have argued elsewhere, swept away older ethics of behavior and ways of seeing and evaluating social reality and its moral issues.[8] A focus on business ethics without an analysis of how bureaucracy shapes those ethics is somewhat like producing *Hamlet* without the role of the Prince of Denmark.

MANAGERS

Corporate managers are the quintessential bureaucratic work group in our bureaucratic society. They not only fashion bureaucratic rules but they are also bound by them. Typically, they are not only *in* big organizations; because their administrative expertise constitutes their livelihood, they are also *of* the organization. They need maintain no pretenses of allegiances to civil service codes nor to an ethic of public service. Their allegiances are to the principle of organization itself and to the market, itself bureaucratically organized. Their conservative public and personal style and conventional demeanor belie their thoroughgoing transforming role in our society. They are, rather, the principal carriers of the bureaucratic ethos in our era. Their pivotal institutional position not only gives their decisions great reach but also links them to other important elites; as a result, their occupational ethics set both the framework and the vocabularies of discourse for a great many public issues in our society. In this essay, I want to examine how the social and political context of managerial work shapes managers' moral rules-in-use and the way they come to see the world. To do this, I will discuss materials gathered during field work in several large corporations.[9]

"What is right in the corporation," a former vice president of a large company says, "is not what is right in a man's home or in his church. What is right in the corporation is what the guy above you wants from you. That's what morality is in the corporation." The hierarchical authority structure central to bureaucracy comes to dominate the way managers think about their world and about themselves. Managers do not see or experience authority in any abstract way; rather, authority is embodied in their personal relationships with their immediate bosses and in their perceptions of similar links between other managers up and down the hierarchy. When managers describe their work to an outsider, they first say: "I work for Bill James" or "I report to Harry Mills" of "I'm in Joe Bell's group," and only then proceed to describe their official functions. Such a personalized statement of authority relationships exactly reflects the way authority is structured, exercised, and experienced in corporate hierarchies.

American businesses, typically, both centralize and decentralize authority; responsibility for reaching objectives—say, profit targets—is pushed as far down the ladder as possible, while the basic direction of the corporation is set from the top. In the large corporations that I studied, this results in a structure where there are independent divisions or companies, each headed by its own president with his own staff and line hierarchy, all monitored by a central corporate staff that reports directly to the chief executive officer (CEO) of the whole corporation. The system is linked together by an intricate series of "commitments" to specific objectives; each subordinate pledges the accomplishment of certain goals to his own boss, who gathers up the commitments of all his subordinates and makes his own commitment to his boss, and so on up the ladder. Each president of each division or company finally makes his own commitment to the CEO based on the promises of his vice-presidents. The CEO locks the entire system into place not only symbolically but also because he has the power to determine whether or not these commitments have been satisfactorily met. In practice, of course, the CEO frames and paces the whole process by nearly always applying pressure for higher goals and greater commitments; the decentralized structure, in fact, actually increases the CEO's centralized power.

This interlocking series of commitments shapes not only a pyramid of promises but also an intricate system of fealty between bosses and subordinates. Bosses depend on subordinates for realistic estimates of goals to avoid "getting on the hook" for commitments that cannot be met and for crucial information to avoid being "blindsided," especially in public. They extend to subordinates, in return, a measure of protection and to a favored few the promise of promotion when and if their own fortunes improve. In this sense the commitment system also constitutes a series of conspiracies between bosses and subordinates. Bosses are, of course, subordinates to still other bosses; thus, the personal links and ties of reciprocal obligation extend from the bottom of the managerial ladder right up to the chief executive officer. Overlaying and intertwined with this formal monocratic system of authority are patron-client relationships. Patrons are usually powerful figures in the higher echelons of management. Depending on one's location in the hierarchy, one's patron might be one's boss. If, however, one is farther down the ladder, one's patron can be several levels higher up the chain of command. In such cases, one is still bound by the immediate formal authority and fealty patterns of one's position, but one also acquires new—though more ambiguous fealty relationships with one's highest ranking patron.

This system of fealty, of patrimony, thus meshes intimately with formal bureaucratic authority. It is important to note that a managers' fealty is *not* to offices as such, as Weber argued in contrasting bureaucracy with feudalism, but to persons who hold offices. This seems to be a peculiar characteristic of business hierarchies, at least in the United States; I do not wish to make a general statement about other, say governmental, bureaucracies, though there is some evidence that similar structures prevail there as well. These fealty relationships in business need not be accompanied by affection or other personal sentiment, though they sometimes are; they do, however, seem to require a degree of personal comfort between boss and subordinate or between patron and client—that is, a meshing of personal styles and the familiarity, predictability, and ease that come from a sharing of taken-for-granted frameworks about how the world works.

Managers draw elaborate cognitive maps to guide them through the thickets of their organizations. Because they see authority in such personal terms, the singular feature of these maps is their biographical emphasis. Managers carry in their heads a thumbnail sketch of the occupational history of virtually every other manager, of their own rank or above, in their particular organization. If a rising star appears below them, they take care to "get a fix" on him, to discover and add to their knowledge all important items about him. Such knowledge begins with the star's occupational expertise but focuses especially on his previous and present reporting relationships, his patrons higher in the organization, his alliances among his peers, and the general estimate of his abilities and prospects. This is not to say that these sketches are accurate or fair; they are, in fact, often based on the flimsiest of evidence. Managers trade sketches of others within their circles and often color the sketches to suit their own purposes. This is one reason why it is crucial for the aspiring young manager to project the right image to the right people who can influence others' sketches of him. Whatever the accuracy of these vocabularies of description, managers' penchant for biographical detail and personal histories is quite remarkable, especially since they evince little inclination for other kinds of history and still less for details in general. Details are usually pushed down to subordinates, and a concern with history, even of one's own organization, constrains the cheerful optimism highly valued in most corporations. Biographical detail is, however, crucial knowledge because managers know that, in the rough-and-tumble politics of the corporate world, individual fates are made and broken not by one's accomplishments but by other people.

Political struggles are central to managerial work and shape managers' consciousness and outlook in fundamental ways. The political structure of organizations is most observable during periods of internal upheaval, a regularly recurring phenomenon in American business. The large conglomerate, of which the Chemical Company that I studied is a part, has been in turmoil for the last few years and presents a focused, indeed sharply drawn, case study of political processes basic to all big corporations. I have taken liberties with dates and with some details.

THE CHEMICAL COMPANY: A CASE STUDY

In 1979 a new CEO took power in the conglomerate. His first move was to restructure the organization into five free-standing companies, each with a different business area—energy, chemicals, metals, electronic equipment, and precision instruments. He dismissed the top leadership of the old organization and personally selected the new presidents for each of the five independent companies. The new presidents each had a relatively free hand in restructuring their organizations, although it seems, in retrospect, that the CEO insisted on certain high-level appointments. What happened in the Chemical Company in this early stage was typical of the pattern in the other companies. The newly appointed president—let's call him Smith—came from a marketing background in a small but important product group in a specialty chemicals division of the old organization. Upon ascending to the presidency, he reached back into his old division, indeed back into his old product group, and systematically elevated his old colleagues, friends, and allies. Powerful managers in a rival process chemical group were demoted, sidetracked, or fired outright. Hundreds of people throughout the whole corporation, a great many in the Chemical Company, lost their jobs in what became known as the "October Revolution" or, in some circles, the "Octoberfest."

The Chemical Company had a good financial year in 1980. Smith consolidated his power and, through his top subordinates, further weeded out or undercut managers with whom he felt uncomfortable. At the end of the year, the mood in the company was buoyant, not only because of high profits but also because of the expectation of massive deregulation and good times for business following President Reagan's election. The day after Reagan's election, by the way, saw managers, in an unusual break from normal decorum, literally dancing in the corridors.

Financial disaster struck the Chemical Company in 1981, however, as it did much of American industry. Smith, elated by his success in 1980 and eager to please the CEO, was, it seems, the victim of his own marketing optimism. He overcommitted himself and his company, and the Chemical Company reached only 60 percent of its profit target for the year. By the end of 1981, then, a sense of gloom and incipient panic pervaded the organization. Rumors of every sort flourished: Smith was on his way out and would take the whole structure of the Chemical Company with him. In fact, it was said, one of the CEO's most trusted troubleshooters, a man who "eats people for breakfast," was gunning for Smith and his job. Smith would survive but would be forced to sacrifice all of his top people, alter his organization's structure, and buckle under to the now vigorous demands of the CEO. The CEO was about to put the whole Chemical Company on the block; at the least, large portions of the company would be sold, wreaking havoc with support staff at corporate headquarters. There were disturbing rumors, too, about growing personal tension and animosity between Smith and the CEO; managers up and down the line knew instinctively that, if the personal relationship between Smith and the CEO were to erode, the inevitable period of blame and retribution for 1981 might engulf everyone, not just well-targeted individuals. Managers mobilized their subordinates to arrange their defenses, tried to cement crucial alliances, and waited. In the meantime, they updated their resumés and responded graciously to the phone calls of headhunters.

The next act of the drama unfolded in February of 1982 with a new reorganization. Smith got rid of his executive vice president—let's call him Brown—who was something of an anomaly in the higher circles of the company. His occupational expertise was in finance, rather than in marketing, like Smith and the rest of Smith's circle. Moreover, although his principal rise had been through the old specialty chemicals division, his original roots in the corporation were in the energy division, where he had been a friend and associate of the man who later rose to the presidency of that company in the 1979 shakeup. This history made Brown suspect, especially when the tension between Smith and the CEO intensified and the presidents of the other companies saw a chance to extend their influence. Brown's strait-laced personal style was also an anomaly amidst the bonhomie that marked the Chemical Company's upper circle. The CEO, himself a financial man, saved Brown, however, and appointed him president of the declining Electronics Company, known by this time as a graveyard—that is, a place with decaying businesses that one buries by selling off. Many managers were amused at Brown's reassignment; despite a nominal promotion, he was being told, they felt, to dig his own grave in an appropriate location. Some were more wary and saw the move as a gambit, in fact as a cover-up by the CEO himself, who had invested heavily in several businesses in Electronics only to have them expire. Brown had not been popular in the Chemical Company, and his departure was greeted, as one manager describes it, "by a lot of people standing on the sidelines, hooting, and hollering and stamping our feet. We never thought we'd see old Brown again." In Brown's place, Smith appointed two executive vice-presidents, one a trusted aide from the old specialty chemicals division and the other an outsider with expertise in selling off commodity businesses—that is, what was left of the old process chemicals division. Blame for 1981 was apportioned to a few general managers, all from that division, and Smith fired them. Other managers felt that not only had Smith reasserted the supremacy of his specialty chemicals alliances, but he had, in addition, bought himself eight months in the process—time enough, perhaps, for the economy to turn around.

As it happened, the economy worsened, and by the fall of 1982, the CEO's pressure on Smith had increased. Smith's men privately referred to the CEO as a "tinhorn tyrant" and muttered about his "henchmen" being sent to extract information from them to be used against Smith. In addition to demanding that some businesses be sold, others cut back, and costs in general reduced, the CEO wanted Smith to dismantle large sections of his staff, particularly in the environmental protection area. In response to a specific environmental disaster in the late 1970s and to the public outrage about chemical pollution in general, Smith had erected upon his ascendency in 1979 an elaborate and relatively free-roaming environmental staff. He felt that this apparatus, though costly, was the best defense against another severely embarrassing and even more costly environmental debacle. The company had, in fact, won an industrial award and wide recognition for its program. The CEO himself had benefited from the public praise for the program on first taking office, and he basked in that attention. Within the Chemical Company, however, as the political atmosphere in the country changed with the conservative legislative, budgetary, and regulatory triumphs in 1981, line managers were chafing under staff intrusions. They blamed the environmental staff for creating extra work and needless costs during a period of economic crisis. The CEO apparently agreed with these sentiments. Smith faced not only relentless pressure because of the company's declining fortunes but public capitulation to the CEO on his preferred organizational design. He chose instead to resign to "pursue other interests," pulling, of course, the cord on his "Golden Parachute" as he left.

The Chemical Company was in a state of shock after Smith's resignation, and the rumor mills churned out names of possible replacements, each tied to a scenario of the future. In such a period, the fealty system of the organization begins to loosen even as it binds people to their pasts. Managers know that others' cognitive maps afford them little escape from their old alliances and associations; at the same time, they realize that they must be poised to form new alliances in a hurry if their areas are targeted for "restructuring."

As it happened, a great many managers found themselves in just that position. To almost everyone's astonishment, and to a great many people's trepidation, the CEO brought Brown back from the Electronics graveyard, after a "thorough assessment of all the candidates," which took two days, and made him the new president of Chemicals. No laughter or jeering was heard in the corridors. Whatever Brown's previous affiliations, there was now no doubt where his fealty lay. He became known throughout the corporation as the "CEO's boy," and people recognized that he had a mandate to wreak whatever mayhem was necessary to prune the Chemical organization and reduce expenditures. Within a short time, he had fired 150 people, most at the managerial level, slashing in the process the environmental staff by 75 percent. Those environmental staff that survived were subordinated to business areas and effectively neutralized. The official rationale was that the company had gone through an extraordinary learning period on environmental issues, benefited greatly from the expertise of the environmental staff, but had by now fully integrated and institutionalized that knowledge into its normal operations. There were, it was argued, no longer any environmental problems facing the company and therefore a modest reduction in this area made good business sense. Privately, among some managers, the assessment is that good staff people simply create work to justify their own existence. Moreover, they feel that work on environmental issues is doubly unnecessary because the only real threat to corporations on environmental issues in the new Reagan era is in the courts; for the most part, however, the courts judge past actions not present practices. By the time the courts get to cases generated by contemporary practices, typically in fifteen years, present executives will have moved on, leaving any problems their policies might create to others.

Brown's purge created extreme anxiety throughout the Chemical organization, even among those who agreed with his attacks on the staff and his pruning of other areas. Some managers expressed astonishment, and indeed outrage, that mostly persons of managerial rank were fired. The normal rule of management is, of course, to fire Indians, not Chiefs. Brown's action seemed to be an unwarranted and ominous violation of the managerial code that management takes care of itself in good times and bad. Those that survived were "looking over their shoulders" and "listening for footsteps behind them." Bitter jokes circulated freely like: "Opening Day at the Chemical Company: Brown comes in and throws out the first employee."

The company staggered into the Spring of 1983, and six months after the national economy began to pick up, its own fortunes began to improve, a typical pattern for industrial supply businesses. Suddenly, the CEO announced another major reorganization, once again dividing the entire corporation into several broad sectors. This time the Industrial Supplies Sector, as it is now called, incorporated Chemicals, Metals, and Plastics. Brown did not get the call to head the whole Industrial Supplies Sector but retained the presidency of chemicals. The leadership of the whole sector was allotted to a man who emerged out of the Metals Company, where he had been president in the old order. He, in turn, gave the presidencies of the other two divisions of the new sector to Metals people, and a new cycle of ascendancy, with its own patterns of fealty, patronage, and power cliques, seems to have begun. Managers noted, with some satisfaction, the irony of Brown being passed over by the CEO for the sector presidency after performing the CEO's dirty work.

HOW TO SUCCEED. . . .

This sequence of events affords a variety of insights into the way managers see and experience their world and shape their rules of behavior. To begin with, managers have an acute sense of organizational contingency. Mistakes, bad judgments, and blunders are as common in business as in any other occupation, although the personal consequences of publicly perceived error are often more severe. However, clear mistakes seen to deserve retribution do not disturb managers; the sense that things are out of their control does. Managers know that a shakeup at or near the top of a hierarchy can trigger widespread organizational upheaval, bringing about startling reversals of fortune, both good and bad, throughout the structure. More to the point, they know that the changes such upheavals bring are often arbitrary, indeed capricious. They depend not on any criteria of merit—although changes are always explained with meritocratic ideologies—but on political connections and such random factors as being in the right place at the right time or the wrong place at the wrong time. Managers in the Chemical Company note that, in fact, their corporation seems to penalize success; only the cream of the managerial crop rises to corporate headquarters, but then, during purges, part of the cream is thrown away. After a certain point in people's careers, managers see success and failure not as achieved or deserved, but as socially defined or dependent on the whims of an irrational market, themselves subject to social interpretations. This sense of uncertainty and lack of control over events generates a profound anxiety in managers, perhaps the key experience of managerial work. This anxiety causes them to turn toward each other to learn and, they hope, to control the process of social definition.

The shaping of alliances is therefore at the core of managerial work and consumes a great deal of managers' time. Alliances are networks of primal loyalties shaped by common work, by common experiences with the same problems or the same enemies, and by favors traded over a number of years. Although alliances are rooted in fealty relationships, they are not bound by them, since fealty shifts with changing assignment and with upheavals. There are any number of criteria for admission to networks. A crucial and universal one is to make sure that one's style—one's personal appearance, way of operating, and mode of self-presentation—meshes with that of powerful members of a clique. Here one must practice, in an unabashed way, what Karl Mannheim calls self-rationalization or self-streamlining.[10] One makes one's self into an object and tailors it to suit the circle, the occasion, the need. An enterprising young manager described his efforts to tailor his external style to criteria valued by the Chemical Company's dominant clique not long after the 1979 reorganization:

There are two aspects which are important—tangible and intangible. First, looks are crucial. The image that they want—if you go to the management committee, they all look the same. They're not robots like a Wall Street firm; but they're clean-cut young executives—short hair, no mustaches, button down collars, Hickey Freeman suits. . . . Then there are the mannerisms. They like you to be well organized, well-spoken. They like presentations, briefings. The greatest thing for your career is to go before the Operating Committee and talk. It's your day in the sun, or rather your five minutes in the sun. What they like are the slick presentations, with slides, with overheads. Short, succinct. Tell them what they want to hear. . . . People who are *comers*—the fair-haired boys—all exhibit the same traits. They are all fast on their feet, well-spoken. They all send *visibility* memos. You know, get your name out, let people know you're managing. Cultivate pseudo-leadership. Develop a habit of calling someone back in a hurry. Wearing your (corporate) tie. . . . The key. . . . is to try to find the right time and place to say something. You gain a lot of respect both for saying something and knowing when to say it. You keep it humorous. The higher up you go, the more people you deal with, and everybody wants something from you. Everybody has a sense of humor, but the top guys can't joke around in their jobs; they can't joke with those above and below them. They can't let their guard down. So if I keep things light, humorous, off-hand, they tend to be open with me. . . . You don't clam up. . . . You keep things rolling and you draw them out of their shell.[11]

With Brown's ascendancy in 1982, the criteria for admission to the dominant circle shifted, and the emphasis was placed on "lean, hungry, and aggressive management." Wise and ambitious managers assessed the situation and adjusted their public faces and styles accordingly. Self-rationalization also demands attitudinal streamlining, a process to be discussed later.

The ability to adapt oneself to a network's criteria is nowhere more important than always to be perceived as a team player. One manager describes team play as "aligning oneself with the dominant ideology of the moment," and it is on this aspect of this multifaceted notion that I will focus here. The sequence of events in the Chemical Company suggests how fraught with conflict and tension corporate life can be. The open power struggles between individuals and between cliques, the bitter clashes within the division between staff and line, and the enmity between the Chemical Company as a whole and the CEO and his corporate staff are simply the public outcome of ongoing guerilla warfare. An identical situation, though considerably less severe at the time of my research, existed in a Textile Firm that was also studied. One gains some idea of the acerbity of managers' views toward rival cliques, factions, and power centers in one executive's definition of an internal auditor. The principal reference here is to the CEO's men, but the sentiment has broader meaning:

Have I ever told you my definition of an auditor? An auditor is someone who situates himself up on a hill overlooking a battle, far from the noise of the guns and smoke of the explosions. And he watches the battle from afar, and when it is over and the smoke is cleared, he goes down into the battlefield and walks among the wounded. And shoots them.

In such a situation, where managers know that "no prisoners are to be taken," leaders of cliques and networks value nothing more highly than unanimity of opinion among their allies and clients. They invoke the ideology of team play to bring their own people into line as well as to cast suspicion on others who pose some threat to them. An upper middle level manager in the Chemical Company demonstrates the rhetoric of team play:

Team play—it's each individual on a team doing his job to the best of his ability and the combination of each person with each other leading to the objective. It means fulfilling your assignment on a project to the best of your ability to the end that the objective is met in a timely and efficient manner. That's team work.

He goes on to discuss the real meaning of the ideology, shifting back and forth between the perspectives of subordinate and boss.

Now what it really means is going with the flow and not making waves. If you disagree with something, bowing to the majority without voicing your disagreement. You can indict a person by saying he's not a team player. That doesn't mean he won't follow directions; it's because he voices an objection, because he argues with you before doing something, especially if he's right. That's when we really get mad—when the other guy is right. If he's wrong, we can be condescending and adopt the "you poor stupid bastard".... tone.

The skillful boss uses ideologies like team play adroitly, counting on subordinates to get the message and choose to do what he wants. The same manager continues:

Another meaning of team play is its use as a club. You use it to jack people into corners without seeming to. If I say to you, do this and you say that you don't really want to, but I insist, well, you've put the guy in an uncomfortable position and yourself too. But if you do it skillfully, the guy is not going to go away boxed. So, on one hand, you can't force them to do something; but you also can't manipulate them to do it. People resent this. What you do is appeal to something like team work and they choose to do it because they know how important and valued it is in the organization. The boss has the extra vote but he has to cast it with some skill.

Younger managers learn very quickly that, whatever the public protestations to the contrary, bosses want pliable and agreeable subordinates, especially during periods of crisis; clique leaders want dependable, trustworthy allies. Those who raise objections to what a boss wants to do or what a clique leader really desires run the risk of being labeled "outspoken" or "naysayers" or "crepehangers." Frank dissent gets interpreted as disloyalty or even betrayal, and bosses and embattled clique leaders apply to such transgressions the accepted norms of warfare.

Managers' insistence on being comfortable with others, their forging of alliances, and their distrust of dissent come into sharper focus in the context of their accountability for decisions. I can only point out here managers' essential rules for making decisions and allocating responsibility. Mythologies about decision making abound in the corporate world. Two widely upheld ideals are the "consensus manager" who can bring his team together to achieve a goal and the "take-charge" guy who exhibits vision and dynamic leadership. Both types are fictions of a sort, even though one can observe marked differences in management style in any hierarchy. Whatever the stylistic differences, however, the reality is that both types of managers try to make things turn out the way they are supposed to—that is, as defined by their bosses. Because managers experience their world as arbitrary, capricious, and fraught with conflict, they recognize that all their decisions are subject to numerous and possibly pejorative interpretations. They try, therefore, to avoid hard decisions; if such decisions cannot be avoided, they involve as many people as possible in the decision-making process in order to spread responsibility and, if things go wrong, potential blame.

Blame is the real issue in big decisions that specific rules or procedures do not cover. Blame tarnishes one's image and reputation and can precipitously limit one's influence and, indeed, one's future. When blame time comes, managers' immediate reaction is, as they put it, to CYA ("cover your ass").

A high-ranking executive says: "The one statement that will paralyze a room is when some guy in authority says: 'Now I'm not interested in a witch hunt, but. . . . ' When those words are uttered, the first instinct of people is immediately to hunker down and protect their own flanks." At the middle levels of the corporation, CYA memos, as they are called, proliferate during a crisis; in fact, it is said that one can gauge the importance of a decision and its potential danger by the amount of paper it generates. Higher-ranking managers know, however, that when disaster strikes, the idea that paper protects anyone is a vain and naive hope. As one executive says, "When things really go peanut butter, all the goddamn memos in the world are not going to help you."

What does matter when things go wrong is agility and political connections. One manager explains the kind of agility that is necessary:

The good manager is always aware and always wary. He knows that he has to be able to point the finger at somebody when things go wrong. And he knows that someone can point the finger *at him* at anytime. There's no accountability in the corporation. People don't want to hear about that shit. What you hope is that no one is after *your* ass. . . . You have to have the political wherewithal to know you're being set up. You have to be able to turn anything around and be able to point the finger at somebody else when they come after you.

He goes on to link this personal skill with the invaluable inclusion in a network of powerful allies:

[And] you need a Godfather. They have to know you. . . . You have to remember that you get to explain things away only *once*. When things get screwed up, you get *one* chance. That's why it's important for everybody to be in bed with everybody else. And if they don't like you from the start, you don't have a chance. Because when things go wrong, what people do is sit down and say—without saying it in so many words—look, our jobs are on the line. Let's make sure that it's not us who gets nailed.

Of course, a less agile individual or less powerful group might get nailed as a consequence, but managers do not concern themselves with this. The fundamental rule of corporate life is to protect oneself and, if possible, one's own.

As a result, the managerial world is not notable for its compassion. Managers know that failure is quite often simply a matter of social definition, but they extend little sympathy to one who "gets nailed" with the blame for a bad decision, or who ends up at the wrong place at the wrong time, or whose business area collapses because of irrational market patterns, or who chooses the wrong network in a political showdown. Such occurrences unsettle managers and remind them that any of these things could easily happen to them. However, they respond by putting as much distance as possible between themselves and one thought to be a failure, particularly if there are known past associations between them. One executive says:

Our motives are purely selfish. We're not concerned about old Joe failing, but we're worried about how his failure will reflect on us. When you pick somebody, say, you invest part of yourself in him. So his failure and what it means to his kids and so on mean nothing. What you're worried about is your own ass with your superiors for having picked him in the first place. . . . What we do essentially when somebody fails is to put him in a little boat, tow him out to sea, and cut the rope. And we never think about him again.

The prevailing view is that managers are big, bossy, well paid, and should be able to take care of themselves. Moreover, those defined as having failed in some major way are expected to be good sports and leave the arena gracefully or, at least, quietly. And, in fact, most do, usually being extended a "Golden Handshake" to speed their departure. Managers see little point in being vulnerable in a world that extols strength and power; it is a dangerous characteristic that can invite only contempt and abuse.

Structures of authority, fealty, patronage, and cliques thus form the basic framework of managerial work, one always subject to upheaval and the consequent formation of new alliances. Each network of affiliation, while it lasts, develops its own criteria for admission and its own etiquette within the general culture of the corporation; the dominant clique in a hierarchy at any given time establishes the tone for other groups. The segmented work patterns of bureaucracy, of course, underlie these larger structures, and managers' cognitive maps to the thickets of their world contain caricatures of the style and ethos of different occupational groups in the corporation. Production types are hard-drinking, raucous, good-time Charlies; accountants are bean counters who know how to play the shell game; lawyers are legal eagles or legal beagles dressed in wool pin-stripes; corporate staff are the king's spies; marketing guys are cheerful, smooth-talking, upbeat fashion plates; financial wizards, who seem to be in the ascendancy everywhere, are tight-mouthed, close-to-the-vest poker players; and outside consultants, who essentially legitimate already desired changes, are people who borrow your watch and then charge you for telling you the time. These different occupational groups meld with each other through regular work assignments, special Task Forces, or through the vagaries of power shifts that subordinate one group to another. Within each grouping, whether based strictly on occupational expertise or emerging as the result of other melding, the more general patterns already described of clique formation, patronage, competition, and power-seeking prevail. The corporation is thus an intricate matrix of rival and often overlapping managerial sodalities. The principal goal of each group is its own survival; of each person, his own advancement. The unintended social consequence of this maelstrom of competition and ambition is the public social order that the corporation presents to the world.

The moral ethos of these managerial sodalities emerges directly out of this social context. It is an ethos most notable for its lack of fixedness. Morality in the corporate world emerges not from some set of internally held principles, but from relationships with some person, some clique, some social network that matters to a person. Since these relationships are always multiple and always in flux, moralities are always situational.

FIXITY AND FAILURE

Bureaucracies thus place a great premium on "flexibility," as it is called. This comes into sharper focus when we analyze, on one hand, a counter case, that of a man who, holding to a different sort of ethic, tried to "blow the whistle" on practices in his firm and, on the other, corporate managers' appraisals of what he did. Here I am using materials drawn from a substudy I am doing on whistleblowers and interviews with some managers in the Chemical Company to whom the case was presented.[12]

Brady (a pseudonym) was educated in England as a Chartered Public Accountant, a profession that he values highly and one that carries considerably more status, respect, and public trust in Britain than the American equivalent—that is, Certified Public Accountant. After a stint with a major auditing firm in England and then in Canada, Brady got a job in the United States as vice president of finance for the international division of a large processed food company. The CEO of the whole corporation was himself a financial man and had initiated a dual reporting system for all of his firm's divisions. All major financial officers, like Brady, had to report not only directly up the line to the president of his division but also laterally to the corporate vice president for finance who in turn reported to the CEO himself. The fundamental rule of the reporting system required any discrepancy in financial figures—budgets exceeded, irregularities in payments, unplanned raises, and so on—to be documented through a Treasurer's Report (TR) that would, in due course, end up on the CEO's desk. The system was stringent and quite unusual in the detail that it required be sent up to the latter. The CEO relished financial detail and, it is said, reviewed every TR carefully.

Brady is a very conscientious man, one deeply imbued with the ethics of his profession. He was disturbed to discover, upon taking office, a number of irregularities in his division, including a bribery payment of some size made to an official of a developing country and, closer to home, a set of doctored invoices done by his peer on the managerial ladder, the vice president of marketing. With the pressure of a federal investigation aiding him, Brady was able to clear up the bribery issue, but when he submitted a TR on the doctored invoices, with his immediate boss's approval, he found that his boss's boss refused to sign off on the report, the requisite procedure before the TR could go over to the corporate vice president for finance on its way to the CEO. The matter languished for some time, despite Brady's repeated efforts to have it go forward. In the meantime, Brady was approached on different occasions by three people in the company, including one friend, and told to drop the whole affair. Brady felt that he was himself in jeopardy from the CEO's scrutiny because he had no verifiable numbers to put in the book to cover the amount. While the matter was unresolved, Brady's immediate boss retired, leaving him in a direct relationship with the man blocking the TR.

Suddenly, Brady found himself demoted, broken in grade and salary, and transferred to the Corporate Division, where he now reported directly to the corporate vice president for finance as assistant treasurer. The change, he feels, was intended basically to keep him under control. As it happened, he soon came across much more serious and potentially more damaging information. Key people in the corporation—at this stage, Brady was not sure just who—were using millions of dollars of the employee pension fund as a profit slush fund—that is, money was not declared as an asset, but concealed. It was moved in and out of the corporation's earning statements each year, as needed, so that the firm always came in exactly on target; in fact, key members of the hierarchy could predict each October the exact earnings per share of the company for the year even though a third of all earnings were in foreign currency. This uncanny accuracy, of course, assured top executives of completely reliable bonus payments, which were tied to meeting profit targets.

This knowledge deeply upset Brady because he saw it as a direct violation of stockholders' trust, a misuse of other people's money for personal gain, and one that could, in hard times, jeopardize the employees' pension fund. He felt that he now had no way of reporting the matter through normal channels; his boss, the corporate vice president for finance, had been hostile to him ever since Brady had come under his control, distrusting Brady, it seems, because of his attempted reporting of the doctored invoices. Brady felt that if the CEO were informed about the manipulation of the funds, he would act decisively to end the violation. Brady discussed the matter with a close friend, a man who had no defined position but considerable influence in the company because of his role as lobbyist, front man, and fixer—in short, an all-around factotum. Brady's information alarmed this man, and with a detailed memo on the slush fund written anonymously by Brady, he approached a key director of the corporation who chaired the Directors' Audit Committee. The director took the memo into a meeting with the CEO and his top aides. Immediately after the meeting, Brady's friend was fired and escorted from the building by guards.

It was only at this point that Brady realized that it was the CEO himself who was manipulating the numbers. The entire dual reporting system that the CEO had personally initiated was, in part, a spy network to guard against discovery of the slush fund manipulation, and perhaps other finagling, rather than a system to ensure financial honesty. The top people still did not know that Brady had written the memo, but he was under suspicion. In time, the pressure on him mounted, and Brady had had enough; he went to the chief lawyer in the whole corporation and laid out the case for him. At that point, Brady was summarily fired, and he and his belongings were literally thrown out of the company building.

It is important to note the sharp contrast between Brady's reasons for acting as he did and corporate managers' analysis of his actions. For Brady, the kinds of issues he confronted at work were distinctly *moral* issues, seen through the prism of his professional code. He says:

So what I'm saying is that at bottom, I was in jeopardy of violating my professional code. And I felt that you have to stick up for that. If your profession has standing, it has that standing because *someone stood up for it.* If the SEC [the Securities and Exchange Commission] had come in and did an analysis and then went into the detail of the case and put me up on the stand and asked me—What is your profession? Was this action right or wrong? Why did you do it then? I would really be in trouble. . . . with myself most of all. I am frightened of losing respect, my self-respect in particular. And since that was tied with my respect for my profession, the two things were joined together.

He goes on to comment further about his relation to professional standards and how those standards contrast with the prevailing ethos of corporate life.

I have fears in a situation like that. . . . It's not exactly a fear of what could happen to me, although that certainly crossed my mind. What it is is a fear of being found out not to stand up to standards that I have claimed as my own. It is a fear of falling down in a place where you have stuck a flag in the ground and said: "This is where I stand." I mean, why is it in life today that we have to deny any morality at all? But this is exactly the situation here. I was just too honest for that company. What is right in the corporation is not what's right in a man's home or in his church. *What is right in the corporation is what the guy above you wants from you.* That's what morality is in the corporation.

For Chemical Company managers, Brady's dilemma is devoid of moral or ethical content. For them, first of all, the issues he raises are simply practical matters, and his basic failing was that he violated the fundamental rules of bureaucratic life: (1) You never go around your boss; (2) you tell your boss what he wants to hear; (3) if your boss wants something dropped, you drop it; (4) you are sensitive to your boss's wishes so that you anticipate what he wants—you don't force him, in other words, to act as boss; (5) your job is not to report something that your boss doesn't want reported, but rather to cover it up. You do what your job requires and keep your mouth shut. Further, these managers feel that Brady had plenty of available legitimations to justify his *not* acting. Clearly, they feel, a great many other executives knew about the pension fund scam and did nothing; everybody, especially the top bosses, were playing the game. There were, besides, a number of ways out of the situation for Brady if he found the situation intolerable, including resigning. Also, whatever action he took would be insignificant anyway, so why bother to act at all? Third, managers see the violations that disturbed Brady—doctored invoices, irregular payments, shuffling numbers in accounts—as small potatoes indeed, commonplaces of corporate life. For them, juggling inventories, post- or pre-dating memos or invoices, tucking large sums of money away for a rainy day are part and parcel of managing in a large corporation where social interpretations, not necessarily performance itself, decide one's fate. Finally, managers feel that Brady's biggest error was in insisting on a moral code—his professional ethics—that had no relevance to his organizational situation. In doing so, he called others' organizational morality—that is, their acceptance of the bureaucratic ethos—into question and made them uncomfortable. They see this as the key reason why Brady's bosses did him in. And they too would do him in, without any qualms. Managers, they say, do not want evangelists working for them.

The finale to the story is worth recounting. After Brady was fired, the CEO of the firm retired and elevated to his position a man known as Loyal Sam who had tracked the CEO throughout his career. The CEO took an emeritus position with the company: Chief of Internal Audit. When the Chemical Company managers hear the outcome, they laugh softly and nod their heads and give even an outsider one of the knowing looks usually reserved only for trusted others in their world.

CONCLUSION

Karl Mannheim points out that bureaucracy turns all political issues into matters of administration.[13] One can see a parallel alchemy in managers' response to Brady's dilemma. Bureaucracy transforms all moral issues into practical concerns. A moral judgment based on a professional ethos has no meaning in a world where the etiquette of authority relationships, nonaccountability for actions, and the necessity for protecting and covering for one's boss, one's network, and oneself supersede all other considerations. As a matter of survival, not to mention advancement, corporate managers keep their eyes fixed on the social framework of their world and its requirements. Thus, they simply do not see most issues that confront them as moral concerns, even when problems might be posed by others in moral terms.

Managers' essential pragmatism, perhaps their most striking characteristic, stems from the priority they assign to the social rules of their bureaucratic context. This pragmatism is the root of the flexibility that I mentioned earlier, and it constitutes a principal criterion for advancement in a corporation. The higher one goes in the corporate world, the more one must rationalize one's self to the norms of flexibility. On one hand, flexibility means a great adeptness at inconsistency, a dexterity at symbolic manipulation. Those adept at inconsistency can freely, and with no qualms, manipulate a variety of rhetorics and vocabularies to meet, as required, the divergent expectations of diverse audiences. On the other hand, flexibility means the capacity to extend the transformation of moral issues into practical concerns to quite far reaches. One might call this an alertness to expediency. In effect, those alert to expediency externalize the objectification of self learned in the course of self-rationalization; they learn to appraise all situations and all people as they come to see themselves, that is, as objects, as commodities, to be rearranged and tinkered with. This is the nub of the moral ethos of bureaucracy and how it affects managers. Some managers pose this "trade-off" between morality and expedience as a question: Where do you draw the line?

Some managers find drawing the line a difficult and anxiety-laden process. They worry in very personal terms about the damage to others' careers caused by purges; they agonize about truth-telling and promise-keeping; they are concerned about the safety of their products and about their corporations' compliance with federal regulations; they find the nonaccountability of the corporation unsettling and troublesome. There is little escape from such anxieties for those who experience them because the press of managerial work, and uncontrollable events as well, always bring new problems to be confronted. More particularly, less-questioning managers intensify the anxiety for those who are uneasy. For these managers, who respond more fully to bureaucratic premiums, alertness to expediency means examining issues not on their intrinsic merits but from the perspective of one's organizational advantage. It means stripping away the emotional and any stated moral aspects of a troublesome problem and asking what outcome will best serve oneself and one's social network. It means, then, working to bring about that outcome without regard for other considerations. They invoke as necessary the numerous vocabularies of accounts that bureaucracy provides managers to excuse or justify nearly any action—whether these are meritocratic ideologies, the need for secrecy or team play, disputed scientific evidence, public ignorance, the myth of better informed and wiser superiors—in short, whatever account is organizationally available and ready at hand. The manager alert to expediency sees his bureaucratic world through a lens that may seem blurred to those outside the corporation; it is, however, a lens that enables him to bring into exact focus the relationships and rules of his world. The alert manager comes to see the misfortunes of others as opportunities for himself. More generally, he measures relationships with others with a utilitarian calculus and forms or breaks friendships or alliances accordingly. He comes, too, to see that the nonaccountability of the corporation is really a license to exert one's own will and to improve one's own fortunes as long as one carefully maintains alliances and does not get caught.

The logical result of alterness to expediency is the elimination of any lines at all. As a practical matter, however, bureaucracies are not self-contained—particularly commercial organizations. They operate in the public arena and are subject to the vagaries and pressures of public opinion. Public outrage about numerous corporate practices can and has posed public issues in specifically moral terms—for instance, on the environment or on worker health and safety—often creating costly dilemmas and public embarrassment for corporate leaders. Public opinion constitutes, in fact, one of the only effective checks on the bureaucratic impulse to translate all moral issues into practical concerns. As one might expect, then, those who have attained the upper reaches of corporations and are imbued with the bureaucratic ethos make every effort to mold public opinion to allow continued uninterrupted operation of business. In this sense, moral issues become issues of public relations.

This equation also emerges directly out of the social context of the corporation that we have described. The politics of the corporation, with its system of fealty, patronage, cliques, and endless power struggles, produces in managers a conception of the public that at bottom is closely akin to the way they see rival managerial groups. For the most part, this view consists of a guarded wariness and a bitterly sardonic appraisal of the shifts in public opinion. Managers are acutely aware of how powerful public opinion can be in turning their world upside down—of how, in fact, it can be used by rival managerial groups for their own ends. Every corporation that I studied has had major confrontations with some outraged publics in the last few years. The big fear is that some action, policy, practice, or product of a corporation will suddenly get caught up in what are seen as unpredictable and irrational waves of hysteria stirred up by self-styled public interest groups. When this kind of catastrophe occurs, not only are huge amounts of time and money wasted, but blame time can suddenly fall like the night within a corporation, bringing shakeups and reprisals with it.

The goal then is to get one's story out to important publics in such a way that the main parameters of public opinion can be shaped and controlled. Most corporations do this on a regular sustained basis, intensifying their efforts during crisis periods. For the most part, corporations allot this work to special practitioners of public relations within the corporation who consult regularly with the highest officials of the firm; these practitioners and, quite often, the highest officials themselves, also work with public relations (PR) specialists based in agencies. The views of PR specialists both in corporations and in agencies correspond closely to views held by corporate managers and executives; generally, specialists are, however, somewhat broader, often more sophisticated, and more detached. In particular, their work gives them a finer appreciation for how the drama of social reality is constructed since they are themselves the stagehands. I will restrict my comments here to how PR people, as a sophisticated proxy for corporate managers, approach all issues, including those fraught with moral implications.

In the world of public relations, there is no ascertainable truth; there are only stories. One takes care to report facts, at least some facts, but one feels free to put any interpretation on facts that one wishes. The task is to work with facts at hand and devise plausible stories that will command the assent, or at least the lack of dissent, of important sectors of the public. It is important to remember that sometimes confusion, as long as it is credibly generated confusion, will serve the same purpose. This means seeing the world as popular novelists do, essentially in broad brushstrokes, boiling down all events to simple understandable drama. Most people's understanding of the world, after all, consists precisely of such little stories. The job then is to present a euphemistically told tale that will enable the corporation to function without undue disruption. Truth and, for that matter, morality are all a matter of perception. One tries, therefore, to engineer moral acquiescence, if not consent, by arranging other's perceptions to suit one's own interest. In short, public relations elevates the bureaucratic virtue of alertness to expedience into a professional calling.

Within this bureaucratic framework, an older ethos like the professional code that Brady tried to assert seems merely quaint, and whistleblowers like him, men engaged in a quixotic search for evanescent absolutist ideals. Bureaucracy makes its own internal rules and social context the principal moral gauges for action. It turns principles into guidelines, ethics into etiquette, responsibility into an agility at avoiding blame, and truth into credibility. Corporate managers who become imbued with the bureaucratic ethos take their world as they find it and pursue their careers as best they can by the rules of that ethos. As it happens—given their pivotal institutional role in our epoch—they help create, as one consequence of their personal striving, a society where morality becomes indistinguishable from the quest for one's own survival and advantage.[14]

8

Bureaucracy and Civil Liberties: The FBI Story

Kenneth O'Reilly

The Federal Bureau of Investigation is almost in a class by itself in eroding American civil liberties.[1] From its origins in the Progressive Era to the unravelling of the Watergate scandals and attendant congressional investigations of the intelligence community in the mid–1970s, the FBI served as an extreme appendage of the discretionary state. Virtually unaccountable outside itself and controlled by a handful of bureaucrats unburdened by traditional legal, constitutional, or moral constraints, the FBI's assumed mission not only included the pursuit of bureaucratic autonomy and empire building, but the advancement of conservative political objectives as well. In both cases FBI officials were remarkably successful. The FBI today remains one of the most prominent and powerful of the federal bureaucracies, and its accomplishments include the legitimization of the domestic intelligence investigation—that is, federal surveillance of politically active Americans suspected of no specific crime.

PROGRESSIVISM AND THE EARLY YEARS

It is hardly coincidental that the Bureau of Investigation (renamed the Federal Bureau of Investigation in 1935) was founded in 1908, at the height of the Progressive Era. The Bureau was established at the direction of President Theodore Roosevelt's attorney general, Charles J. Bonaparte, a grand-nephew of Napoleon I, who acted on his own administrative authority.[2] Although some members of Congress questioned the need for a national police force, citing states' rights traditions and the potential threat to civil liberties (alluding to czarist Russia as the principal model of a nation-state with a national police), Attorney General Bonaparte and President Roosevelt argued that the issue had nothing to do with civil liberties or other abuses of power. It was simply a matter of efficient justice and the need for executive flexibility when attacking political or economic corruption. Though somewhat skeptical of these assurances, and the additional promise that Bureau investigations would be confined to violations of interstate commerce laws, Progressive Era legislators allowed the attorney general's administrative action to stand.

It may appear paradoxical that the institutionalization of federal surveillance can be traced to an era commonly associated with liberal and humanitarian reform. On the other hand, the birth of the Bureau of Investigation was in many ways a typical Progressive Era reform—the creation of yet another "scientific" professional bureaucracy to help manage the complex problems of a rapidly changing society (in this case, the problems of internal subversion and crime). The Progressive Era was captured only in a limited way by such humanitarian reformers as Jane Addams and Robert M. LaFollette's ambitious programs to smash corporate power. Many other progressive reformers emphasized different values—elitism, intolerance, a distrust of mass politics, and an affinity for results, efficiency, and administrative solutions that effectively imposed changes from above. The Progressive era witnessed both the spread of settlement houses and child labor laws and the ascendancy of bureaucracy within the government, the corporation, and much of everyday life. Doctors, lawyers, technicians, economists, intercollegiate and professional athletes, and even sociologists all kept pace by either forming or revitalizing professional societies. The FBI, for its part, stands as a monument to that strain of progressivism that preferred order and stability to the disorder and dissent intrinsic to a less efficient, if more democratic, politics.

Although the Bureau was supposed to fight crime, crime control never fully occupied the federal investigators. Crime control, for the most part, remained the prerogative of state and local government during the Progressive Era, thereby limiting the Bureau's criminal jurisdiction.[3] Bureau agents, in fact, did not have much to do. During World War I, the Bureau began to monitor anti-war activists and other dissidents, eventually basing its authority on the Espionage and Sedition Acts of 1917–1918. The Bureau's main concern, however, was with the Left (communists, socialists, Wobblies, and even liberals—or the "Liberal element," as Bureau officials liked to say) and with Afro-Americans.[4] On August 1, 1919, some nine months after the armistice, the Justice Department formed the General Intelligence Division (GID), specifically to chronicle the activities of racial and political dissidents. Headed by twenty-four-year-old J. Edgar Hoover, a former indexer at the Library of Congress and recent law school graduate, Bureau agents assigned to this unit were specifically directed to gather all possible information regarding sedition "which may be of use in prosecutions . . . under legislation . . . which may *hereafter* be enacted." Among other activities, agents in the field collected books and other literature and forwarded them to the young GID chief. Hoover was busy compiling a "library . . . on 'Liberalism'."[5]

William J. Burns, Bureau chief and former head of the union-busting Burns Detective Agency, said his bureaucracy's mission was to "drive every radical out of the country and bring the parlor Bolsheviks to their senses." As part of this effort, Bureau surveillance was extended to the American Civil Liberties Union, the National Association for the Advancement of Colored People, and dozens of other nonradical groups—including all Afro-American newspapers and all "colored civic organizations." Dossiers were also compiled on such prominent individuals as Felix Frankfurter, with a Bureau report of May 1920 describing the future Supreme Court justice as a member of "the Jewish element furnishing the brains for the radicals." Hoover provided office space and opened GID files to dozens of newspaper reporters and other publicists who had appropriate anti-radical credentials, as well as conservative politicians and such private-sector countersubversives as R. M. Whitney of the American Defense Society and Ralph Easley of the National Civil Federation, in an effort to hype the Red menace.[6]

The Bureau's extensive political spying and crude attempts to shape public opinion did not come under close scrutiny until the congressional investigations of the Warren G. Harding administration scandals. In an effort to depoliticize the Justice Department, in March 1924, President Calvin Coolidge appointed Harlan F. Stone, former dean of the Columbia Law School, attorney general. Stone fired Burns and appointed Hoover acting director of the Bureau. Concerned about the dangers "a secret police" posed to "free government and free institutions," the new attorney general announced that Bureau investigations would henceforth "be strictly limited to" violations of federal statutes and not the "political or other opinions of individuals."[7] To prevent future abuses, Stone implemented a series of specific reforms. These restrictions prohibited wiretaps, dissolved the GID, ended Bureau ties with private detective agencies and patriotic organizations, and forbade the dissemination of anti-radical propaganda. Both the House and the Senate failed to act on pending bills calling for legal rather than voluntary constraints. For the second time in sixteen years, Congress accepted the promise of executive control.

The appointment of J. Edgar Hoover as director of the Bureau was more than a bit ironic. As head of the GID, Hoover was directly involved in many of the Bureau's most blatant political investigations and escapades. He had, nonetheless, kept a low profile and thus was not publicly associated with Bureau abuses. He had also acquired some political capital, so Attorney General Stone's restrictions were simply ignored. Hoover began to solicit reports on radical activities from Bureau field offices even before his appointment was made permanent. He advised Stone to be patient: "Some of these offices," Hoover said in 1924, "have spent considerable time upon investigation of radical matters and seem to be at a loss now as to how to curtail the same."[8] In fact, Bureau officials had been utilizing separate filing procedures and "Do Not File" files to conceal the extent of their anti-radical propaganda activities and their use of questionable investigative techniques since at least 1920.[9] If the new director could only dream about an official Secrets Act, he would raise this simple yet quite effective method of bureaucratic obfuscation to an art form in the coming decades.

THE NEW DEAL

In many ways the modern FBI is a creature of the New Deal. Franklin D. Roosevelt brought the New Deal to federal police power and the Bureau of Investigation's agents just as surely as he brought it to corporate America and the nation's farmers and industrial workers.[10] In response to the exploits of the Depression Era's mobile and opportunistic hoodlums(John Dillinger, et al.), who often exploited the limited jurisdiction of local police simply by fleeing across county or state lines after robbing banks or trains or whatever, President Roosevelt sought to mobilize federal resources for a war on crime. The Justice Department drafted a series of legislative proposals to expand the FBI's criminal jurisdiction, and after an anti-lynching bill was dropped, Congress passed this New Deal crime control package without even taking a record vote. The Roosevelt administration also encouraged the FBI to lead a Madison Avenue-style media campaign to counter the public's supposedly romanticized view of the era's criminal element. President Roosevelt's press secretary, Stephen Early, described this campaign privately as "a plan to publicize and make the G-men heroes."[11]

Shortly after the New Deal crime reforms were passed, President Roosevelt called upon the FBI to provide systematic information about the activities of native fascists and communists. The FBI had the resources to manage this mission well, and from the mid–1930s until the operations of Richard Nixon's "plumbers" sprang leaks in the early 1970s, FBI domestic intelligence investigations were a more or less a regular part of the governing process. Over two thousand FBI domestic intelligence reports were forwarded to the Roosevelt White House alone, with the majority of these detailing the opinions and activities of the President's political "adversaries"—a term that was defined in the broadest sense. Thus the FBI submitted reports on individuals ranging from conservative Republican Congressman Hamilton Fish of New York to March-on-Washington organizer A. Philip Randolph, and on groups and institutions ranging from a committee set up to honor Anton Cermak (the Chicago mayor who helped save President-elect Roosevelt in an assassination attempt and lost his own life in the process) to the City College of New York. The intensity of FBI assistance might have varied from one administration to the next, but in every case Bureau officials proved willing to ingratiate themselves with whoever happened to occupy the Oval Office.

Hoover's FBI was not simply a pliable bureaucratic tool of the executive branch. Domestic intelligence investigations that could escape public or congressional (or, for that matter, judicial) scrutiny could also escape executive scrutiny. FBI officials could, and did, mobilize their investigative resources for the pursuit of independent political objectives. Both Herbert Hoover and Franklin Roosevelt used the FBI to spy on their domestic political adversaries. In Roosevelt's case, this included the solicitation of FBI reports on Herbert Hoover. At the same time, FBI officials held far more alarmist views on internal security issues than President Roosevelt and thus compiled dossiers on a number of prominent New Dealers, since even the New Deal's modest demands for social and economic reform were deemed subversive by the FBI. One FBI burglary (or "black-bag job," in Bureau jargon) in 1942 had as its objective the photographing of Eleanor Roosevelt's correspondence of 1940–1941 with student leaders of the left-wing American Youth Congress.[12] Moreover, the information gathered by the FBI during such unilateral political excursions was sometimes disseminated to the Bureau's ideological allies. The conservative Herbert Hoover, for one, was a frequent recipient of FBI leaks from the 1920s and early 1930s, when he was President, to the 1950s, when as a Stanford University trustee he worked (unsuccessfully) with the FBI director on at least one occasion to deny a faculty member a sizeable grant from the Fund for the Republic.[13]

McCARTHYISM AND MORE

During the New Deal and World War II years such intelligence practices were episodic. With the coming of the Cold War and the first rumblings of McCarthyism, however, FBI officials concluded that their mission in the internal security field required more aggressive methods. Through a series of programs beginning in 1946, the FBI launched an "educational" campaign (the Bureau's word) intended to develop "an informed public opinion" about "the basically Russian nature of the Communist Party in this country." An FBI executives' conference in February 1946 proposed to accomplish this goal by disseminating "educational material" through "available channels"—that is, by leaking derogatory personal or political information on dissident groups and individuals to congressional investigating committees, conservative journalists, and other anti-communist publicists.[14]

Later, in 1951, as the blacklists of the McCarthy era began to harden, yet another FBI program, the Responsibilities Program, was initiated to extend Bureau leaking to the employers of dissidents. When McCarthyism began to dissipate in the mid–1950s, FBI officials responded by launching a counterintelligence program (COINTELPRO) to "expose, disrupt, misdirect, discredit, or otherwise neutralize" domestic communists and those who unknowingly gave aid and comfort to the Communist party. As part of this effort, the Bureau escalated its program to dramatize the Red menace in response to the Communist party's equally dramatic loss of membership and expanded its communist infiltration (COMINFIL) program. Under CO-MINFIL, the FBI began targeting such groups as the Boy Scouts of America on the grounds that "legitimate mass organizations" were sometimes infiltrated by Red agents. These highly structured and institutionalized programs, moreover, were supplemented by thousands of ad hoc actions. When FBI Assistant Director Cartha DeLoach handed Richard Arens, House Committee on Un-American Activities staff director, dossiers on eighty-one California public school teachers, it was not part of any formal FBI program.[15] But the economic carnage from this off-the-cuff leak—resignations, firings, transfers, litigations—was all quite formal and quite quantifiable.

The FBI's attempts to add to the blacklists as well as their other contributions to the cultural pollution of the domestic Cold War scarcely need further documentation. The real question is: how was the FBI able to pursue activities that openly conflicted with (in J. Edgar Hoover's own words) "fundamental principles of common decency and . . . basic American rights of fair play"?[16] At least in part, this success can be understood by FBI officials' cultivation of political constituencies on both sides of the various internal and national security issues of the day, while simultaneously pursuing their own bureaucratic and conservative political interests.

FBI involvement in the domestic communist debates of the early Cold War years and the later controversy symbolized by the junior senator from Wisconsin, Joseph R. McCarthy, provides a fairly clear example of the FBI's political and bureaucratic dexterity. The anti-communist or McCarthyite political style is familiar enough—the reckless charges, myopic focus on the political associations of dissidents rather than on the issues they raised, and tendency to explain the loss of American omnipotence abroad by reference to internal conspiracies at home. The United States emerged from World War II an economic and strategic giant, complete with a nuclear monopoly and the power (or so it seemed) to make the world over in its own image. Yet it was precisely at this time that the United States experienced a series of international shocks: the descending of the Iron Curtain, Mao Tse-Tung's victory in the Chinese civil war, and the Soviets' successful detonation of an atomic bomb.

To explain these troubling developments, McCarthyites raised the specter of treason and simply ignored the very real limits of American power and various external factors. In the McCarthyite view, Eastern Europe had been "sold out" by Franklin Roosevelt and his State Department advisers in 1945 at Yalta. China was "lost" in the same way, and the "secret" of nuclear weaponry was "stolen" by two Jewish members (or former members) of the Communist party and given to Comrade Stalin. Through blunders and betrayals at home, international communism was on the march abroad, and the Democratic administrations of Franklin D. Roosevelt and Harry S Truman were to blame. For Senator McCarthy, as he titled a speech of February 1954 on a tour sponsored by the Republican National Committee to commemorate Abraham Lincoln's birthday, the Democratic ascendancy since the Great Depression signified nothing less than "Twenty Years of Treason."[17]

In the midst of the great domestic communist debates, the FBI publicly allied itself with the presidency, while simultaneously providing covert support for the McCarthyite critique. FBI officials were thus able to strengthen the Bureau's autonomy while pursuing political objectives and engaging in political activities that would have undermined their autonomy if publicly compromised. The FBI accomplished these seemingly conflicting missions by supporting what would become known as the doctrine of "executive privilege."[18] When investigating executive personnel, congressional conservatives on the House Committee on Un-American Activities (HUAC), the Senate Internal Security Subcommittee (SISS), and the Senate Permanent Subcommittee on Investigations (the McCarthy Committee) demanded access to federal employee loyalty files—files that had been compiled principally by the Civil Service Commission and the FBI. When President Truman refused to allow congressional access to these files, conservatives in the Congress and the media charged a cover-up The rationale behind executive privilege was based on expansive national security claims and the need to protect the reputations of innocent persons. J. Edgar Hoover was one of the most effective spokesmen for this argument.[19]

Hoover's rhetoric, combined with the FBI's image of nonpartisanship and professionalism, seemed to offer a compelling alternative to HUAC, SISS, and the McCarthyites. FBI officials, for their part, did not support executive privilege simply to cultivate a liberal constituency. The denial of congressional access to FBI loyalty files enhanced the Bureau's autonomy, creating a political vacuum in which the Bureau could operate with virtually no outside supervision or accountability.

While FBI officials publicly supported executive privilege for reasons of bureaucratic self-interest, the covert and selective support they provided to McCarthyites in the Congress was politically motivated. Hoover and his principal aides did not oppose congressional access to Bureau files. In fact, their political objectives, as outlined at the February 1946 executives' conference and subsequently refined, required it. The FBI was concerned only with the terms of access. Formal Bureau policy required the forwarding of all outside requests for information to the attorney general, with the requestor receiving only the Bureau's "standard claim that the files of the FBI are confidential." In practice, however, the FBI considered all requests of this type "individually" and furnished information "where the best interests of the Bureau would be served."[20]

With McCarthy era Red-hunts and blacklisting extending into the private sector, FBI name checks and other assistance to congressional investigating committees was not limited to federal employees. In 1947 Hoover ordered the Los Angeles field office "to extend *every* assistance to this Committee" as

HUAC was preparing for the so-called "Hollywood Ten" hearings.[21] The FBI sent HUAC the name of Screen Actors Guild President Ronald Reagan and a number of other Hollywood anti-communists, with the suggestion that they be called as "friendly" witnesses. Bureau agents also drew up lists of questions so that the Committee could question the Ten and other "unfriendly" witnesses more effectively.

Yet another FBI private-sector blacklisting effort, the Responsibilities Program, was also launched during McGrath's tenure as attorney general. When initiating this program in 1951, FBI officials based their authority on the recommendations of a delegation of state governors appointed by the executive committee of the 1951 National Governors Conference. Hoover's FBI also discussed the program with McGrath and various White House aides. The delegation of governors met with Hoover in February "for the purpose of developing greater coordination in the field of internal security between the state and Federal governments." According to the director's account of this meeting, the delegation was primarily concerned "about persons teaching in state institutions as well as persons working in key areas for the state who would be considered dangerous to the security of the U.S." Governor Adlai Stevenson of Illinois in particular was troubled by the ongoing (and ultimately unsuccessful) effort to revive the Illinois Seditious Activities Investigation Commission (the so-called Broyles Commission). Although Stevenson was not technically a member of the delegation, he accompanied the other governors to the meeting with Hoover. To guard against "witch-hunting" in state educational institutions and to protect state governors "from ill-considered inquiries by well-meaning legislatures," Stevenson urged the FBI to furnish, "on a strictly confidential basis," reports on the subversive affiliations of college faculty.[22] Following Hoover's meeting with Stevenson and the delegation of state governors, the Responsibilities Program was formally launched.

Responsibilities Program leaks were never confined to the professoriat. Any person who received all or part of his or her income from a government source of any type was a likely Responsibilities Program target. The FBI closely monitored HUAC hearings (and presumably other congressional investigating committee hearings as well) and brought the names of those identified as communists to the attention of their employers or other appropriate officials.[23]

Later, during the Eisenhower years, the FBI briefed Attorney General Herbert Brownell on the Responsibilities Program. Brownell raised no objections at the time, but by November 1954, he was clearly troubled by the political risks involved in the most sensitive aspect of the Responsibilities Program: the FBI's effort to purge the college teaching profession. After discussing his reservations with several Justice Department aides, Brownell ordered Hoover to terminate Responsibilities Program operations aimed at the nation's colleges and universities. The FBI director convinced him to reverse this decision, however, by pointing out that Adlai Stevenson, Democratic party presidential candidate in 1952 (and again in 1956), was on record as supporting the Responsibilities Program operations against subversive faculty. If the Responsibilities Program were somehow publicly compromised and the Eisenhower administration was accused of interfering with academic freedom, Hoover and Brownell apparently felt that Stevenson's involvement would reduce the administration's vulnerability and allow President Eisenhower to point out that the administration was simply continuing a program begun by the Democrats.[24] Stevenson, indeed, was not the only prominent Democratic party liberal who was at least vaguely aware of the Responsibilities Program. FBI Assistant Director Louis Nichols briefed Minnesota Senator Hubert H. Humphrey some two months after the Brownell flap. If Nichols is to be believed, Humphrey thought "it was one hundred percent correct . . . a very proper use of Bureau files."[25]

FBI officials were always interested in obtaining formal authority to conduct domestic intelligence investigations and operations, but at the same time they were willing to circumvent or ignore specific instructions from their ostensible superiors in those cases where such instructions proved a hindrance to Bureau objectives.

To cite a relatively minor and indirect example in conjunction with the Responsibilities Program, the decision to extend the blacklists to public school teachers was a unilateral one. The FBI weighed the risks and decided to do it. Nobody outside the Bureau was consulted. To cite a better known and more explicit example, when Attorney General Francis Biddle ordered Hoover to terminate the Custodial Detention Program in 1943, the director simply changed its nomenclature from that under which it was then known to the Security Index.[26] In 1946, too, when seeking authorization to employ wiretaps in national security investigations, the FBI (or perhaps Attorney General Tom Clark) doctored President Roosevelt's original authorization, leading President Truman to believe he was simply approving a continuation of previous wiretap policy. In fact, the President had unwittingly approved a significant expansion in the use of electronic surveillance. When Truman found out, he blamed Clark, but he did not rescind the directive. Clark, in turn, said Hoover was responsible for the flim-flam.[27]

Similarly, the Responsibilities Program itself was only one of several FBI efforts to police (or extend) blacklisting, and there is no indication that the attorney general or the White House authorized any of these additional programs. Besides the COINTELPROs (which in time went beyond the Communist party to include the Socialist Workers party, the Ku Klux Klan and other "White Hate Groups," the New Left, and "Black Hate Groups"), FBI policy required continuous analysis of "the employment" of Security Index subjects.[28] This policy continued even after the Responsibilities Program was terminated. The Bureau also arranged the subpoenaing of alleged subversives by congressional investigating committees because "experience has proved that in many instances where communists who are employed in key facilities . . . and have taken the Fifth Amendment they have been dismissed from such employment."[29] To insure that sufficient pressure would be brought to bear upon the employers of these people, the FBI routinely briefed "responsible" newspapermen "on the status" of targeted dissidents.

As the "programs of cooperation" with the McCarthy Committee and the SISS, the Responsibilities Program, COINTELPROs, and other less formal operations suggest, FBI surveillance was not an alternative to congressional Red-hunting but an integral part of McCarthyism. From its modest beginnings in the Progressive Era, the FBI attained legitimacy during the New Deal years and consolidation during World War II. For the next twenty-five years, the FBI was for all practical purposes an independent political entity. During the 1960s, it responded to the evisceration of the overt machinery of McCarthyism by radically expanding its intelligence and counterintelligence activities. Eventually, as in the case of the COINTELPRO against the Black Panther party and other militant black groups, these activities included (often successful) efforts to incite violence—"shooting and the like," in the words of one FBI official.[30]

The FBI preference for intelligence investigations and counterintelligence operations over criminal investigations and more mundane police work was most visible during this decade. When asked, for example, to *protect* civil rights activists from the Ku Klux Klan or to throw even one racist southern sheriff in jail, Hoover's FBI claimed limited jurisdiction, warned about the constitutional dangers of a national police force (a "Gestapo," to use the director's favorite specter), and posed as a disinterested, apolitical, fact-gathering investigative agency. The image of FBI agents standing across the street taking notes and refusing to make arrests while Klan thugs were chasing Movement people down the street or much worse is as timeless as that of G-men shooting it out with Dillinger or "Baby Face" Nelson. The FBI would not enforce federal civil rights law or protect civil rights workers, but it would wiretap the telephone of the father of one murdered rights activist and launch formal counterintelligence programs and community surveillance programs (Ghetto Informant Programs, BLCKPRO informants, COMINFIL investigations, and Rabble Rouser Indices) that were, at best, implicitly racist and, at worst, completely outside the bounds of the law.

If the FBI is now more restrained, it is only because of former President Nixon's inadvertent discrediting of "executive privilege." The careless, crude meanderings of the "plumbers" at the Watergate and untenable "national security" claims by White House patriots destroyed the surveillance consensus that Hoover's FBI had worked so tirelessly to build and exploit. 1974 amendments to the Freedom of Information Act have for the first time opened at least part of the FBI archive to the public, providing the type of access to Bureau files that McCarthy had once demanded of Truman. As we now know, these files *are* explosive—but not because they reveal much about the adventures of Red agents, or the complicity of the "party of treason," or the nation's teachers, or Martin Luther King in an international communist conspiracy. Instead, the files reveal the FBI's shameful and at times criminal record of disdain for the constitutional rights of Americans. Also, just as the Bureau of Investigation was temporarily deterred from its bureaucratic assault as a result of the mistakes of the Harding administration only to bounce back with new vigor as the FBI, so the currently more curtailed activities of the Bureau may not mean the end of its attempt to attain bureaucratic hegemony over domestic intelligence.

Since the Watergate era, there have been attempts at controlling the authoritarian tendencies of the FBI. The Freedom of Information Act has allowed individuals and groups to look into and litigate against FBI abuses of constitutionally guaranteed freedoms. The Congress has also appointed watchdog committees to oversee FBI programs.

However, the after-the-fact nature of these regulatory controls still allows the FBI far more leeway in its operations than a legal democracy can legitimately accept. The need for secrecy and for undercover operations inhibits the regulatory potential of the courts and the Congress. Yet no modern polity can do without an efficient national police force.

Therefore, the dilemma remains: how much control over the FBI is necessary for the maintenance of democracy, and how much independence of control is necessary for the effective functioning of the FBI? As long as interstate kidnapping, organized crime, violent political groups, and so on, exist, the FBI will exist. As long as the FBI exists, the threat to democracy exists. The growth in the size of the FBI over the years and the continuing increase in bureaucratization make it more and more difficult to pinpoint responsibility for unlawful acts.

Like any giant bureaucracy, the FBI will continue to exhibit authoritarian tendencies that are anathema to democracy. However, unlike most giant bureaucracies, this one is heavily armed and trained for secret intrusions into the lives of our citizens. Democratic nations must always remember that there is a fine line between a "Federal Bureau of Investigation"—absolutely essential for the modern democratic state—and a "Secret Police"—the backbone of all dictatorships.

9

Bureaucracy and Rationalization in the Soviet Police

William M. Jones

Frederick W. Taylor, the high priest of the scientific management school, has had legions of admirers in the capitalist world. Unlikely though it may seem, V. I. Lenin, founder of the Soviet state, was also an enthusiast who was quite conversant with Taylorism and specifically advocated using its "progressive" aspects to teach Soviet workers how to work.[1] In a broader sense, too, Taylorism is suggested in those famous passages in Lenin's *State and Revolution* which argue that state functions in the socialist society of the future could be made so simple that all workers could perform them with a minimum of training and on a part-time basis, thus ultimately obviating the need for a state bureaucracy.[2] Lenin went to his grave deploring the growth of bureaucracy in the new Soviet state, believing to the end that the political will of the Communist Party and the people united would dictate to the remnants of the state bureaucracy as the state itself "withered away."[3]

That Lenin desired efficiency without bureaucracy is less surprising than his rather un-Marxist desire to substitute political will for historical evolution as the vehicle for social change. Nevertheless, these apparent dualities or paradoxes in Leninism help explain, at least from the perspectives of doctrine and the cult of Lenin, why subsequent Soviet leaders have found it possible to stress efficiency over politics and vice versa at various times in charting Soviet progress toward the one goal that has remained relatively constant since Lenin's time—economic progress. The nature of the Soviet regime itself—especially its legitimacy—rests upon the fulfillment of the ultimate promise of Communism: the equitable distribution of the abundance of material wealth made possible by mass production. George W. Breslauer, among others, has noted that through a kind of "social contract" the Soviet people grant continuing legitimacy to their elite oligarchy in the expectation of a constantly improving standard of living.[4]

Josef Stalin fashioned Lenin's concept of political will into his own cult of personality, eventually destroying both the Communist Party of the Soviet Union (CPSU) and the mass of the Soviet people as independent political actors in order to achieve his own vision of the path of Soviet development. His successor Nikita Khrushchev appeared, on the other hand, to be genuinely interested in restoring, at least to a limited degree, the political power of the rank-and-file of the CPSU and even making new progress toward encouraging the long-awaited transition to public self-administration.[5]

THE BREZHNEV ERA

During the past decade many specialists in the study of the Soviet regime have attempted to identify the social and political contours of the transformation effected by the Brezhnev group after it seized power from Nikita Khrushchev in October, 1964. Although different analysts have identified different trends within the Brezhnev regime as focal, most acknowledge the relative importance of the shift away from Khrushchevian "voluntarism" and "populism" toward CPSU control, professionalism, and bureaucratic structures and processes. Whereas Khrushchev stressed the deprofessionalization of various state functions and the use of volunteers to achieve the "self-regulation" of some aspects of the Soviet regime, Brezhnev reestablished the dominance of the central apparatus of the CPSU, returned to scientists and other experts a significant voice in policy making, and engaged a new professional approach to using organization theory and advanced management techniques in most sectors of the Soviet regime.

An examination of changes made in the Soviet public order apparatus in the formative years of the Brezhnev era reveals in that sector as well this characteristic shift away from antibureaucratic policies toward political strategies that reflect key bureaucratic values—particularly enhanced rationality in organizational structures and processes, professionalism in police cadres, reliance on advanced law enforcement technology, and increased observance of socialist legality—the Soviet version of the rule-of-law principle.

The agency that bears primary responsibility for routine police work in the Soviet Union—law enforcement and the maintenance of public order—is the Ministry of Internal Affairs, or MVD. Although at various times the MVD has been tied to or had included the political police, since 1954 the two have been institutionally separate at the government ministry level, with the latter known as the KGB, or Committee for State Security.[6] The agency within the MVD performing most police functions is the militia, although other MVD agencies, such as the Criminal Investigation Administration, work closely with the militia and are discussed below. Finally, from the early days of the Soviet regime to the present, brigades of volunteers for assistance to the militia, known as *druzhiny*, have played a greater or lesser role in maintaining public order in the Soviet Union.[7]

Beginning in the mid–1950s, as he struggled to consolidate his leading position in the Soviet regime, Krushchev oversaw several key changes in the public order apparatus. First, as noted, the MVD was separated from the KGB. Subsequently a major decentralization of the MVD and militia was carried out, with regional and local Soviets gaining greater authority over police agencies. By 1960, the national-level MVD was completely eliminated, and its functions assigned to the fifteen union-republic MVDs, or in some cases to other ministries. In 1962, in a major public relations campaign, the name of the ministry itself was changed to the Ministry for the Protection of Public Order, or MOOP, and annual observance of Militia Day initiated. On these occasions, massive publicity in virtually every popular Soviet periodical extolled the activities, virtues, and professional experiences of the militia. It seemed fairly clear that the Khrushchev regime, through these 1962 changes, was attempting to communicate to the Soviet people that the police would thereafter concern themselves with socially beneficial law enforcement and public order maintenance functions and eschew those nasty political tasks previously associated in Stalin's time with the dread initials MVD or NKVD (People's Commissariat For Internal Affairs). Finally, under Khrushchev's aegis, the role of the volunteer brigades—the *druzhiny*—was greatly enhanced.[8]

Anti-hooliganism measures enacted in 1966 (less than two years after Khrushchev's ouster) signaled a clear reemphasis on the MVD and the militia, but it was not until 1968 that several trends toward the substantive "improvement" of these agencies became manifest. In November of that year the CPSU Central Committee and the USSR Council of Ministers issued a decree which changed the name of the Ministry for the Protection of Public Order to the Ministry of Internal Affairs. The decree went far beyond simply changing the ministry's name, however. It marked the beginning of a new personnel policy within the militia, a policy that was to be the basis for improvement in the militia in other respects as well. From the late 1960s through the early 1970s, the militia would be considerably altered in three general areas—personnel, organization and operations, and technology—to the extent that its quality as a "professional organization" would be greatly enhanced.

Extensive organizational and operational improvements were made. Within the MVD staff several new units were added: Information and Analysis subdivision, Organization-Inspection subdivision, Scientific-Technical department, and a USSR MVD Main Computer Center. Evidence shows that their creation was motivated by a desire for greater efficiency in data gathering, manipulation, and analysis.

New units and operational techniques were added to the militia as well. A permanent duty staff was placed on twenty-four-hour duty at militia offices down to the city and county level. The Night Militia was created for the purpose of assuming, eventually, the function of guarding public places, a task performed heretofore by the organizationally diffuse departmental militia. Additionally, the Prevention Service was established to forestall recidivism, domestic crime, and job-related crimes. Mobile militia groups, radio-dispatched vehicular patrol units with a fixed beat, were inaugurated in 1973, while operative groups of investigative personnel from both the MVD investigation administration and the militia operative services came to be used in the speedy investigation of crimes by teams of investigators drawn from agencies responsible for dealing with various types of crimes.

Organizational improvements were only one aspect of the Brezhnev reforms in the militia. The 1968 decree also stressed upgrading militia personnel. Articles in the Soviet press have borne out continued stress on two key items: cooptation of individuals who have already proved themselves in other careers and reliance upon the recommendation of the collective.[9] In addition, however, the decree called for "improving the schooling and training of specialists for the militia agencies."[10] In articles appearing since this decree was issued, not only has specialized training been highlighted, but also the general educational level of militiamen, both officers and rank-and-file, has been raised. *Leningradskaia pravda* pointed out on Militia Day of 1972 that the militia no longer accepts recruits without a secondary education. According to Deputy Minister of Internal Affairs, K. I. Nikitin, writing in *Trud* on November 8, 1973:

Practically all chiefs of county and city departments of internal affairs have a university education: two-thirds of the inspectors of criminal investigation and the GAI, and almost 90 percent of the investigators and employees of the BKhSS have higher and secondary specialized educations. . . . Concerning our personnel, there has been a new replenishment. This has been the graduates of higher and secondary educational institutions of the USSR MVD, and also workers at industrial enterprises, specialists of the people's economy with higher and secondary educations. The majority of them are communists and komsomols. Life itself demands from militia personnel not only a clear professional record, but also a profound understanding of an intricate complex of social problems, without which successful prevention work would be impossible.[11]

That the post–1968 militia received a strong infusion of Party and Komsomol members as a part of its upgrading of personnel is also noteworthy. Minister of Internal Affairs N. A. Shchelokov pointed out in a 1974 Militia Day interview with *Sovetskaia Rossiia* that "Representatives of workers, communists and komsomols constitute the professional nucleus of the militia."[12]

The quality of militia personnel was improved in yet another way beginning in 1969. By order of the Minister of Internal Affairs, militia personnel were instructed to pay better attention to relations with citizens and to improve their level of "culture," that is, tact and courtesy. Said Deputy Minister Nikitin:

We are convinced that improving the standard of courtesy in the militia and increasing the exactingness made on every militiaman directly influence the status of legality and level of the safeguarding of public order. It must be admitted that there is still criticism from citizens of the insufficiently high standard of conduct of our staff members and that there are still instances of thoughtless and even rude treatment of citizens by militiamen. We are resolutely stopping such occurrences and reacting sharply to instances of tactless treatment of citizens.[13]

In addition to prescribing these improvements in personnel, the 1968 decree promised technological changes in the militia as well. The resolution defines a number of measures for equipping the militia with technical resources and for improving material conditions for personnel of the militia and other services of the Ministry of Internal Affairs. As I. Glebov, head of the MVD militia's Administration for Administrative Services described it in 1973, substantial progress had been made toward the fulfillment of this objective:

The material-technical base of the militia has changed in a fundamental way. Even at the precinct level its subdivisions employ contemporary criminological technology, two-way radio equipment, burglar alarms, specially equipped automobiles. In its technical equipment is included isotopes and photoelectric technology. . . .

Only in the last five-year-plan, the organs of internal affairs have increased their communications equipment three times, their operative-criminological equipment twice, and their special transport one-and-a-half times.[14]

RATIONALITY AND LAW ENFORCEMENT

The values both implicit and explicit in these changes in the public-order apparatus are: efficiency in organization and work, professionalism and specialized training in personnel, a clearer delineation of roles and spheres of authority within organizational subunits, and technological modernization—all of which seem to resemble a sort of Weberian process of rationalization and bureaucratization taking place within the public-order apparatus.

According to Gerth and Mills, rationality, as Weber typifies its manifestation in both state and corporate bureaucracy,

promotes rational efficiency, continuity of operation, speed, precision, and calculation of results. And all this goes on within institutions that are rationally managed, and in which combined and specialized functions occupy the center of attention. The whole structure is dynamic, and by its anonymity compels modern man to become a specialized expert, a "professional" man qualified for the accomplishment of a special career within pre-scheduled channels.[15]

Such rationalization is accompanied by the "de-mystification of the world in man's thinking and with what Weber called the 'routinization of charisma.' "[16]

Applied to the Soviet experience, such a process would mean an increased role for the state bureaucracy and managerial elite and a reduced role for ideology and the Party. In fact, such a process was envisaged in the early 1950s by Barrington Moore, who speculated on the possibility of the development of a rational-technical society in the post-Stalin Soviet Union. This process could be called the "rationalization of dictatorship," with rationalization defined in terms of "some degree of clarity and regularity in the allocation of rights, duties, and functions." Moore visualized a "technocracy—the rule of the technically competent" as a result of this process, a reduction in the role of the Party and the secret police, and an increase in the roles of the engineer and the manager.[17]

Although Moore speculated that "the technical-rational and formal legal features that exist in the Soviet system might come to predominate over the totalitarian ones," in such a way that political criteria and arbitrariness would be displaced in decision making by rational and technical criteria, others came to differ at least in part with this view. Zbigniew Brzezinski argues that totalitarianism and rationality were not necessarily incompatible; that in the goal-oriented Communist system a political movement such as the CPSU, possessing the will to control a rationalized administration, can continue to do so in pursuit of those goals, which, it should be added, are ideologically rather than rationally derived.[18]

As Jerry Hough points out, Moore's model of the Soviet system as a rational-technical society was very successful in accounting for the directions of post-Stalin change. Yet Moore's model did not account for continuing administrative deviations from established law and delineations of bureaucratic competence, "the continuing vigor of the local Party organ's participation in industrial decision-making," and the continuing use by local Party officials of "non-technical," or political criteria in personnel selection, if, in fact, it appears necessary to assure the loyalty of the person chosen to do the job.[19]

Thus, ideology may also influence attitudes and behavior in the pursuit of goals as well as goal formation. There are limits to the application of rational-technical standards in the decision-making process. Experts may disagree, and when they do, the conflict seldom can be settled by applying rational-technical standards. Nearly all such situations ultimately involve fundamental conflicts in values, professional standards, and interests, and they have no rational-technical answer at all.[20]

In the absence of definitive rational-technical criteria for resolving conflicts, therefore, decisions may be made through the use of bargaining and incrementalism, facilitated by an "instrumental style" of decision making. Most important, however, these decision makers—who in this case are local Party officials—are fully capable of varying their style from instrumental to ideological, depending upon the context of the decision. The nonrational components—power and tradition—impinge upon the decision-making process in ways similar to the operation of this process in other societies.[21]

It could be suggested that the changes in the public order apparatus might lend support in a narrow way to a rationalization hypothesis in seeking a general explanation of the Soviet system. The "rationalization" of the MVD and the militia and the reorganization of the volunteer public order agencies only indirectly indicate the possibility of rationalization in the decision-making process itself, being only the fruits of the decision. The changes described seem to fit a humbler category of rationalization, denoted, according to Paul Cocks, by the Russian word *ratsionalizatsiia*:

Defined as the process of improving the organization of activity, rationalization [*ratsionalizatsiia*] is applied generally to administration and economic production. Concerned narrowly with techniques, not politics, and making a cult of efficiency, it is geared to perfecting, not to liquidating, existing machinery. Its focus is strictly on modifying administrative means, not political ends. As in Western organization theory, then, rationality in its Russian context is a virtual synonym of efficiency and economy.[22]

Efficiency alone, however, poses a problem as a criterion for good police work. In his *Justice Without Trial*, Jerome Skolnick states quite clearly the fundamental contradiction in Western police work between the "ideal of legality" and the criterion of "managerial efficiency" which dominates the policeman's view of his professional obligations. To the extent that the policeman sees himself "as craftsman, rather than as legal actor, as a skilled worker rather than a civil servant obliged to subscribe to the rule of law," he is less likely to be constrained by the principles involved in the latter.[23] Several characteristics of the environment of police work reinforce this tendency. First, "an effort to introduce fairness, calculability, and impersonality" into an American system of the administration of criminal justice that was often corrupt produced a "concept of 'professionalism'... associated with a managerial view emphasizing rationality, efficiency, and universalism." This view envisages the professional as a bureaucrat, almost as a machine calculating alternative courses of action by a stated program of rules, and possessing the technical ability to carry out decisions irrespective of personal feelings.[24] Whereas "the rule of law emphasizes the rights of individual citizens and constraints upon the initiative of legal officials," it tends to place restrictions on the police in meeting these standards of professionalism, especially as the rule of law is embodied in a code of criminal procedure. Indeed, as Skolnick puts it, "Law is not merely an instrument of order, but may frequently be its adversary."[25]

The conflict between the policeman as craftsman and as an adherent to the rule of law is illustrated in police dealings with suspects, the cultivation of informers, and the operation of the clearance rate as a standard for the evaluation of police activity. In each case, expediency in the service of operational efficiency serves to compromise the civil rights of the persons who are the subjects of police work.[26] The problem is compounded by the tendency on the part of the community to support an "official perspective" on law reflecting the interests of those in political authority rather than those who are the "consumers" of police services. This "official" point of view supports the policeman's tendency to emphasize administrative regularity in opposition to due process of law, a tendency which negates the presumption of innocence. Furthermore, the power structure of the community tends to stress order maintenance in its demands upon the police with little countervailing support for the rule of law.[27]

Skolnick himself is aware of how this dilemma is compounded in the Soviet system, where the tradition of the rule of law has only the most tenuous hold on the official consciousness.If a return to socialist legality—the Soviet approximation of the rule of law—was to be the ultimate objective for the Soviet system of the administration of justice under Brezhnev, as it was under Khrushchev, one might seriously question an efficiency campaign in the Soviet police as the most suitable avenue for achieving that goal. Skolnick's analysis points up quite clearly the need for a professionalism based upon a "deeper set of values" than those of managerial efficiency or "technological proficiency."[28]

The conflict in the Brezhnev regime between efficiency and respect for a "deeper set of values"—in this case respect for socialist legality rather than the Western concept of the rule of law—was reflected in the continuing squabble between the MVD, including both the militia and the MVD Investigation Administration, and the Procuracy over the issue of who should conduct the pretrial investigation. The Procuracy was accused by the MVD of conflict of interest, while the MVD was regarded as only marginally competent. The true dimensions of this conflict are difficult to extract from ambiguous and oblique discussions of it in the Soviet press, appears that Procuracy claims to conduct the pretrial investigation were based upon assertions of superior professional competence, whereas MVD claims were based on similar assertions plus their allegation that the Procuracy's involvement in prosecution as well as investigation established a fundamental conflict of interest jeopardizing the ultimate value of socialist legality. This position was ironic in two respects. First, it was the Procuracy, whose fundamental mission in the Soviet system is the safeguarding of socialist legality, which was being called to account by the police, the customary offender in breaches of procedural legality, for failure to respect socialist legality. Second, neither of these agencies gave serious consideration to the alternative solution employed most successfully in Western Europe and the United States, namely, making the independent judiciary the bearer of responsibility for insuring legality in criminal procedure.

Another issue is raised by the post-Khrushchev changes in the volunteer public order agencies—the more general topic of public participation in the Soviet system. The Krushchev regime, under which the great movement for securing widespread public involvement in the maintenance of public order began, has been characterized as anti-bureaucratic and populist, thus reviving a characteristic of the early Leninist period of Soviet government. According to Paul Cocks, "deeply rooted in Lenin's ideas on the state, administration, and bureaucracy was the notion that direct democracy and popular participation in administrative affairs provided the best antidote to bureaucratism."[29] Although Stalin effectively buried this approach, his successors, in Cocks's view, have taken two different approaches to the problem of de-Stalinization and the rationalization of totalitarianism:

For Khrushchev—the impulsive adventurer, fervent ideologue, "democratic popularizer," and restless pragmatist—the means of socio-political organization and advance emphasized public-spiritedness and participation in societal and administrative affairs. By contrast, for the more cautious, faceless, and systematic Brezhnev and Kosygin, who have been fittingly called the "grey directoire of post-revolutionary administrators," the solution lies in bureaucratic instrumentalities perfected according to the principles of scientific Communism and laws of economic development.[30]

The 1974 laws relating to the *druzhiny* certainly represented a victory for the Soviet state apparatus and for the Soviet legal establishment, in that the *druzhiny* were brought under the control of the local soviets and the militia. On the other hand, the role of the *druzhiny* was expanded, rather than circumscribed, and there was certainly no indication in the 1974 laws or in articles discussing them that the Brezhnev regime sought to reduce the public participation in the maintenance of public order. Furthermore, the creation of the public order bases beginning in 1973 appears to have been the start of a new campaign to enlist public participation, even though this format seemed to be characterized by a high degree of organization and systematic supervision by state and soviet agencies.

It is difficult, then, to argue as Cocks does, that the Brezhnev regime has turned its back on public participation as a strategy for Soviet political development.[31] Hough finds great continuity between the Khrushchev and Brezhnev regimes and that, in fact, public participation has continued to be a very important aspect of the Soviet political system. This is especially true in the case of making suggestions in the press and offering testimony before policy-making councils.[32] Hough's suggestions are an invitation for scholars to seek out the essential characteristics of political participation in both the Soviet Union and the democratic governments of the West in order to provide a basis for meaningful comparison.

One such comparison would be between local soviets' Standing Committees for Socialist Legality and the Maintenance of Public Order and citizen police advisory boards and review boards in the United States. If, in fact, the membership of these standing committees means anything, people with significant local influence meet regularly to discuss police matters. It could be that these groups imply only increased Party participation in police policy making, but it would be valuable to examine the entire issue of the role of the local soviets' standing committees. It is one thing for the Brezhnev regime to encourage mass participation in the *druzhiny*; it would be quite significant if the standing committees meant greater expert and public participation in policy making.

CONCLUSION

Under the Brezhnev regime the public order apparatus was transformed from a haphazard concatenation of state and volunteer agencies to a carefully structured alliance in which professionally staffed and managed police units received measured and specified assistance from volunteer groups operating under closer supervision. Impressive efforts were made to define through enacted law and regulation the organizational structure, prerogatives, responsibilities, and standards of professionalism for the Soviet public order police. Moreover, the campaign initiated by Khrushchev in 1962 to create a better public image for the militia was refocused on improving the professional qualities of the militiaman and his capacity for service. New police and volunteer units were created, and efforts (though not entirely successful) were made to delineate the areas of responsibility for all public order agencies. Finally, new emphasis was placed on upgrading the technology of Soviet police work. While it seems clear that efficiency and rationality were the intended effects of these changes, there is no evidence that these objectives were achieved. Soviet statistics on police work published during the period under review are sparse and essentially useless.

In one sense, of course, the entire ruling elite in the Soviet Union, with its centralist tendency, systems for specialized training, intermingling of party and state functions, and elaborate *nomenklatura* appointment lists, is a giant bureaucracy, as Rolf Theen has asserted. Theen acknowledges, however, variation from the classic bureaucratic model, which is an essential and, one might add, distinctive feature of the Soviet regime: the tendency of the entrenched upper echelon of the ruling elite to hedge economically rational performance-oriented decision-making criteria with those derived from

Marxist-Leninist doctrine as well as their personal concerns for keeping power.[33]

This important reservation imposes a regime-based limit to the extent of full bureaucratization somewhat analogous to the barrier set by democracy in liberal regimes. Weber predicted that eventually the relentless inner dynamics of bureaucratization would sweep aside democratic processes, and Soviet leaders since the Bolshevik Revolution itself have fought to stave off this unwanted side effect of economic development. Lenin, as noted at the outset of this essay, believed one could enjoy the efficiency of Taylorism while escaping the capitalistic exploitation that accompanied it in other systems. More recently, the Brezhnev regime revived Soviet fascination with organizational theory and "scientific decision-making."[34] Changes in the public order apparatus reflected this trend, but by 1975, substantive rationality in the Soviet police had not yet achieved ascendancy over party values. Thus, rationality was attenuated, and the police establishment continued to serve objectives defined in Marxist-Leninist terms. In the Soviet police system, appointment, tenure, career, and compensation all could be interrupted by ideologically derived concerns.

What is evident, however, is an ongoing struggle between those elites who wish to reduce the role of the state in police work and encourage more local responsibility for and public participation in maintaining order, and those elites who, in the pursuit of efficiency, stability, and so on are inclined to bureaucratize the Soviet police even further.

PART III

Solutions in Service to Democracy

10

Power versus Liberty in the Welfare State: A Bill of Rights for Social Service Beneficiaries

Ira Glasser

The United States Constitution's Bill of Rights was devised to protect individual rights against the excesses of well-intentioned, democratically elected political rulers. Rights were defined rather simply as limits on governmental power. To say a citizen had the right to distribute a leaflet or worship freely literally meant that the government was without the legal power (i.e., authority) to stop him. "Over himself," wrote John Stuart Mill, "over his own body and mind, the individual is sovereign," and it was precisely to define and construct legal protections for personal sovereignty that the Bill of Rights was added to the fledgling United States Constitution in 1789. The Bill of Rights focused not upon the good intentions of democratic rulers, but rather upon the harm to individual rights that might flow from their excesses. In fact, the Bill of Rights *assumed* their excesses and sought to limit them.

THE RISE OF SOCIAL SERVICES: HOW LIBERTY WAS SEDUCED AND RAVAGED BY GOOD INTENTIONS

In eighteenth-century America, "the government" consisted of the political institutions of the state. The individual whose liberty needed protection against those institutions was the citizen. Two hundred years later, "the government" has become much more than the political institutions of the state. It now also includes the social institutions of caring: public schools, mental hospitals, public housing authorities, developmental centers for the retarded, foster care agencies for homeless children, nursing homes for the aged, and welfare agencies for the poor.

A common phrase—"social services"—arose to describe these institutions, and they came to be widely perceived, especially by political liberals, as entirely humanitarian and benevolent. If there were problems, in this view, with public social services, they were largely problems of money. Liberal society, which is to say "caring" society, came mostly to believe that the only difficulty with social services was that there were not enough to go around; the public sector, they argued, was being starved in the midst of private affluence.

This undifferentiated view of social services, and the political context in which the struggle to provide social services took place, tended to blind liberals to some unintended consequences of their good works. Because their motives were benevolent, their ends good, and their purpose caring, they assumed the posture of parents toward the recipients of their largesse. *Dominion* became legitimate: those who managed social services—not infrequently liberals themselves—came to enjoy a degree of discretionary power over their clients that normally only parents are allowed over their children. As a result, they infantilized those they intended to help and denied them their rights.

Not until the clients of service institutions rebelled in the 1960s did anyone begin to look with skepticism upon these good works. We all trusted the social services and did not fear service professionals. We built no legal restraints into the delivery systems of social services. We became oblivious, in the context of social services, to the adversarial relationship between power and liberty, and we assumed that the interests of clients were not in conflict with the interests of social service agencies.

Vast discretionary power thus came to be vested in an army of civil servants, appointed by examination and organized into huge service bureaucracies, which began quietly and silently to trespass upon the private lives and rights of millions of citizens. If any of those citizens complained about such trespass, for a long time no one listened.

Many people, though decidedly not children, came routinely to depend, as if they were children, upon social services provided by the state for their daily sustenance, and sometimes for survival itself. From a direction wholly unanticipated by early Americans, government power thus came to touch millions of people heavily, and in ways that clearly violated the Bill of Rights. Sometimes the violations were substantial and the intrusions nearly total. Nursing homes are one example of this.

Most of the relatively recent public debate over nursing homes has concentrated upon the poor quality of care provided or upon fiscal fraud. Somewhat obscured has been the quality of life that results from institutional pressures inherent even in "good" nursing homes, when the interests of the home conflict with the interests of the patient. For example, the nursing home may have an interest—a legitimate interest—in getting paid for the services it provides, which should disqualify it from being an impartial protector of the aged patient's assets. Nonetheless, nursing homes often control the assets of their patients and manipulate those assets to their own ends and to the detriment of their patients. Similarly, the patient may desire the freedom to come and go, to socialize, to have visitors and activities, to retain privacy, while the home's interests may run more to administrative convenience and order. When such conflicts of interest arise, the nearly parental powers of the "home" can quickly suffocate the basic rights of individual patients.

As a result, many nursing home patients find themselves in a desperate position, stripped of power and desolate of dignity. They are, most of them, competent in the eyes of the law. They have not been convicted of any crime or adjudged insane. They are adults. Their rights and freedoms cannot legally be denied through any ad hoc informal decisions by nursing home officials or even by well meaning family members.

Yet despite their legal status as free citizens, nursing home residents share much with children, mental patients, and even prisoners. The control of individuals' lives in nursing homes is pervasive. The elderly person is dependent upon the institution for food, clothing, medical care, recreation, companionship—in short, for all the physical and emotional elements of survival. The home exercises complete discretionary power over the aged person. It decides whether the patient is capable of receiving mail or of handling spending money. It decides whether the patient can walk in the neighborhood or even its halls. It decides who will be allowed to visit the patient and when. It decides whether the patient shall stay or leave.[1]

Perhaps the best way to appreciate the degree of control in such service institutions is to compare them to the military and prisons. The new arrival is "shaped and coded into an object that can be fed into the administrative machinery of the establishment, to be worked on smoothly by routine operations." Afterward there are various "abasements, degradations, humiliations and profanations of self": meaningless make-work, denial of sex, forced deference, penalties for self-expression, unfair procedures. The entire process resembles nothing as much as basic training in the military, the purpose of which is concededly to abolish individuality. The reach of the institution extends to the most personal aspects of one's life and, perhaps most significantly, to aspects that are meaningless to anyone else—dress, style, personal appearance, and deportment. In the end, Erving Goffman tells us, "the inmate cannot easily escape from the press of judgmental officials and from the enveloping tissue of constraint."[2]

Similar intrusions flowing from similar discretionary powers are also to be found, though to lesser degrees, in the administration of public schools, public housing, and public welfare. For many years no one thought to question such intrusions or to limit the discretionary powers of public servants providing social services to the needy. Violations of individual rights that would have created an instantaneous political and legal clamor had they been perpetrated by the police went unrecognized when they were perpetrated by social service "professionals." Because such professionals were presumed to be acting in the "best interests" of their "clients," no one thought to question the excesses of their power.

In some institutions service professionals actually and explicitly claimed the legal powers of surrogate parents. In schools, for example, teachers and principals have tried to justify their discretionary power over students by the doctrine of *in loco parentis*. According to this doctrine, parents—simply by sending their children to school (which they are required to do under penalty of the law)—delegate their powers to school officials, who are then permitted to act in the place of the parent. Child-care agencies literally and legally assumed complete parental powers over their wards. Under certain conditions, so did mental hospitals and nursing homes. Other services, like public housing, often treated their clients like children, even though they did not claim the legal power of surrogate parents.

So a tradition grew up; the Bill of Rights existed, but it did not apply to "service" institutions. Yet until the rights revolution of the 1960s, no one saw it that way. Most professionals defended their own discretionary power—and therefore opposed the rights of their clients—with variations on the following argument:

1. I provide an essential and benevolent service. I am a helping professional: I teach. I heal. I rehabilitate. I provide shelter.

2. In order to provide my service well, it is necessary that I be allowed wide discretion. I am an expert. I know how to run schools, hospitals, children's shelters, housing programs, and I must be left alone to apply my special knowledge.

3. The adversary process is inappropriate to the service I provide. Lawyers are an intrusion. They lack my expertise and don't know how to run a specialized institution. The very notion of legal "rights" hampers my ability to provide my service effectively. The Bill of Rights is disruptive.

Thus we have traditionally been seduced into supposing that because they historically represented charity, service professionals could speak for the best interests of their clients. By now we should know better. Power is the natural antagonist of liberty, even if those who exercise power are filled with good intentions.

LIBERTY IN THE WELFARE STATE: THE DOCTRINE OF LEAST HARM

First Principle

The Bill of Rights applies to social institutions of caring and limits the powers of those institutions and their employees over the lives of the dependent.

Six important rights that do not now exist for nursing home patients are illustrative of what yet needs to be accomplished:[3]

1. The right to control personal property. Unless residents of total institutions can exercise control over their personal property, they will be at the mercy of the institution. Often, for example, an elderly person's sole or primary source of income is Social Security. Yet it is not unusual for Social Security checks automatically to be endorsed over to the home or the state as a condition of continued care.

Another important patient property interest is the right to privacy. Perhaps the most poignant loss suffered by nursing home residents is the loss of self, which results from a thorough stripping away of privacy. Nursing home residents should have a guaranteed place to keep their personal belongings. The disappearance of personal property is endemic in nursing homes, which are not now legally liable for lost property. Finally, most nursing homes make private contact between members of the opposite sex impossible, perhaps the most degrading intrusion of all.

2. *The right to control one's own body.* The general law of torts, which basically regards as an assault any medical procedure carried out on an individual against his will, has been expanded to include the individual's right to receive all relevant information he or she would want to know before consenting to medical treatment. The tort law has thus been a vehicle for defining and enforcing the right to informed consent.

For nursing home patients, who often live in relative isolation, and who frequently are assaulted by the gross overuse and misuse of prescription drugs, the right to informed consent is crucial. Yet few, if any, cases raising a claim of informed consent on behalf of a nursing home patient can be found.

3. *The right to come and go freely.* Since nursing home residents are, generally, competent adults, they are entitled to the same rights to freedom from restraint as other citizens. Hence the nursing home resident's claim to freedom from bodily restraint is fundamentally different from that of convicted prisoners or even of young children. Nursing home residents should have the right to come and go as they please, but they do not. Neither physical nor pharmaceutical restraints should be used except perhaps for brief periods during real emergencies. There have been virtually no cases litigating this right.

4. *The rights to free speech, association, petition, and counsel.* The rights of speech, association, and petition are essential to nursing home residents. These rights would enable residents to band together to seek improvement in conditions in the institution and to support one another.

5. *Access to information.* The right to information is crucial to serious reform. Total institutions typically protect themselves from scrutiny and criticism by strictly controlling information and limiting public knowledge to self-serving press releases. A broad right to information about the operation, ownership, and financing of nursing homes and the degree to which they are in compliance with legal requirements is necessary for patients and their representatives to hold institutions accountable. Nursing homes should also be required to print and distribute, in appropriate languages, a Bill of Rights for residents. Rights are never enforceable unless people know about them.

6. *Due process.* The mortality rate for elderly people transferred from one

institution to another is very high. It is sufficiently well documented to have received a name: transfer trauma. The likelihood of transfer trauma can be reduced by involving the elderly person in the transfer decision, allowing it to be contested by the patient, and familiarizing the client, in advance of any move, with the range of alternatives and the characteristics of the new environments.

The foregoing list, sketchy though it is, describes an institution whose residents are still virtually barren of rights. Most other caring institutions, subjected to sustained litigation during the past decade, are today substantially more limited, at least theoretically, in the discretion they are permitted to exercise. Yet even in these institutions, large areas of discretion continue to exist and encroach upon the rights of the dependent. Though the general principle that the Bill of Rights should apply to caring institutions is no longer in jeopardy, this principle still needs to be substantially extended; and where it has been established, it needs to be enforced.

Second Principle

Enforcement of constitutional limits is not self-executing and therefore requires an external force.

The capacity of bureaucratic institutions to absorb criticism and even court orders without changing is almost inexhaustible. Though examples are numerous, two should suffice. In 1969 advocates for student rights succeeded in establishing significant legal limits upon the discretion of public school principals in New York City to suspend students arbitrarily. At the same time, these limits seemed to entitle students to unprecedented due process rights and were described as a model for the nation. In the year when these limits were first imposed, there were approximately thirteen thousand annual suspensions by principals. Eight years later, there were twice that many. Most suspensions violated the Board of Education's own bylaws and were clearly illegal. Most were below the high school level. Most were part of the pattern of illegal exclusion that had resulted for years in a massive push-out problem reflected in low rates of academic diplomas. One principal even complained that students were being "incited" to exercise their rights!

The extended litigation to establish rights for mentally retarded children at Willowbrook, a state institution on Staten Island, New York, provides another anguished example. In March 1972, Willowbrook had a population of 5,200, which was 65 percent over capacity. Children and adults lived packed together in wards of fifty or more with little supervision and no professional staff.[4]

On March 17, 1972, several public interest law groups sued in federal court in an effort to remedy what one expert called a "major tragedy." Massive testimony was given to prove inadequacies of management, staffing, and budgeting. One witness testified to the inedible quality and insufficient quantity of food. Another found that most accidents and injuries to residents occurred when they were awakened by staff. Horror stories flowed into the trial transcript: deaths by choking that could have been prevented with proper equipment and adequate staffing; a resident with a broken leg in a cast infested with bugs and maggots; another resident with an untended infection in his eye which, when cleaned, was found to have a thumbtack imbedded in it. Additionally, there was routine use of cattle prods on residents, which the "service professionals" at Willowbrook called "aversion therapy."

The lawsuit to end these conditions was vigorously resisted by New York State for over three years. Finally, on April 30, 1975, a consent order was signed by the judge. It ordered extensive relief, requiring immensely detailed changes in staffing, programming, and environment, all to take place within thirteen months. It assured adequate staff/patient ratios, guaranteed standards of privacy, dignity, comfort, and sanitation, reduced the overcrowded population and the maximum number of people permitted in each unit, and set up a review panel of experts to monitor compliance. The incredible amount of time and money spent since 1972 seemed at last to have produced fundamental change.

Yet, two years later, lawyers were back in court seeking contempt citations against state officials for refusal to comply with the court order. Some changes had occurred, they acknowledged, but as one lawyer put it, "Life has not changed significantly for most of the 5,200 plaintiffs."

The mere declaration of a legal principle by a court means little without means of enforcement. Lawyers' victories do not imply clients' victories. The last decade can probably be accurately characterized as the beginning of the legal effort to establish rights for the socially dependent. As that effort moves toward completion, a new one must begin, no less inventive and likely to be even more difficult and to meet with even more resistance, to enforce the rights that have been won.

What is clear beyond any doubt is that strong, independent external adversaries are required if individual rights are to be established and enforced against service institutions. Those who are dependent upon the institution must have easy access to such adversaries, who often will be lawyers, but who do not necessarily need to be lawyers.

Institutional officials do not react kindly to external adversaries. Pseudobureaucratic "discretion" is a flower that flourishes in obscurity and withers under the light of fair procedures and substantive limitations. Most service professionals resist the new adversary system and will struggle bitterly to keep the light out. They claim that the adversary system is no part of caring institutions and that its introduction is an obstacle to service.

The new advocates make the existing adversary system explicit by exposing conflicts of interest between institutions and their clients and by challenging those conflicts openly and directly. The new advocates make the adversary system more fair by evening the odds, and that is why they are resisted. They are a countervailing power, and they are fought by the managers of service institutions for approximately the same reasons that labor unions were fought by the managers of industry. They are also necessary for the same reasons that labor unions were necessary: no one accustomed to unlimited discretion will willingly give it up. General Motors didn't, and neither will the social institutions of caring.[5] Therefore, external adversaries were and remain necessary, both to win and to enforce the rights of dependents.

Third Principle

Every program designed to help the dependent ought to be evaluated, not on the basis of the good it might do, but rather on the basis of the harm it might do. Those programs ought to be adopted that seem to be the least likely to make things worse.

Limits upon the powers of service institutions define individual rights by making certain powers illegitimate. But even when they exercise legitimate powers on behalf of dependent people, service institutions can do—and have done—great harm to those they seek to help. The *principle of least harm*, though less ambitious, offers a better guideline for legitimate social programs. Although a complete analytical description of the impact that this principle would have on the full range of social services is clearly beyond the scope of this essay, it would perhaps be useful to examine one group of dependent people, children, in some detail and describe how the principle of least harm might alter current social programs designed to benefit them. In some respects, programs for dependent children provide the best vehicle for the illustration of this principle, for in such programs the state acts directly as surrogate parent.

The history of public intervention in the lives of children is littered with programs that came clothed in the garb of reform but later were revealed to have resulted in substantial, though perhaps unintended, harm. No better example exists of this unhappy phenomenon than the effort, now a century old, to remove troubled children from their homes and seal them off in an environment sheltered from the harsh world and enriched with programs that promised to heal their souls. In New York such children were called PINS—Persons in Need of Supervision. In other states, they were called CHINS—Children in Need of Supervision. We never lack for acronyms in bureaucratic programming.

Originally the product of nineteenth century liberal reform, the institutionalization of children for the ostensibly benevolent purpose of rehabilitation too often was revealed in fact as an Orwellian nightmare of custody, confinement, and punishment. Words like "training school" were substituted for "prison," "child-care worker" for "guard," "campus" for "prison compound," and "cottage" for "cell block." The language of deception did its work well. It didn't sound so bad when we spoke of children sent to live in cottages on a campus where they would be helped by child-care workers. It sounded worse when we spoke the truth: too often children were sentenced to cells in prisons under the custody of guards. Likewise some "training schools" made liberal use of solitary confinement. They called it "the quiet room." Until protracted legislation struck it down in New York, for example, solitary confinement was a fairly common child-care practice in service institutions.

The traditional answer of reformers to such sorry conditions has been to defend the idea of benevolent institutionalization, cite their lofty goals, advocate the improvement of the institution, and ask for more money. "Do not throw the baby out with the bathwater," they counsel. This solution has not worked.

The principle of least harm would avoid this dilemma. Removal of the child into state custody would no longer be a permissable condition of needed services. Separating the child from parental custody should be viewed as a drastic and harmful step. The avoidance of this step would become the first priority of our social response. The same intended beneficial services would be provided but without transferring the child's custody to the state. The benefit of these services to the child would, of course, remain speculative, precisely as it is now, but the harm that would likely flow from state custody could be avoided.

Perhaps the most harmful thing for a growing child is instability, the lack of a permanent family, the absence of the steady love and support of a particular adult. The principle of least harm would seek above all to avoid such instability, whereas current public policy seems everywhere to encourage it. The right to services—such as homemakers, tutors, psychological assessment and counseling, and the like (which affluent families in trouble can purchase)—provided directly to the family in its home, as an alternative to the removal of the child into state custody, does not exist. As a result, too many children are removed and inappropriately placed into foster care. Once in long-term foster care, the establishment of permanent, loving relationships is actively discouraged. Meaningful relationships with biological parents are rare, because public officials and foster care agencies do not adequately encourage them and do not provide sufficient services to facilitate an early return of the child.

Most children in foster care for more than a year spend their entire childhoods in transit. Of 1,505 children moved from foster care in New York City during 1973–1974, only 202 were returned home, and only 103 were placed for adoption. The remaining 1,200 were shifted to another foster placement. One recent study showed that 60 percent of children in long-term foster care were moved more than once, and almost 30 percent were moved three or more times.

The principle of least harm would minimize these destructive results by limiting the initial intervention. Removal of the child from its biological family would become a last resort, the most drastic step possible when no other alternative will suffice. The biological imperative for caring and benevolence would be left intact, insofar as that is possible, by providing supportive services directly to the child and its family. Once a child is removed from the biological family, foster care would be seen as a highly temporary emergency measure, and the child would not be allowed to drift aimlessly toward the age of majority. Contacts between the child and its biological parents would be encouraged, enabled, and maintained as if the child were in a hospital for a brief illness. Priority would be placed on early return, and services would be provided to facilitate that return and make it permanent.

In those cases where the child had been abandoned or legally surrendered, or when all efforts to keep the family together have failed and the child's ties to its biological family have been irretrievably severed, the creation of a new, permanent, stable home through adoption would be required. Currently, exactly the opposite is true. Services are rarely provided outside foster care, and adoption of long-term foster children almost never occurs. The principle of least harm is nowhere to be found in our child-care systems, any more than it can be found in the systems we have to take care of the elderly, the mentally impaired, or the poor.

In all these systems, the dependent are removed from their homes, from their families, and from their communities. It is simply not possible to avoid doing harm in places like Willowbrook, in most nursing homes, or in the systems we have today to "help" children in trouble. Institutionalization itself must be avoided. To anyone who has stayed in a hospital for even a week and contemplated staying a lifetime, these general goals should be self-evident.

Today our caring systems are a long way from these goals. Virtually every caring system we have keeps its eye on the good it hopes to accomplish and blinks at the harm it is doing. As a result, hundreds of thousands—perhaps millions—of people are violated every day of their lives by the encroachments of their ostensible benefactors.

CONCLUSION

In a curious way the principle of least harm bears a close relationship to the old political dictum: that government is best which governs least. This dictum comes from the time when experience had taught most people to fear the excessive power of government and bridle it with a Bill of Rights. More recently, that dictum has been the battle cry of political conservatives, who seemed always to set themselves against humane public programs. During the middle third of the twentieth century, the United States, increasingly dominated by political liberals, became more inclined to trust government.

Beginning with the New Deal, political benevolence became institutionalized on a scale never before imaginable. The discretion of government in general, and of the federal executive branch in particular, expanded itself beyond all prior limits. Government became our friend, and we grew insensitive to its potential encroachments.

The pathological result of that development was Richard Nixon. Before he was stopped—barely in the nick of time and largely as a result of several fortuitous accidents—he came to believe that in the name of "national security" he could do anything. His doctrine of inherent power—the notion that the law did not limit the president if the ends sought were sufficiently important—effectively removed the limits imposed by the Bill of Rights and left us all without rights, defenseless against the encroachments of what he considered to be in our "best interests."

During the same period of time that the political institutions of government were expanding their discretion, the social institutions of caring were expanding theirs, and with similar results. The reimposition of the Bill of Rights upon the presidency during the 1973–1974 impeachment campaign came precisely at the point when the movement to establish limits on the discretion of social institutions also reached its peak. The reemergence of the original understanding politically came after a decade of effort to apply the original understanding socially. The Bill of Rights seemed finally to overcome the Imperial Presidency precisely when it was struggling to overcome the imperial school principal, the imperial caseworker, and the imperial state psychiatrist.

That we might overreact to Richard Nixon's personal excesses and bridle the presidency too much worries some observers. In a similar fashion there are those social critics who worry that the rights movement will impose too many limits on the social institutions of caring and encourage the neglect of the dependent. Both worries have some merit, since every reform has its own unintended consequences. Few—and least of all political liberals—would wish to return to a time when social programs did not exist and dependent sectors were left to their own agonies, just as few would wish to return to the eighteenth-century version of the presidency. But it is doubtful that we need to worry too much about the powers of government. We have only recently, and incompletely, leavened our trust in government with the fear of its excesses that informed the thought of early Americans. As they knew, and we must constantly remind ourselves, power tends to expand itself voraciously. It is liberty that is fragile and always in danger of destruction. In adopting the Bill of Rights, early Americans hardly rejected the idea of governmental power sufficient to achieve legitimate social ends. The proposed constitution was intended to grant substantial powers to the federal government, and it did. The Bill of Rights was added not to negate those powers but to limit them, not to paralyze the government's ability to meet social needs but rather to guarantee against government excesses. The notion of rights never implied governmental neglect—neither in the eighteenth century or today. Rights merely implied certain limits to the methods government could employ in pursuit of legitimate social ends. It was only during the aberrational period of the Progressives that rights came to be seen as inconsistent with needs, and it is the residue of that view we confront today.

The three principles set forth in this essay seek only to restore that balance between individual rights and social needs that was part of the original understanding of democracy in America (and which Weber recognizes as a uniquely *un*bureaucratic quality in the democratic system of the United States comparatively analyzed[6]). No one ever suggested that the Constitution was an instrument of governmental neglect. Indeed, our history describes a steady expansion of governmental powers and social programs, often at the expense of individual rights, in which neglect abounds. Therefore, the three principles set forth here cannot reasonably be opposed on the ground that they might breed neglect. Certainly, they leave ample room for governmental power to fulfill its legislated obligations. What they do *not* permit is the excessive zeal that often accompanies the agents of governmental power, whether well intentioned or not. What they provide is minimal protection for individual rights—most particularly for those "served" by "professionals" in "service institutions." Therefore these three principles deserve to be repeated everywhere and written into all social legislation.

One pauses, of course, at the prospect of such repetition. How many times do we have to listen to the Bill of Rights refrain? André Gide has the answer: "Everything that needs to be said has already been said. But since no one was listening, everything must be said again." And so once more: The midnight knock at the door is always inherent in governmental power. In one century it comes in the form of a British soldier; in another, a caseworker. The encroachment of power upon liberty has many disguises.

11

"Constitutionalizing" Corporations: An Employee Bill of Rights

Ralph Nader, Mark Green, and Joel Seligman

A basic purpose of the United States Constitution is to distinguish powers of government from rights of individual citizens. Due to the widespread fear in the late eighteenth century of a tyrannical national government, most of its framers agreed with Alexander Hamilton's argument in the *84th Federalist Paper* that the powers of the federal government were limited to those expressly delegated to it by the people in the Constitution, or those "necessary and proper" to its operation.

It is within an analogous framework that the question of corporate power should be assessed. As long as corporations were small, the Constitution's failure to mention them was a minor problem. The Supreme Court in the early nineteenth century reconciled the private corporation to the Constitution by treating incorporation as a personal property right. Later in the nineteenth century, the Supreme Court went so far as to hold that the corporation should be considered a "person" or "citizen" for the purposes of the Due Process and Equal Protection clauses of the Fourteenth Amendment.

This reconciliation broke down as the corporation's size, power, and range increased. No longer was it possible to say that the corporation was a person for certain limited purposes and otherwise ignore it; like the state and municipal governments it overshadows, the giant business corporation *is* a government. By employing thousands of individuals, it possesses the power to rule them. It can establish employment rules restricting their conduct, grant or withhold financial rewards otherwise unavailable, or effectively destroy the career of a specialist in a monopoly or near-monopoly industry. How can a Constitution, which fully restrains all levels of political government from invading the rights of citizens, then permit every business corporation to do so?

With this anomaly in mind, the Supreme Court in 1945 laid the doctrinal foundation for applying certain constitutional restrictions to the operations of giant corporations. In the landmark case of *Marsh v. Alabama*, the question was whether a corporation could refuse to permit an individual to distribute religious literature on the "business block" of a company-owned town. Obviously, explained Justice Hugo Black for the Court, if the town of Chickasaw, Alabama, had been owned by a municipality rather than by the Gulf Shipbuilding Company, defendant Marsh's conviction for criminal trespass would have to be set aside. No state or municipality can bar the distribution of religious or political literature consistent with the First Amendment.

Does the First Amendment cease simply because a single company has legal title to all the town? Alabama argued that the corporation's right to control the inhabitants of Chickasaw was coextensive with the right of a homeowner to regulate the conduct of guests. Justice Black disagreed. "The more an owner, for his advantage, opens up his personal property for use by the public in general, the more do his rights become circumscribed by the statutory and constitutional rights of those who use it." When a private corporation performs a "public function," the same constitutional standards of free speech and equal protection of the law apply as if it were the state.

Almost from the day it was decided, commentators anticipated a swift extension of the *Marsh* doctrine. What made Gulf Corporation's functions "public," Adolf Berle notably argued, was that "one corporation owned the entire town." But there is nothing special about sidewalks. "The prejudice of the owner of 90 percent of the available housing would be a public matter." So would the prejudice of the owner of any other necessary good or service. This led Berle to predict the "direct application of constitutional limitations to the corporation, merely because it holds a state charter and exercises a degree of economic power sufficient to make its practices 'public' rules."[1]

Berle proved a poor prophet. The Supreme Court has repeatedly ruled since *Marsh* that there can be no limitation on a corporation's right to use its property exactly as it chooses, unless the corporation is performing a "public function" or "state action" traditionally performed by government. In one recent case the High Court said that a private utility company does not need to notify a customer before cutting off service—in the same manner that a government agency must provide notice before revoking a privilege—even though the utility company had an absolute monopoly of this essential service. The Court held that the utility company was not performing the equivalent of a government function.[2]

If the courts will not protect the rights of citizens against abuses of corporate power, then Congress should. A primary purpose of the United States Constitution was to avoid the tyrannical use of collective power. It makes no meaningful difference to those who lose their "inalienable" rights to freedom of speech or due process of law that they were victimized by a giant corporation rather than by a giant government. In either case the purpose of the Constitution has been frustrated, and the Bill of Rights reduced to a bill of goods.

Potentially the giant business corporation should be subject to the fundamental restraints that the Constitution places upon state and federal government, including the right of the corporation's citizens, its employees, to participate in the governance of their workplace. But how to structure workers' participation into giant corporations is far from obvious. In the view of Mack Hanan and Isidore Silver in pathbreaking *Harvard Business Review* articles, the key is to establish an internal corporate ombudsman with the authority to intervene on behalf of employees and to dramatize and publicize outside the corporation complaints that do not receive proper management attention.[3] Other advocates of "job power" would go further and replicate Yugoslavia's "workers councils," which possess extensive managerial powers, or they would at least generalize the experiments of corporations such as Norway's Norsk Hydro or American firms such as Corning Glass, Motorola, and Pet Foods, which have given their employees wide-ranging powers to redesign their workplaces.[4]

Yet even short of complete "industrial democracy," Congress can act immediately in three obvious areas of constitutional rights.

FIRST AMENDMENT RIGHTS

Except within the ambit of National Labor Relations law, no present federal law assures that citizens will be as free to express themselves in the workplace as they are in the body politic.

Retaliation against outspoken employees occurs most frequently for "blowing the whistle." The conscientious employee risks losing his job for reporting practices such as the marketing of defective vehicles to unsuspecting consumers, the waste of government funds by private contractors, the industrial dumping of mercury in waterways, the connection between companies and bribery or illegal campaign contributions, or the suppression of serious occupational disease data. What Montesquieu called the basis of all political freedom, the assurance that one can do what one ought to do, and that one will not be forced to do what one ought not to do, has failed for the product testers and junior executives of our largest corporations. Men and women who should be lauded as public citizens have been intimidated and ostracized.

Men and women like George Geary: a sales executive for United States Steel, Geary objected to the sale of a new type of pipe which he believed was inadequately tested and likely to fail under high pressure. For this he was fired for insubordination, even though the company considered Geary's charges so serious that it withdrew the product from sale pending major retesting.

Or like Henry Durham, who was demoted for protesting Lockheed's waste-ridden supply practices on the C–5A transport plane and was later forced out of Lockheed after testifying before Senator William Proxmire's Subcommittee on Economy in Government.

Or Colt Firearms' workers Wayne Henfield and Vic Martinez, who were suspended and threatened with being "blackballed" if they publicized the defects of the M–16 rifle.

Or GM engineers Garl Thelin and George Caramanna, who were pressured not to reveal the structural defects of the Corvair.

Or Carl Houston, an engineer for Stone and Webster Engineering Company, who was fired for voicing criticism of the pipe welding of an atomic power plant even though a defect could have led to a catastrophic meltdown.

Or data analysts Kermit Vandiver and Serle Lawson, who were coerced by B. F. Goodrich executives to falsify laboratory test results on an aircraft brake for an Air Force contracted plane, and later forced to leave after they "went public" with the deception.

In each of these instances, employees were punished for trying to protect the public.

RIGHTS OF PRIVACY

Under the First, Fourth, Fifth, and Ninth Amendments, the state may not invade certain rights of individual privacy. These amendments create "zones of privacy" which governmental officials may penetrate only under the most extraordinary circumstances—such as threats to national security or "probable cause" of the commission of a crime—and evidence must ultimately be produced to justify these penetrations. Otherwise they may not penetrate at all.

Under the First Amendment, the federal government normally may not question a job applicant about religion, political opinions, or past political associations. The Fourth Amendment guarantees "the right of people to be secure in their persons, houses, papers, and effects, against unreasonable searches and seizures." Under the Fifth Amendment, no person shall be compelled in any criminal case to be a witness against oneself—either through direct interrogation or through mechanical testimony compelled by polygraph ("lie detecting") machines. The Ninth Amendment provides that the people retain other residual rights, including, the case of *Griswold v. Connecticut* informed us, an absolute right to be secure in the marriage relationship from police inspection for illicit use of contraceptive devices.

No such niceties apply at the workplace. Eighty percent or more of our largest corporations subject the applicant to a battery of personal and psychological interviews and tests. As a condition of employment, the job applicant must answer inquiries respecting such non-job-related topics as reading or travel habits, nonwork interests ("hobbies"), religious faith, relationship with parents, marital difficulties, homosexuality, sexual fidelity or abnormality, political views, "loyalty," and what Sears, Roebuck once quaintly referred to as "values."

To keep "bad apples out of the barrel," many corporations go much further. Former FBI agents or organizations such as Fidelifacts or Bishop's Service are hired to learn what they can about an applicant by talking with neighbors, former employers, and coworkers. Not only do PEIs (pre-employment investigators) interview outsiders about the future employee's health, records at previous jobs, debts, drinking problems, drug addiction, sexual deviancy, or possible criminal violations, but many search firms and management consultants also feel it is imperative that someone—either with the company or retained by the company—get into the applicant's home for a look around. Such a home interview may establish evidence of an unhappy marriage, neglect of children, or whether the applicant's spouse is domineering or otherwise a "problem."

On the job, surveillance may become even more intensive. Vance Packard interviewed executives at the William J. Burns Detective Agency and Norman Jaspan Associates ("with a hundred clients who are listed on the New York Stock Exchange") to document the extent "of hidden cameras, hidden microphones, one-way mirrors, and peepholes to watch the already well-screened employees."[5]

The rights of union leaders, rival businessmen, and corporate critics are particularly susceptible to abuse. Former Senator Edward Long was impressed by a 1962 survey of industrial espionage conducted by the trade magazine *Industrial Research*:

An interesting paradox was reported: nearly everyone questioned thought that wiretapping was dangerous, and "dirty pool," yet one-third of the firms with formal intelligence operations reported they tapped phones or hired someone to do it for them. Another third of these firms carefully refused to say whether they did or did not tap.[6]

Since 1962 the methods deployed by corporations have become more sophisticated. In the largest corporations, computer data banks frequently include "personal dossiers" containing information on an employee's education, military record, medical history, employment background, aptitude and psychological testing performance, as well as subjective appraisals of his character and skills. A corporation may integrate pre-employment "loyalty" or polygraph checks, conviction and credit records, as well as anonymous or unattributed complaints. Since no safeguards assure "contextual accuracy" and computer dossiers are freely disseminated, the individual's ability to maintain control over personal information has disappeared.

Paralleling the cybernetics revolution has been a "bug boom." Wiretapping, hidden television cameras, spike and parabolic microphones, remote sensing devices, and infrared photography have become less expensive and more effective. Under the 1968 Omnibus Crime Act, wiretapping and electronic surveillance have been made a federal crime. For the corporate employee, however, this is more prayer than law: whereas an elaborate procedural framework regulates federal and state law-enforcement wiretaps, no corporation is compelled to answer a victim's inquiry or preserve its records.

EQUAL RIGHTS

An essential right guaranteed by the Constitution is legal equality. This constitutional principle, unlike those previously discussed, has already been applied to corporations to a limited extent. Title VII of the Civil Rights Act of 1964 forbids employers and unions to discriminate on the basis of race, color, sex, religion, or national origin. But Congress has never fully applied the concepts of equal protection and equal opportunity to the largest corporations.

The Constitution becomes merely a paper right to the extent that we permit crucial aspects of American life to be conducted outside its scope. When we say corporations should be "constitutionalized"—that is, the corporation should be made subject to applicable principles of the Constitution—we are not only asserting that the individual rights of those affected by a corporation are more valuable than certain property rights of the corporation, but also that the legitimacy of the Constitution itself is at stake. The Constitution is the United States' First Law because it reflects a general political understanding about this nation's social values. It is seriously devalued, if not undermined, when important activities of American citizens are not protected by its guarantees.

AN EMPLOYEE BILL OF RIGHTS

The burden should be placed squarely on the giant corporation to justify any act which contravenes basic constitutional rights. Corporations under the Federal Chartering Act, to the same extent that the Constitution requires of the United States Government, should in every transaction, practice, or occurrence:

Observe the First Amendment requirements of freedom of religion, freedom of speech, freedom of the press, and peaceable assembly;

Respect the rights of privacy of its employees and all other United States citizens (as well as the nationals of any other country with which it may be dealing); and

Not discriminate on account of race, religion, creed, or sex.

To elaborate, the First Amendment rights of "whistle blowers" will be defined to prohibit retaliation against any employee who in good faith communicates to the board of directors, the United States Congress, state legislatures, local governments, or any appropriate law enforcement agency information concerning corporate violations of state or federal law; information which would tend to impeach the testimony of corporate representatives before state or federal courts, agencies, or legislatures; information concerning inaccurate public statements of the corporation; or information concerning unethical conduct by the corporation or any of its employees. Thus, a company could not retaliate against an employee who exercises his or her constitutional right to dissent or petition public authorities, without due process of law—such as an impartial grievance procedure.

Second, the rights of privacy of employees should prohibit specific types of pre-employment testing and on-the-job surveillance, such as the use of mandatory polygraph tests and the gathering of confidential credit information. Other pre-employment tests would be permitted only to the extent that the corporate employer can demonstrate a functional relation to the job under consideration. The use of hidden microphones or television cameras, which violate the privacy of numerous innocent employees, would be proscribed. Further, the Federal Chartering Act would allow employees the right to examine their corporate personal files. This proposal is similar to recent federal laws which enable students and citizens to inspect their personal files at universities and federal agencies (including the FBI and CIA) to determine whether the collected information is accurate. Some corporations, including IBM, have already recognized the propriety of this right.

Third, the reach of the corporate equal rights provisions is described by the legal term "every transaction, practice, or occurrence." Although it is impossible to anticipate every instance in which a corporate employee, consumer, distributor, or pensioner might be discriminated against on account of race, religion, creed, or sex, the comprehensive language of this definition indicates that in no instance will such discrimination be permitted.

A fourth section would give teeth to these substantive rights by creating a new federal cause of action. Under present state law, a corporation may dismiss an employee or sever an economic relationship at will. The tenor of state law was succinctly described by a Tennessee court in 1884: all employers "may dismiss their employees for good cause, for no cause, or even for cause morally wrong, without being guilty of legal wrong."[7] The Employee Bill of Rights would reverse this rule only when the corporation fires, penalizes, or intimidates an individual in violation of his constitutional rights to freedom of expression, equal rights, or privacy. In such cases, the injured person could seek monetary damages from either the corporation or the corporate executives or employees involved. If the injured person were an employee or dealer of the corporation, she or he might also seek job protection. To effectuate such suits, the federal courts would be given power to enjoin the corporation from dismissing or penalizing an employee or dealer during the litigation process. The courts would also have the power to award the injured person attorneys' fees and costs and to transfer or dismiss corporate executives or employees who wilfully violate these constitutional rights.

Such a remedy would expand an already existent federal policy of protecting employees from "unjust dismissals." For example, the 1964 Civil Rights Act forbids employers from discriminating against employees on account of race, color, sex, religion, or national origin. The National Labor Relations Act authorizes union members to seek damages (in the form of back pay) and reinstatement if they are discharged because of their involvement in certain union activities. The National Labor Relations Act also enables unions to insert "just cause" provisions in their collective agreements to protect their members from discharges for ulterior purposes, for unstated reasons, or for reasons erroneously believed by the employer to be true. Similar protection is provided by the Federal Fair Labor Standards Act, which prohibits the discharge of employees who complain or testify about violations of federal wage and hour laws; the 1972 Muskie Amendments to the Federal Water Pollution Prevention and Control Act, which prohibits discharge, harassment, or discrimination against an employee for reporting suspected violations of federal water quality to federal authorities; and the Federal Automobile Dealers Franchise Act of 1956, which authorizes automobile dealers to bring a damages action against any automobile manufacturer who attempts to intimidate, coerce, or otherwise threaten them.

By generalizing the selective protection of these acts, the Employee Bill of Rights would fairly balance the corporation's general power to make or sever economic relations against the constitutional rights of those affected by the operations of our largest corporations. This rule would effectively announce that accountability in the workplace is an essential corollary of democracy in society and that corporate tyranny will not be the price of efficient production.

12

Industrial Democracy in the Era of the Corporate Leviathan

Robert A. Dahl

Americans have all but abandoned any serious challenge to the appropriation of public authority by private rules that is the essence of the giant firm.
An important reason is that our history has left us without a socialist
tradition. To be sure, the first labor party in the world appeared in the United
States in 1828, and we have had socialist parties as long as any other country.
But like many a successor, that first labor party vanished completely in a few
years, and the socialist parties never managed to acquire enough of a following to make them a major force in American life. At their peak in 1912, they
won six percent of the total presidential vote. In the depths of the depression
in 1932, the total vote for all socialist parties was less than four percent. Why
the United States was uniquely able to pass through its industrial stage
without generating a major socialist movement is an interesting and complex
historical question. I do not wish to search for an explanation here. Let us
ignore the causes and consider the result.

The consequence is, I think, a serious limit to our capacity for clear-headed
public consideration of how economic enterprises should be governed. Because we have no socialist tradition, our debates about economic institutions
nearly always leave some major alternatives—chiefly the "socialist" alternatives—unexplored.

Not that socialism provides all the answers. Socialists often do not even
seem to ask the right questions. But a socialist tradition helps to fill in some
of the missing shades of the spectrum. If Americans were as pragmatic as they
are supposed to be, and less ideological than they are in fact, they would not
need a socialist tradition to offset their ideological narrowness. But in their
present condition, with a patch over one eye and myopia in the other,
Americans find it more difficult than they should to see the whole range of
possibilities for economic enterprise.

THE ILLUSION OF PRIVATE ENTERPRISE

Philosophers point out that if everything in the universe instantaneously grew or diminished in size, we should have no way of knowing it. Something like this seems to have happened in this country. A nation of farmers with a sprinkling of merchants became a nation of employees, managers, and owners. The small family enterprise run by its owner became the large enterprise in which operation was separated from ownership. The ideology of the private enterprise of the farmer and small merchant was transferred more or less intact to the big corporation. The sanctity of the private property owned by the farmer and small merchant was transferred more or less intact to the big corporation. Because a nation of farmers had believed in the virtue of private enterprise, a nation of employees continued to accept the virtues of "private" corporate enterprise.

The transfer of the old ideology to the new economy required a vast optical illusion, for nothing could be less appropriate than to consider the giant firm a private enterprise. Whatever may be the optimal way of governing the giant corporation, surely it is a delusion to consider it a *private* enterprise. General Motors is as much a public enterprise as the United States Postal Service. With gross receipts approximately equal to Sweden's Gross National Product, with employees and their families about as large as the total population of New Zealand, with outlays larger than those of the central government of France or West Germany, wholly dependent for its survival during every second of its operations on a vast network of laws, protection, services, inducements, constraints, and coercions provided by innumerable governments—federal, state, local, and foreign—General Motors is *de facto* the public's business. It is hardly to be believed, yet it is no less uttered in public, that what is good for General Motors is good for the United States. In these circumstances, to think of General Motors as private instead of public is an absurdity.

It would be more realistic to think of all economic enterprise as a public service. Thought of in this way, a private economy is a contradiction in terms. Indeed, every economy is a public or social (not socialistic) economy. To treat economic enterprise in this way does not automatically answer the question of how an economic enterprise should be governed. But it does compel us to ask the question with a new sense of common interest.

CONVENTIONAL NONSOLUTIONS

How *should* the large corporation be governed? In any modern economy, whether one label it capitalist, socialist, mixed, or whatever, an enterprise is subject to three broad kinds of controls. There are the controls exercised by those who directly manage or run the firm—*internal controls*. There are the controls exercised by other enterprises and economic entities, suppliers, consumers, rivals. These controls sometimes operate through the complex mechanisms of the market, sometimes through bargaining, collusion, collaboration, and so forth. These are *economic controls*. Finally, there are the controls exercised by the various governments of the state—local, provincial, national—*governmental controls*.

The intellectual magicians who manipulated the grand theories about economic enterprises that dominated the public arena for over a century all had a clever way of making one or two of these controls mysteriously disappear. In a magic show, of course, mystification is a good thing; this is just what is supposed to happen. But it is hardly to be expected or commended in an economic program.

The neoclassical economists viewed internal controls, authority within the firm, rather as astronomers regard the gravitational force of the earth. To the astronomer, the earth's gravity is all concentrated at a theoretical point at the center of the globe. From the astronomer's purely professional perspective, all the bustling life, struggle, force, and drama going on at the earth's surface are matters too trivial to be noticed. A revolution, a volcano, a hurricane, an earthquake may destroy his observatory, but *en principe* these things do not matter. In quite the same way, the neoclassical economists reduced the firm to an infinitesimal theoretical point in space where the particularities of Mr. Gradgrind or John D. Rockefeller had no more relevance than the living earth does to the astronomer. The complex government internal to the firm vanished and reappeared theoretically as the single rational entrepreneur pressed on by a lust for profit and an inhuman capacity for responding shrewdly only to the impersonal forces of the market. As a classroom exercise this provided exceptional opportunities for the virtuoso of the blackboard, but it told nothing about how General Motors should be governed or was governed. For that matter, the effects on lung cancer of the "rational" calculations of the cigarette manufacturers are a matter for which a display of fancy cost curves hardly constituted a satisfactory answer.

Great advocates of the division of labor, the neoclassical economists assumed that the government of a firm was a matter for lawyers to handle. As it happens, lawyers have helped to work out an answer, one that seems to be taken for granted by most Americans. This, the orthodox "private property" view, says that the firm ought to be governed by the people who own it. The lawyer's answer may do for small businesses, the famous corner grocery run by Mom and Pop. But as an answer to the problem of the large corporation, it is barely an improvement on the economists' nonanswer: Who owns the corporation? The stockholders. To argue that the large corporation should be governed by the stockholders, however, is highly unpersuasive for two reasons.

First, a moment's thought will show that it is an unreasonable denial of the Principle of Affected Interests. Why should people who own shares be given the privileges of citizenship in the government of the firm when citizenship is denied to other people who also make vital contributions to the firm? The people I have in mind, of course, are employees and customers, without whom the firm could not exist, and the general public, without whose support for (or acquiescence in) the myriad protections and services of the state the firm would instantly disappear. The Principle of Affected Interests—which, for example, strikes down property qualifications in civil elections—gives these people a strong *prima facie* case for corporate citizenship.

That the stockholder has a privileged status in the government of the firm is an anachronistic result of the fact that ownership, authority, and productive work in an enterprise were once united in the same persons. Historically, to own something meant to possess the right to use it as one saw fit under the general protection and regulation of the state. To an America of small farmers and small businessmen, this conception naturally appeared to have great validity. What one owned, it seemed reasonable to suppose, was the product of one's own labor. Elementary justice seemed to support one's authority over it, one's right to do as one pleased with it, subject only to certain legal limits laid down by the state. "In that original state of things, which precedes both the appropriation of land and the accumulation of stock, the whole produce of labor belongs to the laborer." This is not Marx speaking, but Adam Smith in *The Wealth of Nations*.[1] The appropriation of land by private owners, and the need of the laborer for capital which he could not himself supply, created claims against "the whole produce of labor," for rent to landlords and for profits to capitalists. So far, Smith and Marx were in perfect accord. What Marx did, however, was nothing more or less than to interpret rent and profit as illegal seizure of the "surplus value" created by labor. Because they seized this surplus value, landlord and capitalist were not benefactors but exploiters of labor.

The socialist challenge touched off a lasting debate over the proposition that a person is entitled to own something used by another to furnish the owner a profit. Strictly speaking, the affirmative may not have won the debate. But its proponents won the battle of law and policy, and owners preserved the legal right to claim the profits of an enterprise, which was perhaps all most of them really cared about.

Paradoxically, however, not only Marx but also socialists in general helped the defenders of the orthodox view to gain acceptance for one of the great myths of the nineteenth century. This was the myth that ownership, internal control, and legal rights to the profits of an enterprise all *had* to be united in the same persons. The myth obviously served the owners, but it also proved to the satisfaction of socialists that in order to control the firm, and thus acquire the authority to eliminate or otherwise affect profits, ownership had to be shifted to "the public," which in practice means the state.

Neither socialists nor antisocialists seriously challenged the mythology of ownership. Thus one question that desperately needed to be asked was generally passed over: would it not be possible to split apart the various aspects of "ownership," so that internal control of the firm might be split off from those who claimed the profits? If so, why should citizenship in a firm be linked exclusively to the right to receive the profits of the firm?

By now, the first question has been answered by a resounding and incontrovertible *yes*. And that yes is the second flaw in the orthodox view. For orthodoxy is flatly belied by the reality of the modern corporation. Even if the owners of a large firm do have the legal right to run it, everyone knows today that they do not and cannot run it. The question that was not asked during the great debate over socialism versus capitalism has now been answered: ownership has been split off *de facto* from internal control. Every literate person now rightly takes for granted what Adolf Berle and Gardiner Means established four decades ago in their famous study, *The Modern Corporation and Private Property*: increasingly in the large corporation ownership is separated from internal control. To be sure, stockholders do retain a nominal right to participate in governing the firm, but they do not and ordinarily cannot exercise that right. The role of the stockholders in the government of the large corporation is rather like that of the British monarch in investing the prime minister with office: the stockholders serve the purely symbolic function of conferring legitimacy and legality on a government that has managed to acquire power by other means. Unlike the British system since 1688, the American corporation occasionally suffers a palace revolution or *coup d'état*. As in old-fashioned military coups in Latin America, when one group of rulers is exchanged for another, the structure of hierarchic authority under the managers remains the same.

Thus the traditional private property view of authority in the corporation denies the right of citizenship in corporate government to all the affected parties except the one group that does not, will not, and probably cannot exercise that right. If property ownership is necessarily attached to the right of internal control, then the modern corporation must be owned *de facto* not by the stockholders but by the managers. But if property ownership does not carry with it the right of internal control, then the stockholders have no special claim to citizenship—and very likely no reasonable claim at all.

If the orthodox private property answer is inadequate, unfortunately the orthodox socialist answer is no better. Over the period of more than a century since the term has come into use, socialism has meant many things, and I do not want to cavil about definitions. One prominent kind of old-fashioned socialism held that a solution to many problems, including the government of the enterprise, was to be found in "public ownership of the means of production." The usual interpretation of this idea was to have the enterprise owned by the state and managed by state officials. What should have been perfectly obvious, but became so only after some industries were nationalized in a number of European countries, is that this solution left the hierarchical structure of authority intact—or strengthened it. The Postal

Service, after all, is hardly a model of democratic government. Thus the traditional socialist answer ran directly counter to another set of ideas that intersected with socialist thought, the concept of "industrial democracy."

Why socialists were unable to see that "public ownership and operation" might be very different from "industrial democracy" is a fascinating and important chapter in social and intellectual history for which there is no room here. A few aspects, however, are so relevant to the question with which we are concerned that they ought to be emphasized. As we have seen, many socialists had, and continue to have, an exaggerated notion of the importance of "property" in the sense of "ownership." The evils they saw in the business firm seemed to flow from the fact that it was privately owned. *Ergo*: Change enterprises from "private" to "public" ownership, and Presto! All will be well. But, they asked themselves, how can the "public" own anything except through the state? Hence, they reasoned, public ownership means state ownership. And since they took for granted that "ownership" means, among other things, the right to manage the firm, the state would naturally acquire the right to manage the firm. Having that right, it would use it—in the interests, of course, of the public.

But just as we have learned that the private owners of a large corporation do not govern it, even if they have nominal citizenship rights, so we have learned that government ownership does not necessarily mean that the public, or even the part of the public most affected by the operation of a firm, will have very much to do with governing it. In the Soviet Union, for example, the general "public," as distinct from state officials, has no more to say about the government of enterprises than the general "public" in the United States has to say about the government of General Motors; and *Workers* probably have even less to say there than in the United States.

That socialists who sympathized with industrial democracy ended up by supporting bureaucratic centralization was also a result of their fascination with the nation-state. Among those whom Marx contemptuously labeled utopians, like Fourier and Owen, socialism was envisaged as a decentralized system, for the socialist economy was to consist of a multiplicity of small, autonomous associations. After Marx, the tendency was to lean heavily on the state, not perhaps the bourgeois state, possibly a workers' state, a state that might wither away in some remote future, but in any case the state. In countries like England and Sweden, where socialist ideas were not so deeply or exclusively influenced by Marxism, labor-socialist parties nonetheless reflected the general confidence of their fellow citizens that the state was a useful, trustworthy, and effective instrument of rule.

Thus socialists were caught up in the centralizing trends of the nineteenth century. Just as liberal reformers turned to the nation-state as the best instrument of reform and regulation, so the socialist leaders placed their hopes, however much their rhetoric sometimes attempted to conceal it, in the possibility of using the government of the nation-state to run the economy.

Like most reformist liberals, socialists came to see in demands for decentralized institutions of government a mask for privilege and reaction, or the bold, wild face of anarchism, or like the proposals of Guild Socialists in England, quaint ideas of academic intellectuals. Their prejudice was far from absurd, but whatever their intentions, the upshot was that socialism contributed its own thrust toward bureaucratic centralization and away from "industrial democracy." In politics, as we all know, intentions and consequences are poorly correlated, and idealism has never been a protection against that.[2]

Probably nothing strengthened the impetus of socialists toward bureaucratic centralization more than their implacable rejection of economic controls in general and the market in particular. Because they could not envisage a vital coordinating role for economic controls, they were trapped into dependency on the state. Being dependent on the state, they had to reject industrial democracy. For in the absence of economic controls, the only coordinating mechanism that remained was governmental control. But coordination by governmental control was obviously inconsistent with autonomy and self-government in the firm. What would "industrial democracy" do to the sacred central plan?

That the market might be usable under socialism, that if incomes were justly distributed the market might enormously expand opportunities for the exercise of personal choice, that by decentralizing decisions to semiautonomous enterprises the market could provide a powerful force to counter bureaucratic centralization, that far from being the formless, anarchic, anti-social force portrayed by orthodox socialists, the market could be made into a highly sensitive instrument for coordinating myriads of activities too complex ever to be settled wisely by central planners—all this socialists did not understand. They were too perceptive to turn away from industrialization because it was part of the bourgeois order. But in their ignorance they turned away from the market, believing it to be an inherent evil of capitalism that could have no place in a socialist order.

Thus the orthodox socialist answer was, and remains, as full of defects as the other, for it was bound to leave the hierarchical structure of the enterprise intact. What is more, workers confronted by their new bosses, now officials of the state, would henceforth be deprived of the legitimacy, and very likely the legality, of challenging their bosses in the old way by striking. Whether workers might be worse off or better off economically under bureaucratic socialism, one thing is clear: socialism of this kind could never bring "industrial democracy."

SELF-MANAGEMENT VS. INTEREST GROUP MANAGEMENT

If both the "Private property" and socialist solutions are unacceptable, are we stalemated? Understandably, in both the United States and the Soviet Union, defenders of the status quo would like everyone to think so. For in that case the status quo—the pseudo-private corporation in the United States, the pseudo-public enterprise in the Soviet Union—would stand a much better chance of being preserved, as would the military-industrial advantages that accrue from either/or oppositions to those already in power.

Probably the most radical alternative to the American and Soviet status quo is exemplified by the system of self-management that has been developed in Yugoslavia since 1950. Yugoslavia is the only country in the world where a serious effort has been made to translate the old dream of industrial democracy into reality—or into as much reality as dreams can have. Let me add at once that in the government of the *state*, Yugoslavia is hardly a polyarchy. The leadership has not yet permitted an opposition party to exist; as the famous cases of Djilas and Mihajlov attest, merely to advocate an opposition party may land one in jail. Yet if Yugoslavia is less democratic than the United States in the government of the state, it is more democratic in the government of the enterprise. In both respects, of course, it is much more democratic than the Soviet Union.

In fact, it was after Yugoslavia broke out of the Soviet orbit that her leaders introduced social self-management as a deliberate and systematic effort to shift from the orthodox, highly centralized bureaucratic Soviet-style socialism toward a socialism that would be more democratic, liberal, humane, and decentralized.[3] During their brief revolution in 1968, the Czechs also moved rapidly toward decentralized socialism with enterprise councils elected mainly by the workers. But after the Russians moved in, this dangerous challenge to bureaucratic socialism was suppressed, and the radical idea of self-management was attacked as anti-socialist. The only appropriate representative of the workers, was, naturally, the party.

Although in Yugoslavia the most dramatic step toward industrial democracy and the one most relevant here was the introduction of workers' councils throughout all economic enterprises, the principle of social self-management was gradually extended to include practically every kind of organized unit—local governments, rural coops, schools, hospitals, apartment houses, the post office, and telephone services.[4]

Although it would be a gross exaggeration to say that self-management of economic enterprises in Yugoslavia is a complete or wholly satisfactory achievement of industrial democracy, in conjunction with other aspects of the Yugoslav system, the workers' councils seem to have produced not only a relatively decentralized economy but also a substantial amount of participation by workers in the government of the enterprise. To be sure, the workers' councils are by no means autonomous. Here as elsewhere in Yugoslavia organized party opposition is not permitted. Strikes are rare and of doubtful legality, and the special influence of the party is important. Nonetheless, it seems clear that the councils are very much more than a facade behind which the party and state officials actually manage the enterprise.

What happens to "property rights" in such a system? Who owns the enterprise? In this kind of a system, the great myth of the nineteenth century stands exposed: Ownership is dissolved into its various components. What is left? A kind of ghostly penumbra around the enterprise. The enterprise is described in the constitution as "social property." But it might be closer to the mark to say that *no one owns the enterprise*. It is not, certainly, owned by the state or by shareholders. It is not owned by the workers in the enterprise. The point is that "property" is a bundle of rights and obligations. Once the pieces in this bundle have been parceled out, nothing exactly corresponding to the conventional meaning of ownership or property remains.[5]

How well would such a system satisfy the criterion of competence? To be specific, would the employees of large firms in the United States manage their enterprises competently? Would American enterprises be as efficiently run as at present? I think one ought to keep in mind that even a modest decline in physical productivity could be offset by some important gains, of which the most significant would be to transform employees from corporate subjects to citizens of the enterprise. How great a gain this would be depends on how much value we and the employees attach to democratic participation and control, as good both intrinsically and in their consequences for self-development and human satisfaction, quite independently of their outputs. In the absence of strictly relevant experience, predictions about productivity are of course hazardous. Although one can hardly compare Yugoslavia and the United States on this matter, the introduction of self-management in Yugoslavia was followed by a rapid rise in productivity. As to the consequences for productivity of the various schemes of employee participation and consultation that have been tried out in this country and elsewhere, the evidence is inconclusive.[6]

But surely the most relevant consideration is that in the United States management is increasingly professional and therefore available for hire. In fact, the emerging practice in the American corporation is for managers and even management teams to shift about among firms. As Barber writes:

The old notion that a responsible official stays with his company, rising through the ranks and wearing the indelible badge of Ford or IBM or duPont, is quaint and out of tune with a world of skilled scientific business management. It is not that the new executive is any less interested in or dedicated to the success of the company that employs him; rather it is that he sees himself as a specialist whose skills and growth are in no way necessarily associated with any particular enterprise.[7]

I do not see why a board of directors elected by the employees could not select as competent managers as a board of directors selected by banks, insurance companies, or the managers themselves. The board of a self-governing firm might hire a management team on a term contract in the same way that a board of directors of a mutual fund often does now. Surely if the "profit motive" is all that it has been touted to be, who has more at stake in improving the earnings of an enterprise than employees would have if the management were responsible to them rather than to stockholders?

Moreover, the development of professional managers starkly spotlights the old question, *Quis custodiet ipsos custodes?* As Barber again points out:

With corporate managers holding the reins of widely diversified, global firms, but conceiving of themselves essentially as professionals, what are the rules—the standards—with which these men are to be governed in their use of the immense power they possess? As well, how are those within the corporation—especially its multitudinous family of technocrats and middle-level executives—to be protected from encroachment on their legitimate interests?[8]

Although Barber poses the question, he offers no answer. Yet self-management is one solution too obvious to be ignored—except in a country blinded by an unthinking adherence to the absolute conception of a "private" firm "owned" by stockholders.

It is not, I think, the criterion of *competence* but rather the criterion of *personal choice* that raises problems for self-management. These problems arise because of the possibility that many employees may not wish to participate in the government of the firm, while many people not employed in the enterprise could claim a right to participate under the Principle of Affected Interests.

Consider the people who work in the enterprise: while many employees, particularly technicians and lower executives would probably welcome self-management, it is very much open to doubt, unfortunately, whether blue-collar workers want to allocate any of their attention, time, and energy to governing the enterprise in which they work. Although sentimentalists on the Left may find the idea too repugnant to stomach, quite possibly workers and trade unions are the greatest barriers at present to any profound reconstruction of economic enterprise in this country. Several aspects of their outlook militate against basic changes. Along with the officialdom of the trade union movement, workers are deeply ingrained with the old private property view of economic enterprise. What is perhaps more important, affluent American workers, like affluent workers in many advanced countries and the middle class everywhere, tend to be consumption oriented, acquisitive, privatistic, and family centered. This orientation has little place for a passionate aspiration toward effective citizenship in the enterprise (or perhaps even in the state!). The job is viewed as an activity not intrinsically gratifying or worthwhile but rather an instrument for gaining money which the worker and his or her family can spend on articles of consumption. In this respect, the modern worker has become what the classical economists said he was: an economic man compelled to perform intrinsically unrewarding, unpleasant, and even hateful labor in order to gain money to live on. So far as its intrinsic rewards are concerned, work is simply so much time lost out of one's life. The work place, then, is not "society in microcosm." It is simply a place where one puts in time and labor in order to earn money.[9] The union is a necessary instrument, but it is also a crashing bore. Solidarity is a matter of sticking together during bargaining and strikes in order to get better wages, but it is not animated by any desire to change the structure of power within the firm.

The upshot for many workers is that a chance to participate in the government of the enterprise (even during working hours) might very well hold slight attraction. After all, in polyarchies and primary democracies a great many citizens are indifferent toward their opportunities to participate. As long as the enterprise pays good wages, its affairs seem even less interesting than affairs of state. In addition to reflecting these attitudes of their constituents, trade union leaders could easily interpret self-management as a threat to their influence: the consequences for incumbent leaders would at best be uncertain, and like leaders generally, most trade union leaders prefer to avoid risks.

Yet these bleak prospects are by no means the whole story. The impetus toward self-management may not come from the strata which the conventional (old and new) Left have for so long courted with such meager response. It may come instead from the white-collar employees, technicians, and the executives themselves. What is more, there is a good deal of evidence to show that although participation does not guarantee increased output in the conventional sense, it does generally increase the worker's satisfaction with and interest in his work situation. If a significant number of employees, whether white-collar or blue-collar, were to discover that participation in the affairs of the enterprise—or that part of the enterprise most directly important to them—contributed to their own sense of competence and helped them to control an important part of their daily lives, then lassitude and indifference toward participation might change into interest and concern. Of course, we should not entertain excessive expectations. Nor should we reject self-management because it may not measure up to the highest ideals of participation—ideals that are, after all, not met in any democratic association.

The most severe problem raised by the criterion of personal choice is, I believe, the existence of Affected Interests other than the employees of the enterprise: not only the consumers but also many others who may be affected by decisions about location, employment, discrimination, innovation, safety, pollution, and so on. How can these Affected Interests be sure that their claims will be fairly weighed in the decisions of the firm? By focusing attention on the *state* as the best agent of all the Affected Interests, this question often drives the advocate of change straight onto the horns of the old dilemma: either bureaucratic socialism or else the private property solution. It is precisely because self-management enables us to escape this dilemma that it is so hopeful an alternative. But have we now escaped the dilemma only to find it lying in wait farther down the road?

I shall not pause to argue with any reader who is so unworldly as to

suppose that once "the workers" control an enterprise they will spontane-
ously act "in the interests of all." Let me simply remind such hypothetical
readers that if self-management were introduced today, tomorrow's citizens
in the enterprise would be yesterday's employees. Is their moral redemption
and purification so near at hand? If not, must self-management wait until
workers are more virtuous than human beings have ever been heretofore?
For my part, it seems wiser to design a government on the assumption that
people will not always be virtuous and at times surely will be tempted to do
evil, yet where they will not lack for the incentive and the opportunities to act
according to their highest potential.

We can now see how the distinction I made earlier between internal
controls, economic controls, and government controls suggests roughly three
ways—not mutually exclusive—for satisfying the Principle of Affected Interests.

To begin with, in addition to workers, other Affected Interests may be
given the right to participate in internal controls, to have a direct voice in
management, for example through representatives on the board of directors
of the enterprise. I term this solution *interest group management.*

Candor compels me to admit that interest group management seems much
more in the American grain than self-management. It fits the American ethos
and political culture, I think, to suppose that conflicting interests can and
should be made to negotiate: therefore let all the parties at interest sit on the
board of directors. It would be a very American thing to do. Interest group
management is, then, a development much more likely than self-management. It is hard for me to see how American corporations can indefinitely
fight off proposals like those most recently made by Ralph Nader for consumer or public members on their boards. I can readily see how we may
arrive incrementally at interest group management of giant firms. Since this
innovation would probably be enough to deflate weak pressures for further
change, the idea of self-management would become moribund.

Yet even if interest group management is more likely, it is much less
desirable, in my view, than self-management. For one thing, interest group
management does very little to democratize the internal environment of an
enterprise. Instead, it would convert the firm into a system of rather remote
delegated authority. There is no democratic unit within which consumer
representatives, for example, could be elected and held accountable. The
delegates of the Affected Interests doubtless would all have to be appointed
in one way or another by the federal government, by organized interest
groups, by professional associations. There would be the ticklish problem of
what interests were to be represented and in what proportions—a problem
the Guild Socialists struggled with but never solved very satisfactorily. Since
the consequences of different decisions affect different interests, have different weights, and cannot always be anticipated, what particular interests
are to be on the board of management, and how are they to be chosen? Are

the employees to elect a majority or only a minority? If their representatives are a majority, the representatives of other Affected Interests will hardly be more than an advisory council. If a minority, I fear that most people who work for large enterprises would be pretty much where they are now, remote from the responsibility for decisions.

Doubtless interest group management would be an improvement over the present arrangements, and it may be what Americans will be content with, if the corporation is to be reformed at all. Yet it is a long way from the sort of structural change that would help to reduce the powerlessness of the ordinary American employee.

Moreover, interest group management would not eliminate the need for economic and governmental controls. Is it not through these, rather than by participating in internal controls, that the Affected Interests could best be represented and protected in a system of self-management?

I cannot stress too strongly the importance of external controls, both governmental and economic. I do not see how economic enterprises can be operated satisfactorily in a modern economy, capitalist, mixed, socialist, or whatever, without some strategic external controls over the firm. However much the Yugoslavs recoil from the Soviet example of bureaucratic socialism, on this point they have no doubts. Their external controls include the forces of the market and credit, participation of the local government in the choice of the director, norms for salaries and the allocation of revenues, and the ubiquitous presence of the well-disciplined League of Communists.

It is worth keeping in mind, too, that the less effective the external economic controls are—the influence of customers and suppliers on costs and prices, suppliers of capital and credit on interest and terms of borrowing, competing firms and products on the growth and prosperity of the enterprise—the greater must be the governmental controls. Just as much so the extreme limit of economic controls will not be easy to find.

Yet it seems obvious that if we place much value on democracy at the work place, the present arrangement is ludicrously far from optimal. As for alternatives, self-management seems closer to the optimal than bureaucratic socialism or interest group management.

13

Why Democracies Need a Legislative Ombudsman

Donald C. Rowat

As a device for protecting citizens against bureaucratic maladministration and abuses of discretionary power, the ombudsman system is unique. Because of the popularity of the ombudsman idea around the world in recent years, there are by now many complaint-handlers who are called "ombudsmen" but who do not qualify as the genuine article. The so-called "classical" ombudsman system as developed in Scandinavia and then transplanted in the 1960s to other countries, including the United Kingdom, New Zealand, Canada (the provinces), and the United States (several state and local governments), has certain essential characteristics. The most important of these is that it is an arm of the legislature and hence independent of the administrative side of the government. In order to distinguish it from other complaint-handling offices now mistakenly called ombudsmen, it is now referred to as the legislative ombudsman.

THE NATURE OF THE OMBUDSMAN SYSTEM

The essential features of the legislative ombudsman are summed up in the following definition: The legislative ombudsman is an officer of the legislature appointed to investigate complaints from the public against unfair administrative action. This definition encompasses an unusual combination of features that make the office unique among grievance-handling, investigating, and appeal bodies.

An ombudsman is an agent of the legislature, appointed and removed only with the approval of the legislature and the leaders of its main political parties, and is free to report back to it at any time. The appointment is for a fixed term, usually four to seven years, so that an incoming party majority cannot easily use its power to remove the ombudsman, who will often, in fact, be reappointed for a second or third term, and is thus politically independent.

An ombudsman is given special powers by law to get at the facts of a case. One of the serious problems citizens face is that they may not know why a decision was made that affects them adversely, or why a decision was delayed, and may thus suspect that they have been treated unfairly but cannot access the necessary documents. The adoption of access to information laws has helped this situation in some countries, but because of the ombudsman's special powers and facilities for investigation, it is much easier for someone in this position than for a citizen or even a legislative member to find out if the decision or delay was justified. One of the main accomplishments of ombudsmen has been to insist that administrators should give reasons for adverse decisions.

More important, when comparing this office to the courts, the ombudsman's method of handling grievances is direct, informal, speedy, and cheap. All that is required to initiate an appeal is for the complainant to phone or write a letter to the ombudsman's office. As an added protection for the large number of inmates of state institutions now found in the modern welfare state, letters from inmates of prisons, welfare homes, and mental hospitals must be forwarded unopened by the supervisory staff to insure against reprisal. No formal court-like hearings are held, and an ombudsman's work is done almost entirely by phone or mail. A phone call to a department, for example, may result in immediate remedial action, or a request for departmental documents to study may be made, and, if the ombudsman is not satisfied that a complaint is unwarranted, a departmental explanation may be requested. If the explanation is unsatisfactory, the complaint will be found warranted, and remedial action will be recommended. This is nearly always acted on by the department. Because the ombudsmen's method of handling grievances is so informal and simple, they have surprisingly small budgets and staffs in relation to the number of complaints handled. The complainant pays no fees or legal costs.

A very important limitation upon an ombudsman's power —and a key difference from the courts or court-like appeal bodies—is that the ombudsman has no right to quash a decision or issue orders, and has no direct control over the administration. In other words, the ombudsmen have no power to substitute their judgment for that of an expert official who made the decision. They have the power only to investigate and, where injustice or maladministration is found, to propose a remedy. Success is based on the fairness of the recommendations and the power of publicity. An ombudsman's most important power is the threat or actual use of publicity. When a proposed remedy is not accepted by the authorities, the main weapon to secure remedial action is publicity—reports to the legislature and the press. Annually the ombudsman places before the legislature a published report that describes typical cases and comments on more serious cases and

issues. Ombudsmen also have the power to issue special reports on important cases to the legislature and the press. Bureaucracy's fear of public
exposure to wrongdoing exerts a powerful influence toward rectitude,
fairness, and efficiency.

An important result of an ombudsman's work is to detect from the nature
of the complaints, or from a rash of complaints in a particular service, bad
practices or procedures that require reform. The office of the ombudsman in
France is especially known for the large number of its legislative recommendations that have been adopted, including important new laws providing a
right of public access to administrative documents and requiring reasons to
be given for decisions.[1]

WHY THE SYSTEM IS NEEDED

The main reason for the widespread adoption of the ombudsman system
is a need for additional protection against administrative arbitrariness and
bureaucratic bungling in the modern state. Since World War II, the tremendous growth in the range and complexity of government activities has
brought with it the need to grant increasing powers of discretion to administrative authorities. As one of Britain's great constitutional lawyers has
warned, "Wherever there is discretion, there is room for arbitrariness." So
too, bureaucratic bungling.

In this age of the welfare state, thousands of administrative decisions are
made each year, many of them by minor officials, which affect the lives of
every citizen. Some of these decisions are bound to be arbitrary, unfair, or
unjustified, but there is no easy way for the ordinary citizen to gain redress.
A tremendous number of minor complaints arise from sheer bureaucratic
inefficiency and unintentional maladministration.

Particularly in the common-law countries, which do not have a system of
administrative courts like those in Western Europe, it has been found that the
traditional avenues for airing grievances against administrative action are
inadequate. The three main traditional avenues have been complaints to
members of the legislature, publicity in the press, and appeals to the courts
(or, where they are provided, to special administrative appeal tribunals).

The right to take grievances to one's legislative representative has serious
limitations. Citizens often do not know their representative, and even if they
do, they are likely to feel that she or he is not impartial because of party
affiliations. Members are often heavily loaded with requests from their
constituents, and this takes time away from their legislative functions. The
office of ombudsman takes over part of this constituency load and gives them
time to play a more important role in law-making. Experience with ombudsman plans, however, shows that complaints handed on to an ombudsman by members of the legislature are only a small proportion of the

total that are received. This indicates that there is a large need which is not met by complaints to members.

The press is a powerful avenue for airing administrative grievances. But the grievances must be serious enough to catch the public's interest, and airing them in the press may not result in a remedy.

Many large daily papers now have special columnists who receive and investigate complaints against the actions of public or private organizations. They play a role surprisingly like that of ombudsmen when investigating complaints against official action. The main disadvantage of media ombudsmen is that they have no legal power to get at government documents, inspect administrative activities, or report to the legislature. Also, their coverage of the population is spotty, their budgets vary, and their staffs' knowledge of administration and law is erratic. Nevertheless, the hundreds of complaints they receive each year against official actions demonstrate that the job of investigating them is too big for elected representatives to handle by themselves.

In common law countries, formal appeal to the ordinary courts is often regarded as adequate protection against administrative irregularities. But the formality, cost, snail-like pace, and narrow scope of appeals makes the courts an unsuitable avenue for the vast majority of minor complaints and even for many serious grievances. Generally, the courts will review a decision only on a question of legality and will refuse to review its wisdom or even reasonableness. Partly for these reasons, special administrative tribunals have been created for appeals in specific areas. These bodies can cover only a small portion of all administrative action. Because they also have the power to make binding decisions, however, they must still follow elaborate court-like procedures and are often cumbersome, slow, and forbidding to the average citizen.

The reason an ombudsman is free to follow quick and informal procedures is that she or he does not have this power of the courts and administrative tribunals to make binding decisions. The ombudsman does not need to hold hearings or use adversarial court-like procedures. This is also the main reason why it is not necessary for ombudsmen to be trained in law. Some of the most successful American and Canadian ombudsmen have not been lawyers.

DESIRABLE FEATURES OF THE SYSTEM

An important feature of the ombudsman system is that, because of the simple and cheap way in which complaints are handled, many minor complaints can be satisfied that would otherwise never be remedied. Though important to the claimant, they are not worth the effort or cost of an elaborate court procedure even if they can be appealed to a court. Typical examples of minor grievances handled by ombudsmen are complaints about getting no answer to an application, getting insufficient information on a right of appeal, and delay in making decisions. Nevertheless, some of ombudsmen's most valuable work is done on serious cases of illegality involving civil rights, such as the unjustifiable use of handcuffs, the recording of telephone conversations by the police, or an assault by an attendant on a mental patient.

Another advantage of the system is that citizens gain a feeling of security from knowing that there is an impartial authority willing to act on their behalf. Even if the complainant is wrong in suspecting unfair treatment, the assurance by an impartial authority that this is not the case can resolve such suspicions. A large part of the ombudsman's job is to satisfy complainants, through the impartiality of an investigation, that they have been dealt with fairly. This aspect of the position, though not revealed by statistics on the number of complaints found to be justified, is extremely important. Also, the fact that a large proportion of the complaints are shown to be unjustified helps to restore public confidence in government and administration. When an ombudsman plan is being considered, it is typical of the public service to fear that an ombudsman will expose their shortcomings, hence they oppose the plan. After the plan is adopted and implemented, however, they appreciate this point, and understand that an ombudsman is an ally in helping to improve their image and their services, and drop their opposition. It is commendable that, despite such a fear, the Canadian committee of top-level officials appointed to consider the concept, recommended a federal ombudsman in 1977.[2]

Another desirable feature of the office is that the ombudsman can protect the inmates of public institutions. People in prisons, hospitals, and especially homes for the disabled and the aged and psychiatric hospitals are among the most helpless in our society. Some of the American and Canadian state and provincial ombudsmen have revealed shocking cases of the way people have been treated in public institutions, and some of their most valuable work has been to remedy the legitimate grievances of such people. A number of American states that do not have a general ombudsman have created specialized ombudsmen for certain types of public institutions, especially prisons. Likewise, Canada's federal government has an ombudsman-like Correctional Investigator who receives nearly 2,000 complaints a year from prisoners.

A little-recognized advantage of the office is the help given by ombudsmen to the large number of complaints that fall outside their jurisdiction. Often they do no more than pass on the complaint to the authority complained against and request a reply on the action taken, yet they have lent the prestige of their office to the complaint, and are far more likely to get favorable action than if the citizen had complained to the authority as an isolated individual. The American and Canadian state and provincial ombudsmen receive many complaints against federal authorities. This is a good indication of the need for an ombudsman at the federal level in both countries.

The serious limitations on the traditional means of handling complaints against bureaucracy and the desirable features of an ombudsman system lend strong support to the argument that citizens and the legislature need the help of an ombudsman in any attempt to investigate and remedy grievances resulting from maladministration or arbitrary administrative action.

THE SYSTEM'S WORLDWIDE SPREAD

In the advanced common-law countries—Australia, Canada, New Zealand, the United Kingdom, and the United States—the weight of this argument has been recognized. The ombudsman plan has by now been adopted in these countries at either the national, state, or local levels—or a combination, as in Australia and the United Kingdom. In the United States the plan has been adopted by four state governments (Alaska, Hawaii, Iowa, and Nebraska), the Commonwealth of Puerto Rico, and the Territory of Guam. It has also been adopted at the national, state, or local level in most of the developed democracies of Western Europe, and by a number of developing countries, including the largest states in India.[3] There is now a bill before the Indian Parliament to provide a version of the plan at the federal level.

The legislative ombudsman is such an important new addition to the machinery for protecting the citizen against bureaucratic abuse that by 1983 it had been adopted in thirty-five countries around the world. As classified and listed in the worldwide survey by the International Ombudsman Institute, ninety legislative ombudsman systems had been adopted by national and lower-level governments by 1983. Of these, twenty-five were national, forty-four were state or regional, and twenty-one were local (see Table 13.1).[4]

It is not surprising that the vast majority of the state, regional, and local schemes have been adopted in the developed democracies, because they are relatively decentralized. Australia, Canada, the United States, and Italy have most of the state or regional schemes, while the United States has most of the ones for city governments.

Among the twenty most developed democracies, seventeen have one or more systems operating at the national or a lower level of government, and a majority (thirteen) have adopted a general scheme at the national level. It will be noted that the scheme has also been adopted at the national level by twelve developing countries, many of which are former British colonies. Indeed, the spread of the system has been so rapid that it may soon become a standard part of the machinery of government throughout the democratic world.

A FEDERAL-LEVEL OMBUDSMAN?

The six federations among the developed democracies (Australia, Austria, Canada, Switzerland, the United States and West Germany) have general

Table 13.1

General Legislative Ombudsman Systems by Country and Level of Government, 1983

COUNTRY	NATIONAL	REGIONAL	LOCAL	TOTAL
A. DEVELOPED COUNTRIES (17)				
AUSTRALIA	1	7		8
AUSTRIA	1	(2)[A]		1
CANADA		9		9
DENMARK	1			1
FINLAND	1			1
FRANCE	1			1
ISRAEL	1		2	3
ITALY		6		6
NETHERLANDS	1		2	3
NEW ZEALAND	1			1
NORWAY	1			1
SPAIN	1			1
SWEDEN	1			1
SWITZERLAND	1	1		2
UNITED KINGDOM	1	2[B]	3	6
UNITED STATES		6	12	18
WEST GERMANY		1		1
	12	32	20	64
B. DEVELOPING COUNTRIES (12)				
BOPHUTHATSWANA	1			1
FIJI	1			1
GUYANA	1			1
INDIA		3		3
JAMAICA	1			1
MAURITIUS	1			1
PAPUA NEW GUINEA	1			1
PORTUGAL	1			1
SOLOMON ISLANDS	1			1
SRI LANKA[C]				
SAINT LUCIA		1		1
TRINIDAD-TOBAGO	1			1
	10	4		14
TOTAL IN FORCE	22	36	20	78
C. APPROVED BUT NOT YET IN FORCE				
BARBADOS (1980)	1			1
BANGLADESH (1980)	1			1
BELGIUM			1	1
INDIA		1		1
IRELAND (1980)	1			1
ITALY		3		3
SPAIN		4		4
	3	8	1	12
GRAND TOTAL	25	44	21	90

[A]Two states joined the national plan by 1983 but did not have
separate plans.
[B]Northern Ireland; one for departments, one for public corporations.
[C]Listed as an executive ombudsman, but probably should be classed
as a legislative office.

ombudsman plans in some or all of their states. But three of them (Canada, the United States, and West Germany) do not have one at the federal level—although Canada and West Germany have specialized ombudsmen for specific purposes. Because the United States and Canada are federations in which the national and state or provincial public services are quite separate, the existence of state or provincial ombudsmen does little to meet the need at the federal level, where thousands of administrative decisions are made that affect the lives of individual citizens. To the average citizen, furthermore, the federal public services in these countries are bewilderingly big and complex. Canada's federal service, which is much smaller than that of the United States, nevertheless has nearly six hundred thousand employees, more than fifty ministerial departments and department-like agencies, and more than one hundred independent organizations of various kinds and sizes.[5] Since these independent organizations are not directly controlled by an elected minister responsible to Parliament, there is more danger of their officials acting irresponsibly. The federal administration of the United States similarly has many independent agencies over which the elected President and Congress have little direct control.

One can even argue that there is greater need for an ombudsman at the national level in the United States and Canada than in Western European countries or Australia, because many Western European countries already have highly developed systems of administrative courts, and Australia has recently established a special court for administrative appeals. From the viewpoint of dealing fairly with citizens, administration in the United States and Canada has the following weaknesses: many independent agencies with power to decide individual cases; limited opportunities for appeals to the courts; antiquated laws on executive privilege, expropriation, and government liability; and weak arrangements for free legal aid to needy people. In Canada, there is also inadequate legislative prescription of administrative procedures, with no national Administrative Procedures Act as in the United States and several Western European countries. Also, Parliament in Canada has no formal procedure for settling grievances, as it has in other Commonwealth countries or in West Germany. As John Kersell has observed:

Canadians and their representatives in Parliament have no procedure for ventilating grievances which compares with Australian "Grievance Day," or for that matter, with British Question Time or New Zealand public petitions. There is no procedure in the Canadian House which in practice provides the back bench Member of Parliament with an adequate opportunity to air a constituent's bona fide grievance without first gaining the co-operation of his party in Parliament.[6]

Even if there were to be reforms in all of these areas, a federal ombudsman office would still be desirable because of the relative ease and cheapness with which it could settle minor grievances and the impetus it would give to improving administrative action. The adoption of an ombudsman system might also help to bring about other reforms. Most of them are legally complicated and technical, and it is therefore difficult to create an informed public opinion about them. A government does not easily submit to limitations on the free exercise of its executive powers that such reforms imply. The ombudsman system, on the other hand, is simple, easily understood, has great popular appeal, and does not limit a government's powers. The public discussion generated by the creation of a federal office, and later by the office's recommendations for reform, could help to bring about these more technical reforms in the realm of administrative law.

Though the need for the office at the federal level in the United States and Canada appears to be great, there is no easy way of estimating the total number of unsatisfied complaints that citizens have against their federal administrations in these countries. One way of doing this, and at the same time comparing existing systems, is to examine the number of complaints received by some state and provincial ombudsmen, and by some national plans in other developed democracies. A comparison can be made by calculating the total number of complaints per hundred thousand of population for each jurisdiction. I have therefore chosen a representative group of developed unitary and federal countries and states for which reasonably comparable information is available in the 1983 survey by the International Ombudsman Institute, from which the complaint figures for Table 13.2 are drawn.[7] The population figures used in the table are United Nations estimates for 1980, and the complaint figures are for 1980 except where footnoted.

Particularly notable in these data are the following facts: (1) even in developed democracies, there are thousands of complaints each year that are not adequately handled by traditional avenues of appeal; (2) in federations the number of complaints at both levels of government is large; (3) the number of complaints per hundred thousand varies greatly from one ombudsman scheme to another, partly due to differences in accessibility, scope of jurisdiction, and the definition of a complaint; and (4) the number of complaints in France is proportionately extremely low. This is because in France formal complaints must be made first to a member of the legislature. Even if complaints that now go informally directly to the French ombudsman were to be included, however, the number per hundred thousand would still be only a fraction of that for other systems. The same is true of the United Kingdom, where complaints at the national level must also go first to a Member of Parliament. This is further convincing evidence that complaints to legislative members do not satisfy the need.

Therefore if the United States and Canada were to have federal systems which permitted direct complaints, one could expect them to receive large numbers of complaints. The closest parallel is the Australian case. By 1984–1985, the annual number of complaints and inquiries the federal

Table 13.2

Complaints Received by Ombudsmen in Selected Developed Unitary and Federal Countries

	POPULATION (000's)	COMPLAINTS RECEIVED	COMPLAINTS PER 100,000
1. DEVELOPED UNITARY COUNTRIES			
DENMARK	5,120	1,518	29.6
FRANCE	53,480	3,751	7.0
ISRAEL	3,780	7,326	193.8
NEW ZEALAND	3,090	1,592	51.5
NORWAY	4,070	1,573	38.6
SWEDEN	8,290	3,484[B]	42.0
2. DEVELOPED FEDERATIONS			
STATE OR PROVINCIAL LEVEL			
HAWAII	770	1,369[A]	177.8
IOWA	2,913	781	26.8
ONTARIO	8,571	4,022[AB]	46.6
RHINELAND PALATINATE	3,641	2,743	75.3
VICTORIA	3,877	2,541	65.5
ZURICH	1,123	653[C]	58.1
FEDERAL LEVEL			
AUSTRALIA	14,420	11,872[AD]	82.3

[A]Mid-1980 to mid-1981.
[B]There were also 4,687 informal complaints and inquiries.
[C]1978-1979.
[D]Includes informal complaints and inquiries.

ombudsman there receives had increased to over twenty thousand.[8] If the main lines of a federal system in Canada or the United States were the same as in Australia, one can calculate that, on the basis of proportionate populations, a federal system in Canada might eventually receive over thirty thousand complaints and inquiries a year, and in the United States probably ten times that. Since the ombudsmen usually find that ten per cent or more of complaints to them are justified, this means that a federal ombudsman in the United States would receive about thirty thousand justified complaints each year. Such calculations indicate how large the number of genuine grievances against the federal administrations that are never remedied is in Canada and the United States, and overwhelmingly support the need for a legislative ombudsman in these and other democratic states.

14

Quality Circles: Implications for American Management

Lisa K. Armour

During the twenty years between 1947 and 1967, the productivity rate of the United States grew at an annual rate of 3.1 percent. Since 1967, however, productivity has declined, with an average annual growth rate of 1.6 percent. In contrast, during the decade between 1969 and 1979, Japan's annual productivity growth rate averaged over 9 percent.[1] As a result of Japanese success in maintaining a high productivity growth rate, American business executives have begun to examine Japanese management styles in order to identify the elements responsible for this success and to integrate them into American organizations to improve productivity. One of the strategies cited as a key to the success of the Japanese is the *quality circle*. William Ouchi, author of *Theory Z*, claims that "many American managers. . . . have been struck by the effectiveness of these circles and are determined to implement similar techniques in their own companies."[2] A number of problems are encountered, however, when implementation is attempted. The most threatening problem to the successful implementation and survival of a quality circle is the resistance encountered from supervisors and middle management of traditional bureaucratic organizations.

A quality circle can be defined as "a small group of employees, doing similar work, who volunteer to meet periodically to discuss production, quality, and related problems, to investigate causes, recommend solutions, and take corrective actions to the extent of their authority."[3] Generally each group consists of between seven and twelve members. Meetings are usually held weekly at the same time, either on or off company time. Circle members are trained in statistical methods, group dynamics, and group decision-making techniques.[4]

Sud Ingle, quality control manager for Mercury Marine, a division of the Brunswick Corporation, states that "although the basic idea" for quality circles "originated in the United States, the right combination of factors existed only in Japan. The seeds planted by the Americans were accepted by the Japanese and nourished to the fullest extent."[5] The seeds planted in Japan were sown by two Americans, Edward Deming and Joseph Juran.

After World War II, General MacArthur asked that someone be sent to Japan to teach the people better quality control methods, as Japanese products at that time were known for their poor quality. Deming, a government statistician, was sent to Japan to train management people in quality control methods. Between 1948 and 1950, Deming was so successful that he was called on repeatedly to train additional scientists and engineers in statistical methods. His services were so highly regarded by the Japanese that in 1951 the Union of Japanese Scientists and Engineers awarded the first Deming Prizes for corporations and individuals—a practice that continues to the present.

Juran visited Japan during 1954 and 1955. According to his lectures on total quality control, "quality begins in the design stage and ends after satisfactory services are provided to the customer"; thus it is "the total quality that counts for the success of the company."[6] The Japanese were quite receptive to this notion of total quality control, as the government was also concerned with the service aspect of a quality improvement program.[7]

At the time that Deming and Juran were teaching the Japanese better quality control methods, the Japanese government declared better quality a national priority. This commitment to quality improvement, coupled with the willingness of the Japanese workers to learn the statistical methods taught by Deming and Juran, resulted in the establishment of various programs designed to promote quality. These included weekly radio series on quality, the designation of a national quality month, and the introduction of quality circles in 1962.

The original impetus for the creation of quality circles came from industry foremen who were wondering what to do with all their newfound knowledge.[8] The intent was to form small groups in the shop and teach the workers the various statistical techniques that the foremen had been taught. The workers and their knowledge of their jobs were recognized as being an important element in maintaining and improving quality. Three quality circles were registered with the Union of Japanese Scientists and Engineers in May, 1962. By the end of that year, twenty circles had been registered, and by 1979 over 100,000 circles were registered in Japan.[9]

COMING HOME

In 1967 the United States was introduced to the Japanese concept of quality circles through an article written by Juran entitled "The QC Circle Phenomenon." In 1968 a group of quality circle leaders from Japan visited the United States, with each team member presenting a paper concerning quality circle activities. In late 1977 the International Association of Quality

Circles (IAQC) was established to serve as a clearinghouse for quality circle information.

The first American company to introduce quality circles into its organization was Lockheed Missile and Space Company in 1974. "While Lockheed's efforts have since waned, the spread of QC programs throughout American industry is unparalleled by any other organizational improvement program."[10] Other companies that have implemented quality circle programs include Hewlett-Packard, Hughes Aircraft, Northrup, and General Motors. Quality circles have also been introduced into a number of service industries, such as banks, retail stores, and hospitals.

A QC is composed of circle members, a circle leader, a facilitator, and a steering committee. The steering committee, which consists of the plant manager, plant superintendent, quality control manager, manufacturing manager, an industrial engineer, personnel manager, the facilitator, and one of the circle leaders, "oversees the Quality Circle program to insure proper implementation of Circle projects and to promote Quality Circle activities."[11] The most important task of the steering committee is to keep open the lines of communication between workers and management.

The leader of the QC is usually elected by the circle members, although in some cases it may be the workers' manager or supervisor. The circle leader is "responsible for the operation of his Circle and is therefore responsible for the Circle's activities."[12] The leader must see to it that the circle maintains its focus on the problem at hand, while using the relevant statistical techniques to solve the problem.

Working closely with the circle leader is the facilitator. "The facilitator or coordinator is the person who really makes the program work in the United States."[13] The facilitator, who is usually trained by an external training firm, is responsible for training circle members. The following activities have been identified as the key responsibilities of the QC facilitator: "support circles in various stages. . . . keep track of progress. . . . help to put on management presentation. . . . follow-up on projects started. . . . [and] training."[14]

Sud Ingle describes the circle members as "the heart of the program, and proper use of their untapped brainpower is the key to its success."[15] Donald Dewar of Lockheed writes that "the member is that part of the Quality Circle that makes it all worthwhile."[16] The most important aspect of circle membership is its voluntary nature. Membership must be voluntary for a QC to achieve desired results. Workers should never be required to participate in a circle. A successful QC will be composed of volunteer members who participate actively in the problem-solving efforts of the group.

Statistical techniques are used to collect and analyze data. It is recommended that training in these techniques be conducted over a six to eight week period so as not to overwhelm the workers.[17] The following techniques have been identified as the most effective means of collecting data: check sheets, graphs, histograms, control charts, and sampling.

Once the quality circle has collected the data relevant to the problem being addressed, the circle must then analyze the data. QC members are trained in a variety of data analysis techniques. The most common are brainstorming, Pareto analysis, cause and effect analysis, and presentation skills. These last are important since, after data concerning a problem have been collected and analyzed and a solution has been proposed, these findings must be presented to management. Workers are trained in oral and group presentation techniques, project report preparation, and in the use of audiovisual equipment and other visual aids. Management presentations are an integral element of the QC program, as it is during this stage that management recognition and support of the circle is confirmed or denied. For a quality circle to produce any worthwhile results, it must receive support from middle and upper management.

QC AND Z

Quality circles can be described as one element of a larger whole. William Ouchi, in *Theory Z*, argues that "the Q-C Circle cannot be understood in isolation, but only as one part of a larger and more complex organizational system—and such a system as Theory Z offers."[18] Thus to understand the basic premises of the QC concept, it is necessary to consider the major elements of the Theory Z approach to management.

In giving a basic definition of Theory Z, Ouchi states that "quite simply, it suggests that involved workers are the key to increased productivity."[19] Worker participation, then, is central to the Theory Z approach. Three other key elements of Theory Z are trust, subtlety, and intimacy. Management must learn to trust workers to do their jobs, while workers must learn to trust management to treat them fairly. Subtlety involves such things as taking into consideration the personalities of workers when scheduling work assignments. Intimacy refers to a sense of community and belonging among workers. Another important aspect of Theory Z is egalitarianism. "Egalitarianism implies that each person can apply discretion and can work autonomously without close supervision, because they can be trusted. Again, trust underscores the belief that goals correspond, that neither person is out to harm the other."[20] Ouchi describes a Type Z organization as "a community of equals who cooperate with one another to reach common goals."[21] Thus, hierarchical rank in a Type Z organization is much less important than in a typical bureaucratic organization.

While there is certainly more to the Theory Z approach to management than has been described here, the key elements identified are the most important in terms of understanding the relationship of the QC to Theory Z. These elements are the "underlying principles" of a QC that management must "make a commitment to adapting" in order for the QC to produce desired results.[22] Consistent with this argument is the fact that in the United States, quality circles have tended to be most successful in companies Ouchi describes as Type Z organizations.

QC AND AMERICAN MANAGEMENT IDEOLOGY

The number of Type Z organizations in the United States is relatively small; instead, "one of the most basic and widely accepted 'givens' in American business is that large companies are structured in hierarchical fashion, with a heavy concentration of decision-making power at the top."[23] That this is the case would explain the failure of many QC experiments in American companies, as the proper environment needed to foster QC success does not exist. Achieving "long-term success within an organization," for QCs, rather, "will require the commitment on the part of management to a fundamental change away from a 'top-down' management style, greater responsiveness to workers, and a reconceptualization of workers' capabilities and the values of their participation."[24] Many managers, however, are reluctant to make these changes for a variety of reasons.

Janice Klein, writing in the *Harvard Business Review* has identified five types of supervisory resisters and the reasons why they oppose quality circles.[25] First is the Theory X proponent, who believes that workers should be closely supervised and do only that which they are told to do. This resister opposes QCs because there is a lack of close supervision, and workers have an opportunity to make suggestions concerning certain work to be done. The second type of resister is the status seeker. This manager enjoys the prestige associated with his position and is reluctant to give up any of this status. The idea of being a co-equal with other members of the QC—whose jobs may be "lower" on a traditional hierarchy—is less than prestigious.

The third type of resister is the skeptic, who questions whether the QC will receive the necessary support from upper management. If upper management is not going to support the QC program, why should middle management? The fourth type of resister is the equality seeker. He desires equality for himself, but not for the average employee. He desires a greater role for middle managers in the decision-making process but does not wish to see lower-level employees gain more influence at his expense. The last type of resister is the deal maker. Deal makers prefer to deal one-on-one with employees. With the introduction of QCs, the supervisor must deal more with groups than with individuals. With less ability to make deals with individuals, supervisors must look for new ways to influence workers. They resist the QC because they would rather hold on to old forms of influence.

A number of other reasons exist for supervisory resistance to QCs.[26] Some supervisors fear that they will be "shown up" by the QC. For example, a QC might come up with a solution to a problem that middle management could not solve or did not even know existed. Also, a brainstorming session might identify a large number of existing problems after middle management has spent a good deal of time trying to convince top management that no problems exist. Other managers view QCs as just another "of the latest in a series of vogue management techniques."[27]

Concerns about job security and job definition will cause some middle managers to resist QCs.[28] As workers require less supervision under a participative management style, managers begin to wonder if there will continue to be a need for supervisors. Managers also begin to question what the exact nature of their job is and how they will be evaluated: "Lack of a well-defined set of responsibilities also gave special trouble to supervisors who had to balance the egalitarian position required of them by participation in quality circles one hour per week with the authority they exercised on a daily basis."[29] The "parallel organizational structure" created by QCs transcends the traditional roles assigned by the bureaucratic organization.[30]

Perhaps the most important reason that middle managers resist implementation of quality circles is the potential effects that the circle might have on their ability to manage. Inasmuch as most American organizations are managed in a top-down, hierarchical fashion, the implementation of QCs brings "an intervention into the organization itself, and . . . a potentially significant change in the assumptions made about employees and the way they are managed."[31] Any time the level of employee involvement significantly increases, the level of first-line supervisory authority decreases.[32] Thus, research conducted in 1981 revealed that foremen were aware of and concerned about the decrease in authority that would accompany a QC program.[33] Middle managers experience the same concern.[34]

THE QC AND BUREAUCRACY

In terms of the effect of QCs on traditional bureaucracy, the circles pose the greatest challenge to the first two characteristics in Weber's ideal type:

I. There is the principle of fixed and official jurisdictional areas, which are generally ordered by rules, that is, by laws or administrative regulations.

II.The principles of office hierarchy and of levels of graded authority mean a firmly ordered system of super- and subordination in which there is a supervision of the lower offices by the higher ones.[35]

When considering implementation of a QC program, American organizations must recognize the challenge that such a program poses to the bureaucratic structure of the organization. Once this challenge is recognized, management can take the necessary steps to help overcome middle management resistance.

For a QC program to be successful, several key conditions must be met. First and foremost, the QC program must be recognized for what it is. The QC is to be a small group of workers doing similar work who meet regularly and voluntarily to address work-related problems in an effort to produce solutions to these problems. Members are to be given adequate training in a variety of statistical techniques to aid in collecting and analyzing data.

Quality-related problems should not be the only issues addressed by the circle. Circle objectives can also include: "self-development . . . mutual development . . . improvement in communications and attitude . . . waste reduction . . . cost reduction" and productivity improvement.[36]

Simply allowing a QC to exist, however, is not enough. Management must be willing to take seriously the suggestions offered by the group. "If the ideas are never converted into action, Quality Circle programs usually lose their momentum and die."[37] Management must be willing to implement some of the suggestions offered by the group. If workers see that management is unwilling to implement any of their ideas, they soon cease their problem-solving activities, and the circle becomes nothing more than a social hour or gripe session.

Obviously the attitude of management plays a major role in determining the success or failure of a QC program. Some writers argue that QCs should not even be attempted without "full management commitment."[38] Research shows that a management style that is both production and people oriented is generally more supportive of the QC concept than is a production-only oriented style.[39]

Donald Dewar of Lockheed has identified the following elements as those essential for QC success:

Management is supportive.

Participation is voluntary.

There is a people-building attitude.

Training is provided.

Team-work is encouraged.

Recognition is provided.

Members select problems in their area of expertise.

Circles solve problems, not just identify them.[40]

When management is considering introducing QCs into the organization, it must be aware of these essentials. If management is unwilling to promote the type of organizational atmosphere needed to foster the growth and survival of QCs, then it should reconsider implementing them.

QCs represent a fundamental change in the nature of employee-management relations. Middle managers and supervisors often find themselves in the middle of this new arrangement, as they have had little say in the decision to implement QCs, while at the same time they are the ones who have to act on the ideas suggested by the circles. Placed in this rather uncomfortable situation, middle managers and supervisors often resist the efforts of the QC. Managerial resistance manifests itself in a number of forms. Specifically, middle managers resist QCs because they fear the effects that the circle might have on their ability to manage and thus their position in the organizational hierarchy. Without the support of top and middle management, QCs cannot be expected to produce any positive results. Unless management is fully committed to the entire concept of a QC, such a program should not be implemented in the organization.

EPILOGUE
Bureaucracy and Its Discontents

William H. Swatos, Jr.

In a number of respects, neither Marx nor Weber had his hopes for the future realized. The working class, Weber was already able to see, was not going to be the force of revolution of which Marx dreamed. Weber did not live to see liberal democracy's failure to realize his own high ideals for individual freedom and dignity—nor the grotesque *führer*-democracy that occurred in his own country. The peculiar historic irony Weber often pointed to in other circumstances, furthermore, befell his own work. What he intended to be a prophetic warning against bureaucracy became a cornerstone for building the edifice of bureaucratic administration. The perversion of Weber's writings on bureaucracy stands in history with the perversion of Marx by the Soviet Union and with Calvin's perversion by capitalism. What Weber recognized in his philosophy of history—the unintended, unforeseen consequences of idea systems as they are transformed by the concrete factors of human action—he did not see could clearly happen in his own case as well.

Each of the three sections of this book has attempted to look at the problem of the consequences of bureaucratic administration from different, though not unrelated, angles. The first section focuses primarily on theoretical issues; the second, on case studies; the third, on alternatives to or modifications in bureaucratic processes to effect more participatory political-economic structures. In this epilogue I wish to respond to each of these thematic areas, both by offering a critique of some of the proposals advanced and by extending each section into new areas that might be explored in greater depth in future work, building bridges between what has appeared in this collection and a larger world of thought and action, as historical and contemporary phenomena are evaluated in light of the insights our authors have furnished. I offer each of my major sections, then, as a commentary on each of these divisions of the book in order to illustrate how the problems in, practice of, and proposed solutions to bureaucracy interact complexly in the warp and woof of human experience in modern society.

SIN IN THEORY AND PRACTICE

Charles Perrow has written that the "sins" attributed to bureaucracy are frequently either debatable as evils in the first place or are not the result of bureaucracy at all. If we take "the ideal type as ideal," these kinds of things should not happen in bureaucracy. Why, then, do they happen? The simple answer—as any good Weberian knows—is because the model of bureaucracy is not a model *for* organization at all; rather, it is a model for *comparing* organizations to each other.[1] Whether "sin" be defined as "missing the mark" or "separation," what has happened to "Weber's ideal type of bureaucracy" is that it has been severed from the methodological ground of comparative-historical sociology in which it was first developed and pressed into the service of a series of not necessarily consistent political-economic uses.

Whereas people *do* attempt to model organizations in the bureaucratic manner, however, there is also a more complex answer: the ideal type "bureaucracy" is fundamentally *inhuman* in its ontology. This is why, of course, bureaucracy is so dehumanizing in its effects. Modern bureaucracy as a mode of social relationship is based on the machine and machine production. The flaw in bureaucracy as a model *for* organization is that people are not machines. While people may be induced or coerced into behaving like machines, the story does not end here. People always carry an element of intentionality with them. Machines do not. The problems associated with bureaucratic management arise because people are human beings with intentionality who resist being treated merely as machines—even when behaving like machines. The error of bureaucratic administration is to assume that this mechanical model for organizational comparison actually models human beings—or can be made to do so with some minor (often also quasi-mechanical) "adjustments."

It is little wonder that many bureaucratic managers find automation so attractive: they have been using people instead of machines for machine-like jobs for a century or more. Thus there should be no surprise that tasks that can be performed by a machine—i.e., once a machine is invented to do them—are performed more efficiently by a machine than by human beings who carry the baggage of intentionality along with them. At the core of bureaucracy is the evisceration of anything distinctively human: "Bureaucracy develops the more perfectly, the more it is 'dehumanized,' the more completely it succeeds in eliminating from official business love, hatred, and all purely personal, irrational, and emotional elements which escape calculation."[2]

The tragic flaw of bureaucratic impersonality in the service of efficiency is specifically this: It tends to minimize good and promote evil. A good turn done on some*one*'s behalf (an instance of anti-bureaucratic personalism) at the very least is not rewarded and may even be punished. An application of the rules, by contrast, no matter how it hurts the employee, client, or customer is seen as a sign of a conscientious bureaucrat. Since few people are able to keep up with all the rules in a modern bureaucracy, the citation or creation of "rules" by those bent on inflicting harm (or avoiding responsibility) can be easily magnified. By formally discouraging personalism—i.e., personal concern for others—bureaucracy encourages the worst people have to offer, for it denies the most significant rewards people can receive: justice, genuine friendship, admiration, and love. In bureaucracies acts of human kindness or friendship are done by breaking the rules—working against the organization—while acts of meanness are done in the name of the rules and the organization. Bureaucracies are inherently unjust because justice—though rightly "blind" to bribes—involves the application of law taking the circumstances of the person into account. Bureaucratic rules, by being "impersonal," do not allow for the recognition of individual differences. This underlies the significant distinction between the administration of bureaucratic rules and democratic adjudication to which both Ron Glassman and Kathi Friedman referred earlier in this volume.

I raise this point in some detail because a basic error in discussions of bureaucratic administration and its alternatives is what Dennis Wrong has called the "oversocialized" conception of human being.[3] Current emphasis on structure rather than process, a reflection itself of the processes of modernity, has created among many social scientists and their epigones in "management theory" and "industrial relations" an incredible naiveté with respect to "human nature": they deny it! By "human nature" I do not mean those weak ideological conceptions Berger and Luckmann rightly demolish in their work;[4] rather, I refer to the fact that human beings are intentional actors who bring with them specific biographies, hence perspectives and interests (something Berger and Luckmann, in fact, affirm), which incline them to act in a variety of ways in differing times, places, and circumstances.

This "sociological fallacy"—more accurately, the fallacy of a particular kind of sociology that is extremely marketable precisely because it conforms to the mechanistic expectations of modern life—is to deny *psychological anthropology*: not the "pop" psychology of "one minute managers," but the fact that human actors are, as Victor Turner has written elsewhere, "total human beings in full psychological concreteness, not abstract, generalized sociocultural entities."[5] To make such an assertion is not to embrace psychological reductionism but to recognize that "the socialization of people into a social system is never entirely successful," and specifically that "human beings resist cultural indoctrination and consciously develop oppositional views of the social structure" in the face of "a dominant ideology which would attempt to give normative significance to social inequality."[6]

The "sociological fallacy" is to misuse the principle of cultural diversity to pretend that there is nothing distinctive about human being—to forget about intentionality or to reduce it to a mere "possibility" that is easily manipulable or suppressed in social settings. It is to claim that because certain traits are learned, they are not "real"—the very opposite of the burden of *The Social Construction of Reality*. By assuming that people in modern Western culture do not act to maximize their own perceived benefit, we are liable to overrate bureaucracy (either positively or negatively) or its alternatives. The point is not to deny the core sociological principle of "structural effects," but to recall to the discussion of bureaucracy the importance of the personality structures functioning in these organizations. "Bureaucratic personalities" are built upon foundations already laid in modern Western civilization that run deep into our past. Modernity brings special technical developments to our civilizational heritage, and bureaucracies impose a social context in which these are given meaning. We can better use the principle of cultural differences to recognize the richness and diversity of human adjustment to a total field of conditions than as a basis for pretending that in any socio-cultural system people do not bring intentionality to their various social experiences, including the workplace: *action orientations* that can be understood by the very action sociology (Weber's supposed "methodological individualism") that is at the core of Weber's program.

THE UNANTICIPATED AND THE FORESEEN: CASES PAST AND PRESENT

Probably the greatest full-scale attempt to reverse the seemingly all-enveloping tide of bureaucratization was Nazism. Some readers will find this assertion surprising, as the Nazi regime is often associated today with blind obedience to the orders of hierarchical superiors, and this is true. Jeffrey Herf documents quite clearly in his book *Reactionary Modernism*, however, that this was not the way it all began. To the contrary, Nazism was intended as a program to unite irrationality ("real humanity") and modern technology, and in one sense, that is exactly what it did. The obedience phenomenon so prominent in modern characterizations of Nazism is not in conflict with this: what makes Nazi obedience so reprehensible, after all, is the *unreasonableness* of it. That we should associate this with bureaucracy in casual observations rather than with an anti-bureaucratic protest movement shows how far bureaucracy has fallen in modernity from the operational definition of *rationality* that it supposedly was. That Nazism as a historic case should now have this "bureaucratic" image as one of its prime signals also shows the enormous power of bureaucracy to shape movements to its prerequisites.

The emphasis of Nazism upon the mystical, magical, and romantic should not be neglected when viewing anti-bureaucratic proposals in our own time. Nazism gained a great hold on a population by emphasizing precisely those "human" elements it claimed were being denied by rational economics in commerce and industry and rational politics in the state. Emphasis on "blood," sexual myths, "nature," racial mystique, and ethnic differences all coalesced in an ideology that was simultaneously opposed to Taylorism, Fordism, Leninism, internationalism, urbanism, bureaucracy, democracy, and socialism. To take but one specific example of contemporary relevance, Nazis opposed general access to sexually explicit material ("pornography"), emphasizing instead the "mystery" of sex as against its commercialization, rationalization, and perhaps routinization. When Nazi sexual atrocities are laid over against this, we see that the celebration of the irrational—of "feelings"—does not necessarily bring a higher morality.

The results of Nazi "experiments" and "solutions" shocked the world; yet it is not clear that the lessons about the value of rationality that this case has to offer have been adequately recognized. We do not sufficiently recognize, *as Weber did*, the liberating quality of rational social organization. Michels' and others' *ad hominem* references notwithstanding, Weber eschewed any alliance with German conservatives who tried to substitute romantic visions of the past for concrete action in the present. Thus he wrote:

At home the vested interests . . . manipulate the equally hypocritical slogan of the necessity to protect the 'German spirit' from contamination by 'democracy,' or they look for other scapegoats. . . . In Germany we have *demagoguery* and the pressure of the rabble *without democracy*, or rather *because of the absence* of an orderly democracy.[7]

To this may be joined two rather different cases from our own society.

The HMO (health maintenance organization) concept, as a first example, originated via corporate ombudsmen (who are not the same, but are related to, the legislative ombudsmen discussed by Donald Rowat). HMOs were created with the highest motives; indeed, they were intended in part to offset the cart-before-the-horse style of problem solving that Kathi Friedman points to when she notes that our society is often more concerned with sickness than wellness. They were created by people who had nothing to gain personally from them and who were ostensibly responding to the initiatives of clients rather than the reverse. Over time, however, HMOs have become themselves bureaucracies, now frequently existing in an adversarial position to both patient and physician independence, further bureaucratizing health care. Why? A failure of the ombudsman program? Hardly. What the skewed development of the HMO program demonstrates is the power of bureaucracy as an organizational form to shape programs to its prerequisites.

Does this mean that nothing can stop bureaucracy? No. What it means is that enormous vigilance must be taken to foresee consequences. Even when persons affected by programs are involved in their planning, good intentions do not necessarily yield good results One must question, in particular, whether the use of professional managers without employee control—even with employee consent—is not inherently damaging to attempts to offset bureaucratic hegemony. The area of health care and its cost coverage (the welfare-insurance complex) recall a Weberian comment, though made in another context "[T]he sterile complaints about 'Saint Bureaucratius'—instead of positive critique—cannot be overcome so long as the present condition of uncontrolled bureaucratic domination persists."[8] Particularly lamentable in this context are attempts to curb litigious activities as a health care cost-containment strategy. As Glassman, Friedman, Glasser, and others have shown, the ability to *go to law* is one of the strongest democratic bulwarks against total bureaucratic domination of any life sphere.

The second contemporary example I would raise is the crash of the Challenger space shuttle in January 1986 and the events surrounding it. A lengthy report by a special presidential commission has been issued on this tragedy. It was quickly endorsed by the appropriate officials and the President himself.[9] This document both confirmed enormous bureaucratic bungling and accepted it in its conclusion that "no one" could be blamed for the disaster. In simple terms, it recognized and used every bureaucratic maneuver. Internal hearings, reassignments, golden parachutes, sidetracking (if not demoting) of whistleblowers, faulting of "the system" (while maintaining the system), all figured in the process. At the core of the problem, however, was the significant sociostructural distinction within operating bureaucracies between "managers" and "experts."

Ideal typically, the strength of bureaucracy is that it uses persons with expert skills for specific tasks for which they are qualified. In practice, however, "management" has come to be a key bureaucratic function independent of task expertise. Management is not doing a skill function to accomplish a task. Management is perpetuating the organization. The following wisp of testimony clearly indicates this: Robert Lund was vice-president of engineering for Morton Thiakol, an expert. Jerry Mason was senior vice-president of the corporation. Lund initially opposed the launch on technical grounds, but testified that he then changed his mind when Mason asked him to "take off his engineering hat and put on his management hat" in order to review his launch decision. The manager, not the expert engineer, Lund consented.[10] Not expertise, but management, lies at the core of and calls the shots in modern bureaucracy.

This is *not* the employment of rational, technical expertise to achieve efficient production; rather, it is the attempt to use any means available to obtain organizational maintenance. As Robert Jackall has written elsewhere:

[B]ureaucracy erodes internal and even external standards of morality, not only in matters of individual success and failure but also in all the issues that managers face in their daily work. Bureaucracy makes its own internal rules and social context the principal moral gauges for action. . . . [W]hat matters in the bureaucratic world is not what a person is but how closely his many personae mesh with the organizational ideal; not his willingness to stand by his actions but his agility in avoiding blame; not what he believes or says but how well he has mastered the ideologies that serve his corporation; not what he stands for but whom he stands with in the labyrinths of his organization.[11]

Yet it was not possible for the presidential commission's report even to say that bureaucracy was to blame, for perhaps this would have brought the truth too close to home.

The handling of the Challenger accident may be valuably compared to that of the Watergate incident, as illustrative of bureaucratic authority as contrasted to legal authority. The pardon of former President Nixon notwithstanding, individuals were held accountable for breaking laws in the Watergate case. Indeed, this is the whole context that necessitated a pardon for Nixon. Watergate was an embarrassment for the United States but a triumph for democracy and for legal authority. In the case of the Challenger, by contrast, no one was held accountable. This does not mean, of course, that there was not what Jackall terms "blame time" within the various bureaucracies involved. It does mean, however, that legal principles were sacrificed to bureaucratic priorities. As is typical in bureaucratic cases, the Challenger report ignores the human dynamics involved in the interpersonal maneuvering that led to the Challenger's destruction and takes up instead "mechanical" problems—the model of the machine returns. This highlights in a very specific case the theoretical differences between legal and bureaucratic approaches addressed earlier in this volume by Ron Glassman.

While these examples run quite a range and, admittedly, carry some heavy emotional freight, they enable us to confront directly the core problem of bureaucracy: people attempting to gain advantage over other people, whether individually or organizationally. I can see, for example, a physician in a snazzy HMO being told to "take off his doctor's hat and put on his manager's hat" in considering a costly, chancy procedure to save a life. "Consider first the well-being of the patient" seems far away—as, apparently, did "consider first the well-being of the astronauts." Regardless of whether the motivation is "the Program" or "CYA," it is clear that the client-victims are not the first priority. I can see two former astronauts sitting on the presidential panel with the best of intentions, not realizing how their report contributed to the enhancement of bureaucratic control and the undermining of law everywhere by not assigning blame to anyone. I can see Americans seduced into new "mysteries" by bureaucratic control of information necessary for concrete problem solving—responding perhaps too favorably to a state governor who tells them in words that raise an unpleasant specter that old people have a social obligation to die (ageism replaces racism in the bureaucratization of death).

These are not the fault of bureaucracy, but they are not independent from it either, and this is just the point. People attempting to gain advantage over other people, whether individually or organizationally, can use bureaucracy precisely because of its impersonality to mask their true intentions, while bureaucracy seduces people who intend to do good into doing evil because its impersonality gradually dehumanizes all their activities into the application of rules, rather than the doing of justice.

CULTURE-POLITICS AND MANAGEMENT

In this concluding section I wish to focus on a specific management strategy and develop a critical anthropology of it primarily from a Weberian perspective. It relates most specifically to the discussion of quality circles by Lisa Armour. As she addresses the pitfalls inherent in the implementation of quality circles in an American management setting, I wish to suggest that there are additional issues of theoretical concern even if such a program is implemented. I will then examine these for their possible outcomes.

In the midst of a worldwide economic recession, Americans sought an explanation and remedy for the substantial slump in the nation's primary industries. Of particular concern were those sectors of the domestic economy in which American consumers have turned to imported goods in preference to domestic products. The automobile industry is in many ways the most visible and typical. Japanese products have captured a significant share of the market. Except for some voluntary restraints in that country, there is every reason to expect that this would be even larger. Indeed, from one perspective, the United States could even be termed a "colony" of Japan, as we ship them raw materials, while we buy their finished products—with more of our money flowing to them than theirs to us. The preferred explanation for Japanese success is that their labor management process is superior to that in the United States. In an attempt to recoup some of its former strength in the world economy, American industry has spent considerable effort to study and deploy the Japanese model. Developing upon the earlier distinction by McGregor between traditional top-down management as "Theory X" and participative management as "Theory Y," Ouchi has termed this most recently marketed Japanese import *Theory Z*.

A number of authors have critiqued Theory Z in terms of technical matters and general "importability." I will touch on these issues only peripherally. My major concern is not whether Theory Z *can* be employed in American industry, but whether it *should*. In particular, I want to ask questions about the implications of Theory Z for American society and for the world system. I will argue that serious concern for the sociopolitical consequences of Z-type management is a matter of utmost urgency for both American business interests and the larger society. Theory Z's "wholistic concern for people"[12] is not only contrary to the strong American value of democratic individualism, but it also has no inherent claim to humaneness or a "humanistic style." Such assertions largely mask the strongly collectivisitic (but not socialistic) presuppositions upon which Theory Z is based and from which a society that is anything but democratic may grow.

The essential distinction, according to Ouchi, between Z organizations and those under which industry has heretofore operated is that *Z organizations are clans rather than hierarchies.*[13] It is on this basis that both the superiority of Z organizations and their humaneness are justified. It is precisely the significance of this distinction that I wish to raise and challenge.

Historically, the movement from clan to hierarchy has been viewed as a sign of progress. The myth of "Progress" has by now been widely discussed by social scientists and philosophers to the extent that we realize that the term is both value laden and time bound. Nevertheless, it is clear that hierarchical forms of social organization replaced clans in the breakthrough to modernity. The most "efficient" hierarchical organizations are bureaucracies; yet bureaucracies are based on a mechanical model of human behavior that is at variance with lived experience. In the ideal-typical case, bureaucracy is associated with X-type management, while the "work ethic" acts as an intervening variable. Particularly important to this ideology is the predestinarian dogma, which holds that everybody is where she or he is in the social structure by God's inscrutable will. Predestination thus constitutes the *ideological substructure* of the work ethic. Stripped of its religious pretensions, this is a powerful tool for the justification of power by the powerful, even as they exploit the weak. Indeed, dominating the weak is a specific task for which the strong are destined and an obligation of their status.

The supposed essence of bureaucracy is that it is a "rational" form of administration. There is a clearly articulated calculable means-end relationship in both production and values. Impersonality is at the heart of bureaucratic administration, and efficiency is its goal. The clan, by contrast, is a form of irrational organization where "the watchword is *loyalty.*"[14] Clan organization involves a series of personal bonds between members, and in historic clan societies, life outside of a clan was impossible. The impersonal bureaucracy, then, is at clear variance from the clan. The clansman puts the organization above both self-interest and class-interest, not "out of motives that he can defend to his own intellect [i.e., means-end calculation], but rather out of deep irrational urges," security being one of the most notable. Significantly, Kimball and McClellan make this observation specifically in defining a fascist mentality.[15] Significantly, too, it was precisely this supplanting of rationality by irrational "impersonal forces" that Weber warned would condemn post-Protestant ethic modernity to life locked in a mechanical housing—the "iron cage."[16]

Viewed from this perspective, it is difficult to see a form of industrial organization based upon the clan as anything other than reactionary or retrograde. This does not mean, however, that Z organizations will not work. They may work very well. It does mean, however, that Z organizations set the stage for dramatic changes in our culture and politics.

In a well-known essay, Etzioni has distinguished three types of organizational power: coercive, remunerative or utilitarian, and normative.[17] In his discussion itself, no type is urged as morally superior to another, nor is any evolutionary schema introduced. We do learn, however, that coercive power is the least efficient, and normative power is the most efficient. Assuming that one has normative power over another, input effort is minimized in relation to output. Highly motivated volunteers properly trained are the cheapest labor available. Slaves are the most expensive. If we look at Western history, furthermore, we can describe it in terms of a gradual, if unsteady, shift from coercive to remunerative power. The great societies of antiquity were all slave societies. The Judeo-Christian ethic brought a slow moderation of this form, until by the Industrial Revolution, wages generally replaced direct force, as the basis of labor performance, and labor was "formally free."

Examined closely, Z organizations are based primarily on normative power. Unlike coercion and remuneration which use a punishment-reward system potentially susceptible to rational calculation—indeed, one way to understand the transition from coercion to remuneration is that it is easier and more effective to calculate rewards than punishments—normative power is essentially *irrational*. Religious organizations, for example, are textbook cases of normative power. If Z organizations become predominant in social organization, then it may be argued that Etzioni's typology can be used in a developmental framework: from coercion, to remuneration, to normative power.[18] If normative power is most efficient in terms of input-output ratio, furthermore, and efficiency is still accepted as the primary goal of industrial production, then it can be argued that Theory Z is a step forward—"Progress." Z seems to present the "enchanting" possibility of economic growth and humanistic management. One can almost have one's cake and eat it too.

At this point, however, a catch appears. There is no zero point in this developmental sequence. Prior to the great slave societies of antiquity there were clans, which in turn gave way to coercive empires. The Mafia, after all, is clan-based management. The problem with normative power is that it works well only as long as everyone assents to the norms. Once norms break, there is no objective basis upon which to restructure. Whereas coercion is the ultimate foundation of order, the failure of normative power to maintain itself can lead only to coercive power coming in its wake. Theory Z, then, supplants rational management with irrationality. The goal of efficiency is initially advanced, but as soon as the normative power holding the organization together gives way, coercion returns (witness the Mafiosi).

The archaic appeal to the clan, then, can set the stage for traditionalist revolution and a fascist state. "To have a world without marketplace values" such as those that characterize the modern bureaucratic state, one also "must have a world without a marketplace at its center."[19] In spite of Ouchi's distinction of the market from the clan, the introduction of Z management will not alter the fundamental association of modes of value rationality with modes of instrumental rationality. As Z supplants rational management, a counterrevolution based upon coercive power is a likely consequence. The result could well be worse than Weber's "dictatorship of officials." The clan is not a democratic structure, and attempts to graft democratic processes onto clans produce irreconcilable tensions—as Saga Iceland demonstrates.

What seems to make Theory Z particularly attractive to social scientists is that it is a group-based approach to human relations. Unlike earlier management theories, it capitalizes upon basic social scientific research on groups, group dynamics, and individuals in groups. While many earlier management approaches attempted to destroy or frustrate informal groups in the workplace, Theory Z uses the group to enhance productivity. But Z management, however much good it promises, finds its roots in archaic social structures and cultural processes. Instead of hierarchy (X) or independence (Y), Theory Z offers clan bonding. This is not democracy but group dynamics that can easily turn into group pressure, as any social scientist also knows. Clans are participatory, but father figures make decisions after taking clan counsel. Workers may gain some psychological relief, but their actual power in the organization remains uncertain. False consciousness lies waiting at the door. The possibility for harm in such a situation should not be underestimated. Not only are the advantages of industrial democracy lacking, but this is also a far cry from socialism, since a management stratum owning the means of production still exists. Putting on the clothes of the workers and walking among them is one of the oldest tricks in the book of rulership. As a matter of fact, as the need for managerial types ("middle management") is decreased by virtue of successful Z-type management, the real gulf between employees and owners is likely only to widen. If we remember that bureaucracy began not as an outgrowth of Western legal traditions but from oriental despotism (as the essays in Part I indicate), we may wish to think twice about the "creative" potentials of Theory Z.

The solutions presented in this volume stand as efforts to promote democracy and law as positive alternatives to romantic and archaic, let alone "final," solutions. With Weber we recognize the pitfalls of all human institutions and their foundation upon social actors who have many, and mixed motivations, the highest of which do not always take precedence. Nevertheless, we are concerned that the possibilities of some of the alternatives proposed to bureaucracy today—as in Weber's day—must be examined in terms of their consequences for evil as well as good. Ira Glasser's principle of "least harm" can be a tremendous asset. Not how much good might be done, but how little harm can befall us is as good a test criterion to apply to alternatives to bureaucracy as it is to bureaucratic proposals themselves. "[I]t is clear that the Western notion of 'the individual in general' as a source of rational choice has replaced the corporate group as the responsible, even ethical unit, and that it is not really feasible to turn the clock back to cultural forms that are appropriate to preindustrial and nonurbanized societies."[20]

Notes

INTRODUCTION

1. On Marx, *see* Schluchter essay in Chapter 2 of this volume. For the Enlightenment figures, *see* Montesquieu, *The Spirit of Laws*; Rousseau, *The Social Contract*; Saint-Simon, *Social Organization*.

2. Weber, 1978a: 1401–2 (emphasis added).

3. See Mumford, 1966: 188; Mills, 1956.

4. Weber, 1978a: 1408.

5. Weber, 1978a: 267.

6. Weber, 1978a: 1402.

7. Weber, 1978a: 1401–2.

8. Weber, 1978a: 1453.

9. Weber, 1978a: 1454.

10. Or, "dictatorship of the officials"; *see* Weber, 1971: 209; here we use Bendix's translation (1960: 451).

11. Weber, 1978a: 1403.

12. "Heroic pessimism" is Wolfgang J. Mommsen's phrase; *see* his essay, Chapter 3 of this volume.

13. *See* Weber, 1958a: 77–128; Abramowski, 1982; Swatos, 1986.

14. *See* Popper, 1950: 463.

15. Weber, 1958b: 182.

16. Perrow, 1979.

17. A contemporary example is Clark (1985: 46), who writes, with incredible stupidity, "Weber did not expect to see historical instances of his monocratic bureaucracy in pure form, but *he was committed personally to approach the ideal*" (emphasis added). What is so damnable about this line of argument is that it not only misrepresents Weber and serious Weberian scholarship, but it also, as it sets up the groundwork for the remainder of the essays in the collection in which it appears, gives the informed reader good reason to question whether any of what follows should be taken seriously. This is only one of several examples that could be given (a literal textbook case is Daft, 1986: 175–77).

18. Readers who nevertheless wish to consult a superlative "rehabilitation" should *see* Murvar, 1983.

19. *See* Antonio, 1979.

20. Weber, 1958a: 198.

21. Taylor, 1947.

CHAPTER 1

1. In Tucker, 1978: 713.

2. Marx, 1962(IV): 423ff.; *see* Marx, 1951(I): book 1; Marx, 1953: 582ff.

3. In Tucker, 1978: 531.

4. Marx, 1953: 111.

5. *See* Marx, 1951(I): 48ff.

6. *See* Tucker, 1978: 537ff.; Marx, 1953: 375ff.

7. In Tucker, 1978: 52.

8. Marx and Engels, 1975(III) [or "Philosophy of Law"].

9. Hegel, 1967: paragraph 261.

10. Hegel, 1967: para. 279, 273.

11. Hegel, 1967: para. 289.

12. Hegel, 1967: para. 287.

13. Hegel, 1967: para. 289.

14. Hegel, 1967: para. 205, 283, 294–97.

15. Hegel, 1967: para. 297.

16. Hegel, 1967: para. 289, 256.

17. Hegel, 1967: para. 281. Hegel used this argument first of all to forestall any demand for abolishing the dynastic monarchy. Only in rare cases would he consider universal suffrage permissible, as in the articulation of special interests through local corporations.

18. Marx and Engels, 1975(III): 44.

19. *See also* the "Introduction" to the "Contribution," Marx and Engles, 1975(III): 176ff. This critique does not apply, however, to Hegelian analysis as a whole. Marx said, after all, that Hegel's "German philosophy of right and of the state is the only German history which is *al pari* with the *official* modern reality" (p. 180).

20. Marx and Engels, 1975(III): 45.

21. Marx and Engels, 1975(III): 45–46.

22. Marx and Engels, 1975(III): 45–49.

23. Marx and Engels, 1975(III): 172.

24. Marx and Engels, 1975(III): 168.

25. Marx and Engels, 1975(III): 153.

26. Marx and Engels, 1975(III): 166.

27. Marx and Engels, 1975(III): 166.

28. Marx and Engels, 1975(III): 46.

29. In Tucker, 1978: 475.

30. Marx and Engels, 1975(III): 156–57.

31. Marx, 1967: 15.

32. Marx, 1967: 8.

33. Marx, 1967: 7.

34. Marx, 1967: 25.
35. Marx, 1967: 27.
36. Marx, 1967: 47.
37. Marx, 1967: 62.
38. Marx, 1967: 67.
39. Marx, 1967: 49.
40. Marx, 1967: 104–5.
41. Marx, 1967: 106.
42. Marx, 1967: 121–22.
43. Marx, 1967: 35.
44. Marx and Engels, 1975(III): 74.
45. Marx, 1967: 75.
46. Marx, 1967: 77.
47. Marx, 1967: 122.
48. Marx, 1967: 123.
49. Marx, 1967: 124–25.
50. Marx, 1967: 127, 129, 131.
51. Marx, 1967: 133.
52. Marx, 1967: 135.
53. Weber, 1978a: 164ff.
54. Marx, 1967: 18. In style and composition, Marx resorts extensively to the literary thesis that in human history all tragedies repeat themselves as farce.
55. Marx, 1967: 131.
56. In Tucker, 1978: 631.
57. *See* Marx and Engels, 1964(XVII): 542.
58. Marx and Engels, 1964(XVII): 518.
59. In Tucker, 1978: 631.
60. *See also* Engels' introduction to "The Class Struggles in France," in which he admitted that a new constellation had completely changed the conditions for the new class struggle. There he advanced his famous thesis that new tactics were necessary under the conditions of organized capitalism. *See* Tucker, 1978: 621, 627ff.
61. Marx and Engels, 1964(XVII): 610.
62. On this score Engels differs from Marx. Even in Engels' later writings, bureaucratic rule is the exception, possible only in periods "in which the contending classes are so close to an equilibrium that for a short time the state gains a certain independence as apparent mediator." For Engels, therefore, the most consistent form of bourgeois rule continues to be the democratic republic. *See* Engels, 1967: 157. Marx, too, later seems to have returned to this view; *see* Tucker, 1978: 538. These differences are not important, however, because for both Marx and Engels the defense of bourgeois class interest remains the ultimate content of bourgeois class rule.
63. Marx and Engels, 1975(VI): 79.
64. Marx and Engels, 1975(VI): 79.
65. Marx and Engels, 1975(VI): 84–88.
66. Marx and Engels, 1960: 574.
67. In Tucker, 1978: 477.
68. In Tucker, 1978: 470.
69. Marx and Engels, 1968: 680.

70. In Tucker, 1978: 631.
71. In Tucker, 1978: 632.
72. *See* Weber, 1978a: 1015ff.
73. In Tucker, 1978: 632–33.
74. In Tucker, 1978: 633–34.
75. In Tucker, 1978: 643.
76. In Tucker, 1978: 635.
77. Marx, 1951(I): 55; 1951(III): 671.
78. Marx and Engels, 1968: 339.
79. Marx, 1951(III): 672.
80. In Tucker, 1978: 634.
81. In Tucker, 1978: 529.
82. Marx, 1973: 592.
83. In Tucker, 1978: 530.
84. Marx, 1953: 89.
85. In Tucker, 1978: 530.
86. Marx, 1973: 705.
87. In Tucker, 1978: 531.
88. Engels, 1969: 93; Marx and Engels, 1964: 543–44.
89. Marx, 1973: 700, 706.
90. In Tucker, 1978: 529.
91. Lenin, 1969: 26.
92. Lenin, 1969: 16.
93. Lenin, 1969: 38.
94. Lenin, 1969: 38.
95. Marx, 1953: 111.
96. Grateful acknowledgment is made by the author, translator, and editors to Guenther Roth for reading, correcting, and encouraging this translation.

CHAPTER 2

1. Weber, 1978a: 987.
2. Weber, 1958a: 214.
3. Weber, 1978b: 283.
4. Weber, 1958a: 234.
5. Weber, 1978a: 988–89.
6. Weber, 1971: 197.
7. Weber, 1971: 199.
8. Weber, 1971: 202–23.
9. Weber, 1971: 209–10.
10. Weber, 1971: 215.
11. Weber, 1971: 197.
12. Weber, 1971: 197.
13. Weber, 1971: 198.
14. Weber, 1971: 199.
15. Weber, 1971: 201.
16. Weber, 1971: 205.

17. Weber, 1971: 209.
18. Weber, 1971: 211.
19. Weber, 1978b: 341.
20. Weber, 1978b: 344.
21. Weber, 1976: 234.
22. Weber, 1976: 234.
23. Weber, 1976: 234.
24. Weber, 1947: 343.
25. Weber, 1978a: 1145.
26. Weber, 1976: 389–411.
27. Antonio, 1979.
28. Beetham, 1974: 86–87.
29. *See* Mueller, 1982.
30. Weber, 1978a: 1402–1403.
31. *See* Abramowski, 1982.
32. *See* Weber, 1978a: 1403; *see* Löwith, 1982.
33. Weber, 1958a: 128.

CHAPTER 3

1. Weber, 1924a: 227; *see* Weber, 1978a: 1156–57.
2. Mommsen, 1974a: 24; *see* Swatos, 1986.
3. Weber, 1958b: 181.
4. Weber, 1958b: 181.
5. Weber, 1958b: 182.
6. Weber, 1958b: 64.
7. Weber, 1978a: 1156–57.
8. Weber, 1978a: 138.
9. Weber, 1971: 205.
10. Letter to Michels, August 4, 1908 (Fondazione Luigi Einaudi, Turin, no. 5912):

There are two possibilities:. . . . 1) "My kingdom is not of this world" (Tolstoy) or a syndicalism which has been brought to its logical conclusion which, when translated into a revolutionary ethical personal stand means, "the final end means nothing to me, the *movement* is everything.". . . . *or* 2) Culture, that is, *objective* culture which externalized itself in *technical* and other "achievements," *the affirmation* in and through *adaptation* to the sociological conditions of *all* "techniques," be they economic, political or what have you. . . . If one chooses the second alternative, then all the talk about "revolution" is a farce, *any* thought of abolishing the domination of man over man through *some kind* of "socialist" system or through any contrived form of "democracy" amounts to nothing more than a *utopia.*

See Weber's basic acceptance of the principle of domination of man over man, even within a legitimate democratic system in 1958a: 77–128.
11. Weber, 1971: 204.
12. Letter to Michels, August 4, 1908; *see* Mommsen, 1974b: 122 (also available in English [Mommsen, 1984]).
13. *See* Hufnagel, 1971: 148–54. When Hufnagel attributes the fact that Weber refused to develop an alternative prescription for ending alienation "to the caution of

the scientist" and to "the critic's bias not to go beyond the negative activity of critical destruction" (p. 152), I am unable to follow him. It is not "caution," nor is it mere critical negativity, but rather realistic insight into the conditions of industrial societies that made Weber come to the realization that there was no quick solution to the question that Marx raised. It led him to develop a range of strategies designed to make the best of a situation that was in and of itself irreversible.

14. "Only political democratization is perhaps achievable in the foreseeable future, and it is not such a small thing. I cannot prevent you from believing that there may indeed be more to it, but neither can I force myself to think so." Letter to Michels, November 6, 1907 (in Mommsen, 1974b: 114).

15. *See* Weber's contribution to the discussion at the 1905 convention of the *Verein für Sozialpolitik* (Social Policy Association) held in Mannheim (Weber, 1924b: 396–97); *also see* Mommsen, 1974b: 125.

16. Weber in 1909 referred to the state as "the seat of political power which dominates national society" (in Shils, 1973: 20); *see* Weber, 1978a: 975, 983–90.

17. *See* Mommsen, 1974a.

18. Letter to Michels, August 4, 1908, in Mommsen, 1974b: 201.

19. *See* Mommsen, 1974a.

20. *See* Röhrich, 1972: 143–44.

21. *See* the Vocation essays, Weber, 1958a: 77–156.

22. This essay represents a reworking and translation of materials originally published in Mommsen, 1974c.

CHAPTER 4

1. Weber, 1978a: 956–98.

2. Weber, 1978a: 956.

3. *See* Glassman, 1986.

4. Human sacrifices were a regular occurrence in ancient Egypt, for instance. *See* Frankfort, 1978.

5. Weber, 1951.

6. Weber, 1951.

7. Weber, 1978a: 990, 1006, 1403.

8. Wittfogel, 1981.

9. Weber, 1978a: 1212–1372.

10. Weber, 1978a: 1212–1372.

11. Weber, 1978a: 1212–1372.

12. Polanyi et al., 1957.

13. Polanyi et al., 1957.

14. Ferguson, 1918.

15. Aristotle, *Politics. See also*, Weber, 1978a: 1301–39.

16. Weber, 1978a: 809–31.

17. Aristotle, *Politics*.

18. Weber, 1958b.

19. Polybius, *Histories*. The volume on the theory of the "mixed polity" is book 6. *See also* Fritz, 1954. Polybius uses the term "mob rule" to criticize Athenian democracy. Polybius, like Aristotle, preferred a form of mixed constitution in which the   rich

and cultured played a greater role than that allowed in Athens. Polybius thought that Rome exhibited the perfect mixed constitution. Yet, the Roman Republic collapsed not long after Polybius' death, and the Gracci revolts of the plebians were already dawning in Polybius' lifetime.

20. Weber, 1978a: 1212.
21. Weber, 1978a: 641.
22. Weber, 1978a: 956.
23. Mills, 1956.
24. *See* David Hume, *Political Essays* and Jean Jacques Rousseau, *The Social Contract.*
25. Marx (*Communist Manifesto*) in Tucker, 1978.
26. Alexander Solzhenitsyn, commencement address, Harvard University, Cambridge, Massachusetts, June 8, 1978; for excerpts *see* New York *Times*, June 13, 1978: A18.
27. *See* John Locke, *Treatise on Civil Government.*
28. B. Wootton, 1945; *see* Ward and Dubos, 1966; Myrdal, 1963.
29. *See* Mommsen, 1974a.
30. *See* Glasser's essay, Chapter 10 of this volume.
31. *See* O'Reilly's essay, Chapter 8 of this volume.
32. *See* Glassman, 1978.
33. *See* Antonio, 1979.

CHAPTER 5

1. Weber, 1978a: 667.
2. This development is traced in detail in Friedman, 1981.
3. Durkheim, 1964.
4. This essay is based principally on my earlier work (Friedman, 1981), but has benefitted from the comments of Stephen L. Esquith (*Contemporary Sociology,* 1983: 242–43), which alerted me to opportunities to improve and refine my treatment of the adjudication/administration distinction and its implications. In addition, my perspective has been broadened and sharpened by working for four years (1981–1985) on Capitol Hill since I completed that manuscript in 1980; *see also* Friedman, 1987.

CHAPTER 6

1. Rosen, 1963.
2. Reiff, 1961: 390.
3. Hummel, 1982: 3.
4. N. Long, 1952: 810.
5. Hobbes drew his impression of the terrible Behemoth from the fortieth chapter of the Book of Job.
6. Arendt, 1959: 24.
7. Freidson, 1970: 48
8. Hummel, 1982: 81.
9. American Hospital Association, *Hospital Medical Records: Guidelines for Their Use and the Release of Medical Information* (Chicago: AHA, 1972), p. 3.

10. Ontario Council of Health, *Medical Record Keeping* (Toronto: Ontario Council of Health, 1978), pp. 8–9.

11. Rozovsky, 1974: 64.

12. Klugman, 1983: 1350.

13. Canadian Medical Association, *Code of Ethics* (December, 1984).

14. Freidson, 1975: 171.

15. *See* "Doctors v. lawyers: 'A real nasty fight,' " New York *Times*, February 14, 1986: A18.

16. Weber, 1958a: 221.

17. Weber, 1958a: 233.

18. Klugman, 1983: 1350.

19. Knoppers, 1982: 412.

20. Horace Krever, *Report of the Commission of Inquiry into the Confidentiality of Health Information* (Toronto: Queen's Printer, 1980), 3 vols; hereafter cited as *Report*.

21. Westin, 1976: 27.

22. Klugman, 1983: 1358–59.

23. *Report*(II): 100.

24. Rozovsky and Rozovsky, 1984: 65–66.

25. Steiner, 1978: 78.

26. Golodetz et al., 1976: 78.

27. But even here evidence exists—contrary to conventional psychiatric opinion—that mental patients can benefit by reading their records; *see* Stein et al., 1979: 327–29.

28. Ellison and Beldner, 1984: 50.

29. Ellison and Beldner, 1984: 51.

30. Rozovsky, 1974: 14.

31. Berenato, 1984: 6.

32. Berenato, 1984: 5.

33. Westin, 1977: 23.

34. Klugman, 1983: 1363 (n.84).

35. *See* Shea and Margulies, 1985.

36. Scrivens, 1985: 292.

37. *Report* (II): 157.

38. *Report* (II): 158.

39. *Report* (II): 158.

40. *Report* (II): 158.

41. *Report* (II): 158.

42. Miller, 1983: 276; *see also* Picard, 1984: 339.

43. Brannigan and Dayhoff, 1986: 143.

44. Brannigan and Dayhoff, 1986: 143.

45. Brannigan and Dayhoff, 1986: 143.

46. *Report* (II): 260.

47. Brannigan and Dayhoff, 1986: 145.

48. Brannigan and Dayhoff, 1986: 145.

49. Brannigan and Dayhoff, 1986: 145.

50. *Report* (I): 10.

CHAPTER 7

1. For a comprehensive listing of these works, *see* D. Jones, 1977; D. Jones and Troy, 1982.

2. These include the Center for the Study of Applied Ethics at the Darden Graduate Business School, University of Virginia; the Center for the Study of Values at the University of Delaware; the Center for Business Ethics at Bentley College; the Center for the Study of Ethics in the Professions at the Illinois Institute of Technology; the Ethics Resource Center in Washington, D.C.; and the Center for Applied Philosophy at the University of Florida.

3. *See,* for instance, the *Report of the Committee for Education in Business Ethics,* sponsored by the National Endowment for the Humanities (1980).

4. For a useful listing of some of the main works in this tradition going back to 1900, *see* Christian and Hicks, 1970.

5. Casuistry emerges whenever men and women try to establish rules to guide themselves through the moral quandries of everyday life; it is, of course, as ancient as human thought itself. For two fine summaries of the main historical developments in moral casuistry, *see* Wenley, 1910; Nelson, 1973.

6. The exception to this in the sociological literature is Bensman, 1983.

7. Lederer, 1918–19.

8. Jackall, 1983.

9. During 1980–1983, I did field work in several corporate settings. These included: the chemical company of a large conglomerate, a large textile firm, a small chemical firm, a large defense contractor, and a large public relations firm. My basic methodology was semi-structured interviews with managers and executives at every level of management. The interviews usually lasted between two and three hours, but, especially with reinterviews, some went on much longer. I interviewed more than 125 managers. In addition, I gathered material in more informal ways—for example, through nonparticipant observation, over meals, and by attending various managerial seminars in the companies studied. I am indebted to the National Endowment for the Humanities, which provided me with a Fellowship for Independent Research in 1980–1981 and to Williams College for several small research grants that have facilitated my work.

10. Mannheim, 1940: 55ff.

11. Emphasis in field notes.

12. The field work with organizational dissenters or whistleblowers began in the summer of 1982 and is still continuing. To date, I have completed nine case studies, interviewing thirteen dissenters in the process. I have also done a number of other case studies, which have proved to be too ambiguous to help much in understanding the nature and motivation of organizational dissent. I am indebted to the Wenner-Gren Foundation for Anthropological Research for its financial support of this phase of my research. The Educational Fund for Individual Rights in New York City and the Governmental Accountability Project in Washington, D.C., have given me considerable help in this project.

13. Mannheim, 1936: 118.

14. I wish to thank Joseph Bensman, Arthur Vidich, Stanford Lyman, Michael

Hughey, and Janice Hirota for reading a draft of this paper and for making many helpful comments on it.

CHAPTER 8

1. *See*, for example, Powers, 1987; Donner, 1980; Theoharis, 1978, 1982, and 1988; Ungar, 1975; Sullivan and Brown, 1979; Watters and Gillers, 1973; Halperin, 1976; and Garrow, 1981. This essay is based on O'Reilly, 1983a; *see* O'Reilly, 1988.

2. The events leading to Attorney General Bonaparte's decision are summarized in U.S., Congress, Senate, Select Committee to Study Governmental Operations with Respect to Intelligence Activities, *Final Report—Book VI, Supplementary Reports on Intelligence Activities*, 94th Cong., 2nd sess., 1976, pp. 73–74.

3. A notable exception was the Mann (or White Slave Traffic) Act of 1910. Based on the Constitution's interstate commerce clause, the Mann Act made it a federal crime to transport a woman across a state line for immoral purposes.

4. The postwar Red scare included a brief black scare during the summer of 1919.

5. *See* Letter, William J. Neale to all Special Agents in Charge, October 2, 1920, FBI Special Agent in Charge Letter File.

6. For Frankfurter, *see* Williams, 1981: 572–74. For the GID, *see* Lowenthal, 1950: 89–92; and Senate Select Committee, *Final Report—Book VI*, pp. 98–101. Burns is quoted in Goldstein, 1978: 175.

7. In Goldstein, 1978: 176.

8. Memo, J. Edgar Hoover to Attorney General, November 5, 1924, FBI Special Agent in Charge Letter File. *See also* letter, Hoover to all Special Agents in Charge, November 5, 1924, FBI Special Agent in Charge Letter File.

9. For an early example, *see* letter, Edward J. Brennan to Franklin L. Dodge, Jr., November 22, 1920, Investigations, Dept. of Justice (1), Thomas J. Walsh Papers, Library of Congress; *see also* O'Reilly, 1983c.

10. O'Reilly, 1982.

11. Memo, Stephen Early to Lowell Mellett, July 30, 1940, Official File 880, Franklin D. Roosevelt Papers; and memo, Early to the President, July 12, 1940, President's Personal File, Franklin D. Roosevelt Presidential Library, Hyde Park, New York. The New Deal crime reforms included the Fugitive Felon Act (prohibiting suspected felons from fleeing across state lines to avoid prosecution); an amendment to the Lindbergh Law (allowing the FBI to enter kidnapping cases automatically after seven days); the Stolen Property Act (prohibiting the interstate transportation of stolen property valued at $5,000 or more); the Anti-Racketeering Act (criminalizing the extortion of money or other valuables by telephone or through the mails); an amendment to the federal bank robbery statute (expanding FBI jurisdiction to any bank insured by the Federal Deposit Insurance Corporation); and the National Firearms Act (authorizing the collection of a federal tax on machine guns, silencers, sawed-off shotguns and rifles, and the licensing of arms dealers and the registration of weapons). Bureau agents also gained full arrest power and the authority to carry any kind of firearm.

12. Internal FBI documents regarding this burglary, and copies of Mrs. Roose-

velt's correspondence, are in the American Youth Congress folder, Nichols Official and Confidential FBI Files.

13. Letter, J. E. Hoover to Herbert Hoover, September 8, 1955, Post-Presidential Papers—Individual, Herbert Hoover Papers, Herbert Hoover Presidential Library, West Branch, Iowa; also memo, *re* Fund for the Republic, September 6, 1955.

14. U.S., Congress, Senate, Select Committee to Study Governmental Operations with Respect to Intelligence Activities, *Final Report—Book II, Intelligence Activities and the Rights of Americans*, 94th Cong., 2d sess., 1976, p. 66; and *Final Report—Book III, Supplementary Detailed Staff Reports on Intelligence Activities and the Rights of Americans*, 94th Cong., 2d sess., 1976, p. 430.

15. Memos, James F. Bland to Alan H. Belmont, May 6, 1959, no. 61–7582–4143, and June 2, 1959, no. 61–7582–4172, FBI House Committee on Un-American Activities (HUAC) File.

16. Hoover is quoted in Whitehead, 1963: 353–54.

17. *See* Cabell Phillips, "One-Man Task Force of the G.O.P.," New York *Times* (Magazine), October 24, 1954; and Brown, 1961: 72–73.

18. For an excellent discussion of the executive privilege issue, see R. Berger, 1974.

19. *See* Hoover in Whitehead, 1963: 353.

20. Memo, FBI Executives' Conference to FBI Director, October 14, 1953, no. 61–7582-not recorded, FBI HUAC File.

21. For Hoover's order, *see* the handwritten notation on memo, Louis B. Nichols to Tolson, May 13, 1947, no. 61–7582–1464, FBI HUAC File. *See also* O'Reilly, 1983b.

22. For Stevenson on the FBI, *see* W. Johnson, 1974: 126, 135, 138; Cochran, 1969: 257–58.

23. Memo, FBI Executives' Conference to FBI Director, October 14, 1953, no. 61–7582-not recorded, FBI HUAC File.

24. Referred to in correlation summary memo, March 22, 1956, no. 2, in Adlai E. Stevenson folder, J. Edgar Hoover Official and Confidential FBI File.

25. Memo, Nichols to Tolson, January 17, 1955, no. 62–77485-not recorded, Hubert H. Humphrey FBI File.

26. The Security Index File has been declassified and can be consulted in the reading room at the J. Edgar Hoover FBI Building, Washington, D.C.

27. Theoharis, 1978: 256–57 (n.15).

28. Memo, Bland to William C. Sullivan, June 6, 1961, no. 100–358086–2924, FBI Security Index File.

29. Memo, FBI Director to Special Agent in Charge (SAC) Boston, January 23, 1958, no. 61–7582–3636, FBI HUAC File; and memo, SAC Boston to FBI Director, March 5, 1958, no. 61–7582–3710, FBI HUAC File.

30. *See* Donner, 1980: 177–240; and Senate Select Committee, *Final Report—Book III*, pp. 185–224.

CHAPTER 9

1. Meyer, 1957: 205–207; *see also* Fischer, 1964: 258. Herf (1984: 225) specifically contrasts the association between Lenin and Taylorism with Nazi "philosophical irrationalism"; *see also* Bailes, 1978.

2. Lenin, 1969: 42–44.

3. Ulam, 1965: 528–35.

4. In Hoffmann and Laird, 1984: 220–21.

5. *See* Hoffman, 1984: 6–8.

6. For a detailed account of this history, *see* W. Jones, 1976: esp. chapter 1.

7. *See* W. Jones, 1976: chapter 7.

8. W. Jones, 1976: 22–36.

9. *See* "In the CPSU Central Committee and the USSR Council of Ministers," *Pravda* and *Izvestiia*, November 29, 1968, trans. in *CDSP* 20/48, p. 3; *Spravochnik partiinogo rabotnika*, no. 8 (1968), pp. 445–46; B. A. Viktorov, "Chovye pravo poriadka," *Krasnaia zvezda*, November 8, 1970; N. A. Shchelokov, "Today is Soviet Militia Day: On Guard over Order," *Pravda*, November 10, 1970; trans. in *CDSP* 22/45, p. 14.

10. "In the CPSU Central Committee and the USSR Council of Ministers."

11. Iu. Stvolinskii, "Postovye," *Leningradskaia pravda*, November 11, 1972. N. K. Nikitin, "Vsegda na postu," *Trud*, November 8, 1973. GAI and BKhSS stand for the State Automobile Inspectorate and Combating the Theft of Socialist Property and Speculation, respectively.

12. N. A. Shchelokov (interview), "Sluzhit narodu," *Sovetskaia Rossiia*, November 8, 1974.

13. N. K. Nikitin, "On Guard over Order," *Izvestiia*, November 10, 1971; trans. in *CDSP* 23/45, pp. 21–22. Similar sentiments were voiced by a Moldavian SSR Minister of Internal Affairs, N. Bradulov, in a Militia Day article appearing in *Sovetskaia Moldaviia*, November 10, 1971. In the Kirgiz SSR the Ministry of Culture issued in 1971 a statute on "Cultural Tutelege of Organs of the MVD." *See* V. Smorygo, "Na strazhe poriadka," *Sovetskaia Kirgiziia*, November 10, 1972.

14. I. Glebov, "Vsegda nacheku," *Sovetskaia Rossiia*, November 8, 1973. *See also* "Today is Soviet Militia Day: On Guard over Order."

15. In Weber, 1958a: 49.

16. In Mesa-Lago and Beck, 1975: 222.

17. Moore, 1954: 188–89.

18. Brzezinski, 1962: 28–35.

19. Hough, 1969: 282–84.

20. Hough, 1969: 307–10.

21. Hough, 1969: 311–18.

22. In Mesa-Lago and Beck, 1975: 222.

23. Skolnick, 1966: 230–31.

24. Skolnick, 1966: 236.

25. Skolnick, 1966: 6–7.

26. Skolnick, 1966: chapters 5–8.

27. Skolnick, 1966: 240–42.

28. Skolnick, 1966: 239.

29. In C. Johnson, 1970: 161.

30. In C. Johnson, 1970: 165.

31. Hough, 1969: "The Brezhnev Era." Hough uses the phrase "Khrushchevism without Khrushchev" to summarize his point that the Brezhnev regime has pursued a number of Khrushchev's policies rather than abandoning or even reversing them

(*see* especially, p. 8). For a recent overall appraisal of the Khrushchev regime, *see* Breslauer, 1976.

32. Hough, 1976.

33. In Hoffman and Laird, 1984: 135–36.

34. In Hoffman and Laird, 1984: 331–58; *see also* Breslauer in Hoffman and Laird, 1984: 224–31.

CHAPTER 10

1. Nursing homes are not directly run by the government. However, that does not mean that they are any less public institutions. Whenever the government undertakes an obligation, for example, to provide education at public expense, to provide care for foster children at public expense, or to provide care for the elderly at public expense, it normally does so in one of two ways: either the public service is provided directly through public institutions like schools, or it is provided indirectly through public subsidies as in the case of nursing homes or child-care agencies. Such public subsidies may come in the form of medicaid payments or direct payments on a contractual basis from the government to the institution for each person served. Normally, there are government restrictions on how such payments may be used, and the "private" agency becomes an agent of the government. In the latter instances, the government discharges its obligation through such "private" agencies, but it is still a government-provided service.

2. Goffman, 1961: 16.

3. The following discussion relies heavily on the work of Professor Sylvia Law of New York University Law School; *see* Law and Neuborne, 1974.

4. *See* Hansen in Wortis, 1977.

5. Ironically, some labor unions joined their managerial adversaries in a kind of Hitler-Stalin pact against their clients. In many schools, for example, teachers' unions, which had so recently won their own fight to limit managerial discretion, often joined forces with principals and boards of education to resist similar demands by students. Teachers who had justly disrupted entire school systems by strikes in order to force contracts upon school officials that limited managerial powers and thereby secured teachers' rights, now linked arms with their former adversaries and accused students who sought the same rights of disrupting the school. Those who managed the schools and those who worked there thus came to find a common cause in oppressing those whom the schools were designed to serve.

6. Weber, 1978a: 267.

CHAPTER 11

1. Berle, 1952: 933.

2. *See* New York *Times*, December 24, 1974: Al.

3. *See* Silver, 1967; Hanan, 1971.

4. *See*, especially, *Work in America*, Report of a Task Force to the Secretary of Health, Education, and Welfare (1973).

5. Packard, 1964: 25, *see also* 49–59, 68–71.

6. E. Long, 1966: 208.

7. *Payne v. Western & A. R. R.*, 81 Tenn. 507 (1884).

CHAPTER 12

1. Smith, 1793: 96.
2. *See* Weber, 1958a: 77–128 [eds.].
3. "Social self-management" is the English translation of the Serbo-Croatian term used to cover the various forms of participatory authority at the lower levels. Thus the workers' councils are said to represent workers' self-management; at the municipal level (the commune) the term "self-government" is often used. *See*, for example, *Constitution of the Socialist Federal Republic of Yugoslavia*, Ch. II, Art. 6, and Ch. V, Art. 96.
4. Every person working in an enterprise is entitled to participate in the choice of the workers' council. In an enterprise with fewer than thirty people, the council consists of everyone in the enterprise except the director. In firms with more than seventy people, they must elect a council. In firms with between thirty and seventy persons, they opt for one solution or the other. The workers' council elects an executive body, the managing board, and together with an equal number of representatives of the municipality (commune), members of the workers' council choose the director, who is also *ex officio* a member of the managing board. The director has a four-year term, cannot be a member of the workers' council, and is typically a professional; thus the relationship between workers' councils and directors is not unlike that between city managers and councils in manager-council government in the United States. Members of the Board are elected for one year and cannot serve for more than two years in succession; three-quarters of the members must be production workers. Readers looking for information about Yugoslavia's experience with self-management may wish to consult Furubotn and Pejovich, 1970; Garson in Vanek, 1975; Horvat, 1976. The best critical account to come to my attention is by a Swiss sociologist, Albert Meister (1964), though it goes barely beyond 1960. Hugh A. Clegg (1963) and Adolf Sturmthal (1965) place workers' control in Yugoslavia in a comparative context of movements toward industrial democracy. The most perceptive treatment of citizenship and democracy I know is G. Wootton, 1966. A skeptical but not wholly unsympathetic treatment of industrial democracy from the perspective of a Swedish professor of business administration is found in Eric Rhenman, 1968.
5. *See* Patterson, 1982: 18–21 [eds.].
6. *See*, for example, Rhenman, 1968: 83–84.
7. Barber, 1970: 97.
8. Barber, 1970: 98.
9. The best evidence on this point of which I am aware comes from a study of attitudes of affluent workers in Britain, *see* Goldthorpe et al., 1968–69.

CHAPTER 13

1. Rowat, 1984a: 66.
2. Committee on the Concept of the Ombudsman, *Report* (Ottawa, 1977).
3. *See* Rowat, 1984b.

4. These figures are compiled from: International Bar Association Ombudsman Forum and International Ombudsman Institute, *Ombudsman and Other Complaint-Handling Systems Survey* 13 (Edmonton, 1983), chapters 5 and 10. For more complete information on the worldwide spread of the institution, *see* Rowat, 1985; Stacey, 1978; Caiden, 1983: especially vol. 2, the country studies.

5. Sutherland and Doern, 1985: 90.

6. Kersell, 1960: 149.

7. *See* n. 4.

8. Jack E. Richardson, "Having a Federal Ombudsman," a paper presented by the Australian Commonwealth Ombudsman to the Canadian Bar Association Conference, Halifax, Nova Scotia, 1985, p. 3; *see also* Commonwealth Ombudsman and Defence Force Ombudsman, *Annual Reports, 1984–85*.

CHAPTER 14

1. Boyce, 1985: 67.
2. Ouchi, 1982: 223.
3. Blair et al., 1982: 9.
4. Boyce, 1985: 70.
5. Ingle, 1982: 13.
6. Ingle, 1982: 8.
7. Ingle, 1982: 8.
8. Ingle, 1982: 10.
9. Dewar, 1980: 8.
10. Blair et al., 1982: 10.
11. Ingle, 1982: 43.
12. Ingle, 1982: 44.
13. Ingle, 1982: 49.
14. Ingle, 1982: 52–54.
15. Ingle, 1982: 47.
16. Dewar, 1980: 183.
17. Ingle, 1982: 89.
18. Ouchi, 1982: 229.
19. Ouchi, 1982: 4.
20. Ouchi, 1982: 68.
21. Ouchi, 1982: 70.
22. Ouchi, 1982: 223.
23. Macleod, 1985: 31.
24. Blair and Whitehead, 1984: 22.
25. Klein, 1984: 89–92.
26. *See* Collard and Dale, 1985: 28.
27. Collard and Dale, 1985: 28.
28. Klein, 1984: 89.
29. Klein, 1984: 88.
30. Lawler and Mohrman, 1985: 66.
31. Blair and Whitehead, 1984: 18.
32. Klein, 1984: 91.

33. Zahra, 1984: 28.
34. Harmon, 1984: 30.
35. Weber, 1958a: 196–97.
36. Ingle, 1982: 27.
37. Lawler and Mohrman, 1985: 68.
38. Collard and Dale, 1985: 28.
39. O'Donnell and O'Donnell, 1984: 51.
40. Dewar, 1980: 91.

EPILOGUE

1. Perrow, 1979. Perrow understands the proper use of ideal types and raises this point to clarify the problem.

2. Weber, 1978a: 975.

3. Wrong, 196.

4. P. Berger and Luckmann, 1967: 48–49.

5. V. Turner, 1985: 186.

6. B. Turner, 1986: 25.

7. Weber, 1978a: 1405, 1451; *see* Herf, 1984. Griffin's (1981) attempt to associate modern sexually explicit media with Nazism is groundless in the light of history. The Nazi regime may well be termed "pornographic," but it was clearly "anti-porn," as the phrase is generally used.

8. Weber, 1978a: 1419.

9. Presidential Commission on the Space Shuttle Challenger Accident, *Report*, June 9, 1986 (Washington, D.C.).

10. Storer Rowley and Michael Tackett, "NASA waived own guideline, panel told." Chicago *Tribune*, February 28, 1986:1/13.

11. Jackall, 1983: 130.

12. Ouchi, 1982: 44.

13. Ouchi, 1982: 70. Clans also contrast with *markets*.

14. Fisk and Barron, 1983: 82.

15. Kimball and McClellan, 1962: 156.

16. "Iron cage" is Parsons's rather poetic translation of Weber's *ein stahlhartes Gehäuse* (1958b: 181). Although it is captivating, this rendering is hardly accurate and may well convey the wrong sense: a prison cell of solitude. The phrase is probably better rendered "steel housing" or "machine casing," and the allusion is to something like the housing of an electric motor or an automobile transmission in which there is constant activity but no escape. *See* Kent, 1983. I have also come to agree with Kent (contrary to my earlier position, e. g., Swatos, 1986: 217 [n. 41]—based on Giddens) that the famous "specialists without spirit" that follows in Weber's essay is a Weberian construction, not a direct quote from anyone. This is also supported by Sica, 1985: 73–74.

17. Etzioni, 1975: 3–67.

18. In doing this, of course, there is a change in the methodological structure of the argument. Since the function of typological analysis is to permit comparisons of empirical cases to each other, the types cannot be developmental. I am simply using

these terms in this way to illustrate what might happen should the scenario described here be true.

19. Genovese, 1969: 242.
20. V. Turner, 1985: 150.

Bibliography

Note: Primary documents, newspaper articles, agency reports, and so forth are cited in full in the Notes.

Abramowski, Günter. 1982. "Meaningful life in a disenchanted world: Rational science and ethical responsibility—an interpretation of Max Weber." *Journal of Religious Ethics* 10: 121–34.

Antonio, Robert J. 1979. "The contradiction of domination and production in bureaucracy: The contribution of organizational efficiency to the decline of the Roman empire." *American Sociological Review* 44: 895–912.

Arendt, Hannah. 1959. *The Human Condition.* Garden City, NY: Doubleday.

Bailes, Kendall. 1978. *Technology and Society under Lenin and Stalin.* Princeton, NJ: Princeton University Press.

Barber, Bernard. 1970. *The American Corporation.* New York: Dutton.

Beetham, David. 1974. *Max Weber and the Theory of Modern Politics.* London: Allen & Unwin.

Bendix, Reinhard. 1960. *Max Weber: An Intellectual Portrait.* Garden City, NY: Doubleday.

Bensman, Joseph. 1967. *Dollars and Sense.* New York: Macmillan.

Berenato, Mark A. 1984. "Keeping your patients' medical records." *Legal Aspects of Medical Practice* 12(March): 5–7.

Berger, Peter L., and Thomas Luckmann. 1967. *The Social Construction of Reality.* Garden City, NY: Doubleday.

Berger, Raoul. 1974. *Executive Privilege.* Cambridge, MA: Harvard University Press.

Berle, Adolf A. 1952. "Constitutional limitations on corporate activity—Protection of personal rights from invasion through economic power." *University of Pennsylvania Law Review* 100: 933–55.

———. 1967. *The Eighteenth Brumaire of Louis Bonaparte.* New York: Interna Property. New York: Harcourt Brace Jovanovich.

Blair, John D., Stanley L. Cohen, and Jerome Hurwitz. 1982. "Quality circles:

Practical considerations for public managers." *Public Productivity Review* 6 (May/June): 9–18.

Blair, John D., and Carlton J. Whitehead. 1984. "Can quality circles survive in the United States?" *Business Horizons* 27 (September/October): 17–23.

Boyce, Michael T. 1985. "Can quality circles be applied in the public sector?" *Journal of Collective Negotiations* 14: 65–75.

Brannigan, Vincent M., and Ruth E. Dayhoff. 1986. "Medical Informatics: The Revolution in Law, Technology, and Medicine." *Journal of Legal Medicine* 7 (1): 8–12.

Breslauer, George W. 1976. "Khrushchev reconsidered." *Problems of Communism* 25 (September/October): 18–33.

Brown, Stuart Gerry. 1961. *Conscience in Politics: Adlai E. Stevenson in the 1950s.* Syracuse, NY: Syracuse University Press.

Brzezinski, Zbigniew K. 1962. *Ideology and Power in Soviet Politics.* New York: Praeger.

Caiden, Gerald E. (ed.). 1983. *The Ombudsman: An International Handbook.* Westport, CT: Greenwood.

Christian, Portia, with Richard Hicks. 1970. *Ethics in Business Conduct: Selected References from the Record—Problems, Attempted Solutions, Ethics in Business Education.* Detroit: Gale Research.

Clark, David L. 1985. "Emerging paradigms in organizational theory and research." Pp. 43–78 in Yvonna S. Lincoln (ed.), *Organizational Theory and Inquiry.* Beverly Hills, CA: Sage.

Clegg, Hugh A. 1963. *A New Approach to Industrial Democracy.* Oxford: Blackwell.

Cochran, Bert. 1969. *Adlai Stevenson: Patrician among Politicians.* New York: Funk and Wagnalls.

Collard, Ron, and Barrie Dale. 1985. "Quality circles: Why they break down and why they hold up." *Personnel Management* 17 (February): 28–31.

Daft, Richard L. 1986. *Organization Theory and Design.* St. Paul, MN: West.

Dewar, Donald. 1980. *The Quality Circle Guide to Participation Management.* Englewood Cliffs, NJ: Prentice-Hall.

Donner, Frank J. 1980. *The Age of Surveillance.* New York: Knopf.

Durkheim, Emile. 1964. *The Division of Labor in Society.* New York: Free Press.

Ellison, Julius, and Rhonda Beldner. 1984. "Hospital records: What do they tell attorneys?" *Trial* 20(October): 50–51.

Engels, Friedrich. 1967. *The Origin of the Family, Private Property, and the State.* New York: International Publishers.

————. 1969. *Socialism.* New York: International Publishers.

Etzioni, Amitai. 1975. *Comparative Analysis of Complex Organizations.* New York: Free Press.

Ferguson, W. S. 1918. "The Zulus and the Spartans." *Harvard African Studies* 2: 197–234.

Fischer, Louis. 1964. *The Life of Lenin.* New York: Harper & Row.

Fisk, Jim, and Robert Barron. 1983. *The Official MBA Handbook.* New York: Simon and Schuster.

Frankfort, Henri. 1978. *Kingship and the Gods.* Chicago: Chicago University Press.

Freidson, Eliot. 1970. *Profession of Medicine.* New York: Dodd, Mead.

————. 1975. *Doctoring Together*. New York: Elsevier.

Friedman, Kathi V. 1981. *Legitimation of Social Rights and the Western Welfare State*. Chapel Hill: University of North Carolina Press.

————. 1987. *Beyond the Welfare State*. Chapel Hill: University of North Carolina Press.

Fritz, Kurt von. 1954. *The Theory of the Mixed Constitution in Antiquity*. New York: Columbia University Press.

Furubotn, Eiric G., and Svetozar Pejovich. 1970. "Property rights and the behavior of the firm in the socialist state." *Zeitschrift für Nationalökonomie* 30: 431–54.

Garrow, David J. 1981. *The FBI and Martin Luther King, Jr.* New York: Norton.

Genovese, Eugene D. 1969. *The World the Slaveholders Made*. New York: Random House.

Glassman, Ronald M. 1978. "Rational and irrational legitimacy." Pp. 49–73 in Arthur J. Vidich and Ronald M. Glassman (eds.), *Conflict and Control*. Beverly Hills, CA: Sage.

————. 1986. "Manufactured charisma and legitimacy." pp. 115–28 in Ronald M. Glassman and William H. Swatos, Jr. (eds.), *Charisma, History, and Social Structure*. Westport, CT: Greenwood.

Goffman, Erving. 1961. *Asylums*. Garden City, NY: Doubleday.

Goldstein, Robert J. 1978. *Political Repression in Modern America*. New York: Two Continents/Schenkman.

Goldthorpe, John H., David Lockwood, Frank Bechofer, and Jennifer Platt (eds.). 1968–69. *The Affluent Worker*. 3 vols. Cambridge: Cambridge University Press.

Golodetz, Arnold, J. Ruess, and R. L. Milhous. 1976. "The right to know: Giving the patient his medical record." *Archives of Physical Medicine and Rehabilitation* 57: 78–81.

Griffin, Susan. 1981. *Pornography and Silence*. New York: Harper & Row.

Halperin, Morton H., Jerry J. Berman, Robert L. Borosage, and Christine M. Marwick. 1976. *The Lawless State*. Harmondsworth, England: Penguin.

Hanan, Mack. 1971. "Make way for the new organization man." *Harvard Business Review* 49 (July/August): 128–38.

Harmon, James F. 1984. "The supervisor and quality circles." *Supervisory Management* 29 (February): 26–31.

Hegel, G.F.W. 1967. *The Philosophy of Right*. London: Oxford University Press.

Herf, Jeffrey. 1984. *Reactionary Modernism*. Cambridge: Cambridge University Press.

Hoffman, Erik P. 1984. *The Soviet Union in the 1980s*. New York: Academy of Political Science (Proceedings).

————, and Robbin F. Laird (eds.). 1984. *The Soviet Polity in the Modern Era*. New York: Aldine.

Horvat, Branko. 1976. *The Yugoslav Economic System*. White Plains, NY: Sharpe.

Hough, Jerry F. 1969. *The Soviet Prefects*. Cambridge, MA: Harvard University Press.

————. 1976. "Political participation in the Soviet Union." *Soviet Studies* 28: 14–19.

Hufnagel, Gerhard. 1971. *Kritik als Beruf: De Kritische Gehalt im Werk Max Webers*. Frankfort: Propyläen.

Hummel, Ralph P. 1982. *The Bureaucratic Experience*. New York: St. Martin's.

Ingle, Sud. 1982. *Quality Circles Master Guide*. Englewood Cliffs, NJ: Prentice Hall.

Jackall, Robert, 1983. "Moral mazes: Bureaucracy and managerial work." *Harvard Business Review* 61 (September/ October): 118–30.

Johnson, Chalmers (ed.). 1970. *Change in Communist Systems*. Stanford, CA: Stanford University Press.

Johnson, Walter (ed.). 1974. *"Let's Talk Sense to the American People"* (vol. 4 of *The Papers of Adlai E. Stevenson*). Boston: Little, Brown.

Jones, Donald G. 1977. *A Bibliography of Business Ethics, 1971–1975*. Charlottesville: University of Virginia Press.

————, and Helen Troy (eds.). 1982. *A Bibliography of Business Ethics, 1976–1980*. Charlottesville: University of Virginia Press.

Jones, William M. 1976. *Maintaining Public Order in the Soviet Union*. Unpublished Ph.D. dissertation, Duke University.

Kent, Stephen A. 1983. "Weber, Goethe, and the Nietzschean allusion." *Sociological Analysis* 44: 297–320.

Kersell, John E. 1960. *Parliamentary Supervision of Delegated Legislation*. London: Routledge & Kegan Paul.

Kimball, Solon T., and James E. McClellan, Jr. 1962. *Education and the New America*. New York: Random House.

Klein, Janice. 1984. "Why supervisors resist employee involvement." *Harvard Business Review* 62 (September/October): 87–92.

Klugman, Ellen. 1983. "Towards a uniform right to medical records." *UCLA Law Review* 30: 1349–77.

Knoppers, Bartha Maria. 1982. "Confidentiality and accessibility of medical information." *Revue de Droit Université de Sherbrooke* 12: 395–431.

Law, Sylvia, and Burt Neuborne. 1974. *The Rights of the Poor*. New York: Avon.

Lawler, Edward E., III, and Susan A. Mohrman. 1985. "Quality circles after the fad." *Harvard Business Review* 63 (January/February): 65–70.

Lederer, Emil. 1918–19. "On the socio-psychic constitution of the present time." *Archiv für Sozialwissenschaft und Sozialpolitik* 56: 114–39.

Lenin, V. I. 1969. *State and Revolution*. New York: International Publishers.

Long, Edward V. 1966. *The Intruders*. New York: Praeger.

Long, Norton E. 1952. "Bureaucracy and constitutionalism." *American Political Science Review* 46: 808–18.

Lowenthal, Max. 1950. *The Federal Bureau of Investigation*. New York: Sloane.

Löwith, Karl. 1982. *Max Weber and Karl Marx*. London: Allen & Unwin.

Macleod, Jennifer. 1985. "Changing power relationships within corporations." *Employment Relations Today* 12: 31–35.

Mannheim, Karl. 1936. *Ideology and Utopia*. New York: Harcourt, Brace and World.

————. 1940. *Man and Society in an Age of Reconstruction*. London: Kegan Paul, Trench, Trubner.

Marx, Karl. 1951. *Das Kapital*. Berlin: Dietz.

————. 1953. *Grundrisse der Kritik der politischen ökonomie*. Berlin: Dietz.

————. 1962. *Werke-Schriften-Briefe*. Darmstadt: Wissenschaftliche Buchgesellschaft.

_____. 1967. *The Eighteenth Brumaire of Louis Bonaparte*. New York: International Publishers.

_____. 1973. *Grundrisse*. New York: Random House.

_____, and Friedrich Engels. 1960. *Ausgewählte Schriften*. Berlin: Dietz.

_____. 1964. *Werke*. Berlin: Dietz.

_____. 1968. *Selected Works*. Moscow: Progress Publishers.

_____. 1975. *Collected Works*. New York: International Publishers.

Meister, Albert. 1964. *Socialisme et Autogestion, L'Experience Jougoslave*. Paris: Editions du Seuil.

Mesa-Lago, Carmelo, and Carl Beck (eds.). 1975. *Comparative Socialist Systems*. Pittsburgh: University Center for International Studies.

Meyer, Alfred G. 1957. *Leninism*. New York: Praeger.

Miller, Robert D. 1983. *Problems in Hospital Law*. Rockville, NY: Aspen.

Mills, C. Wright. 1956. *The Power Elite*. New York: Oxford University Press.

Mommsen, Wolfgang J. 1974a. *The Age of Bureaucracy*. Oxford: Blackwell.

_____. 1974b. *Max Weber und die Deutsche Politik*. Tübingen: Mohr.

_____. 1974c. *Max Weber*. Frankfort: Suhrkamp.

_____. 1984. *Max Weber and German Politics 1890–1920*. Chicago: University of Chicago Press.

Moore, Barrington, Jr. 1954. *Terror and Progress USSR*. New York: Harper & Row.

Mueller, Gert H. 1982. "Socialism and capitalism in the work of Max Weber." *British Journal of Sociology* 33: 151–71.

Mumford, Lewis. 1966. *The Myth of the Machine*. New York: Harcourt, Brace and World.

Murvar, Vatro. 1983. *Max Weber Today—An Introduction to a Living Legacy*. Brookfield: Max Weber Colloquia and Symposia at the University of Wisconsin-Milwaukee.

Myrdal, Gunnar. 1963. *Challenge to Affluence*. New York: Pantheon.

Nelson, Benjamin 1973. "Casuistry." *Encyclopedia Britannica* 5: 51–52.

O'Donnell, Merle, and Robert T. O'Donnell. 1984. "Quality circles—the latest fad or a real winner?" *Business Horizons* 27 (May/June): 48–52.

O'Reilly, Kenneth. 1982. "A new deal for the FBI." *Journal of American History* 69: 638–58.

_____. 1983a. *Hoover and the Un-Americans: The FBI, HUAC, and the Red Menace*. Philadelphia: Temple University Press.

_____. 1983b. "The FBI and the origins of McCarthyism." *Historian* 45: 372–93.

_____. 1983c. "Herbert Hoover and the FBI." *Annals of Iowa* 47: 46–63.

_____. (forthcoming) *Racial Matters: The FBI and the Struggle for Black Equality*.

Ouchi, William G. 1982. *Theory Z*. New York: Avon.

Packard, Vance. 1964. *The Naked Society*. New York: McKay.

Patterson, Orlando. 1982. *Slavery and Social Death*. Cambridge, MA: Harvard University Press.

Perrow, Charles. 1979. *Complex Organizations*. New York: Random House.

Picard, Ellen I. 1984. *Legal Liability of Doctors and Hospitals in Canada*. Toronto: Carswell.

Polanyi, Karl, Conrad M. Arensburg, and Harry W. Pearson (eds.). 1957. *Trade and Market in Early Empires*. Glencoe, IL: Free Press.

Popper, Karl. 1950. *The Open Society and Its Enemies*. Princeton, NJ: Princeton University Press.

Powers, Richard Gid. 1987. *Secrecy and Power: The Life of J. Edgar Hoover*. New York: Free Press.

Reiff, Philip. 1961. *Freud*. Garden City, NY: Doubleday.

Rhenman, Eric. 1968. *Industrial Democracy and Industrial Management*. London: Tavistock.

Röhrich, Wilfried. 1972. *Robert Michels, vom Soziologisch—Sydikalistischen zum Faschistischen Credo*. Berlin: Duncker & Humblot.

Rosen, George. 1963. "The hospital: Historical sociology of a community institution." Pp. 1–36 in Eliot Friedson (ed.), *The Hospital in Modern Society*. Glencoe, IL: Free Press.

Rowat, Donald C. 1984a. "The ombudsman in France." *Canadian Public Administration* 27: 66–86.

———. 1984b. "The state ombudsmen in India." *Indian Journal of Public Administration* 30: 1–32.

———. 1985. *The Ombudsman Plan*. Lanham, MD: University Press of America.

Rozovsky, Lorne E. 1974. *Canadian Hospital Law*. Toronto: Canadian Hospital Association.

———, and Fay A. Rozovsky. 1984. *The Canadian Law of Patient Records*. Toronto: Butterworths.

Scrivens, Ellie. 1985. "The protection of personal data in the NHS." *Political Quarterly* 56: 290–94.

Shea, Steven, and David Margulies. 1985. "The paperless medical record." *Social Science and Medicine* 21: 741–46.

Shils, Edward A. 1973. "The power of the state and the dignity of the academic calling in imperial Germany." *Minerva* 11: 18–23.

Sica, Alan. 1985. "Reasonable science, unreasonable life: The happy fictions of Marx, Weber, and social theory." Pp. 68–88 in Robert J. Antonio and Ronald M. Glassman (eds.), *A Weber-Marx Dialogue*. Lawrence: University Press of Kansas.

Silver, Isidore. 1967. "The corporate ombudsman." *Harvard Business Review* 45 (May/June): 77–87.

Skolnick, Jerome. 1966. *Justice without Trial*. New York: Wiley.

Smith, Adam. 1793. *An Inquiry into the Nature and Causes of the Wealth of Nations*. London: Strahan and Cadell.

Stacey, Frank. 1978. *Ombudsmen Compared*. Oxford: Clarendon.

Stein, Eugene J., R. L. Furedy, M. J. Simonton, and C. H. Neuffer. 1979. "Patient access to medical records on a psychiatric inpatient unit." *American Journal of Psychiatry* 136: 327–29.

Steiner, Penelope. 1978. "Patient access to the medical record." *Medical Record News* 49: 77–78, 80–81.

Sturmthal, Adolf. 1965. *Workers' Councils*. Cambridge, MA: Harvard University Press.

Sullivan, William C., and Bill Brown. 1979. *The Bureau: My Thirty Years in Hoover's FBI*. New York: Norton.

Sutherland, Sharon L., and G. Bruce Doern. 1985. *Bureaucracy in Canada*. Toronto: University of Toronto Press.

Swatos, William H., Jr. 1986. "The disenchantment of charisma." Pp. 129–46 in Ronald M. Glassman and William H. Swatos, Jr. (eds.), *Charisma, History, and Social Structure*. New York: Greenwood.

Taylor, Frederick W. 1947. *Scientific Management*. Westport, CT: Greenwood.

Theoharis, Athan. 1978. *Spying on Americans*. Philadelphia: Temple University Press.

———— (ed.). 1982. *Beyond the Hiss Case*. Philadelphia: Temple University Press.

————. 1988. *J. Edgar Hoover: A Biography*.

Tucker, Robert C. 1978. *The Marx-Engels Reader*. New York: Norton.

Turner, Bryan S. 1986. *Equality*. Chichester, England: Ellis Horwood.

Turner, Victor. 1985. *On the Edge of the Bush*. Tucson: University of Arizona Press.

Ulam, Adam. 1965. *The Bolsheviks*. Toronto: Collier.

Ungar, Sanford J. 1975. *FBI*. Boston: Little, Brown.

Vanek, Jaroslav. 1975. *Self Management*. Baltimore: Penguin.

Ward, Barbara, and René Dubos. 1966. *Only One Earth*. New York: Norton.

Watters, Pat, and Stephen Gillers (eds.). 1973. *Investigating the FBI*. Garden City, NY: Doubleday.

Weber, Max. 1924a. *Gesammelte Aufsätze zur Sozial- und Wirtschaftsgeschichte*. Tübingen: Mohr.

————. 1924b. *Soziologie und Sozialpolitik*. Tübingen: Mohr.

————. 1947. *Theory of Social and Economic Organization*. New York: Oxford University Press.

————. 1951. *The Religion of China*. New York: Free Press.

————. 1958a. *From Max Weber*. New York: Oxford University Press.

————. 1958b. *The Protestant Ethic and the Spirit of Capitalism*. New York: Scribners.

————. 1971. *The Interpretation of Social Reality*. New York: Scribners.

————. 1976. *The Agrarian Sociology of Ancient Civilizations*. London: NLB.

————. 1978a. *Economy and Society*. Berkeley: University of California Press.

————. 1978b. *Weber: Selections in Translation*. Cambridge: Cambridge University Press.

Wenley, R. M. 1910. "Casuistry." *Encyclopedia of Religion and Ethics* 3. Edinburgh: Clark.

Westin, Alan F. 1976. *Computers, Health Records, and Citizen Rights*. Washington D.C.: Department of Commerce.

————. 1977. "Medical records: Should patients have access?" *Hastings Center Report* 7(December): 23–28.

Whitehead, Don. 1963. *The FBI Story*. New York: Pocket Books.

Whyatt, John. 1961. *The Citizen and the Administration*. London: Stevens.

Williams, David. 1981. "The Bureau of Investigation and its critics." *Journal of American History* 68: 560–79.

Wittfogel, Karl A. 1981. *Oriental Despotism*. New York: Random House.

Wootton, Barbara. 1945. *Freedom under Planning*. Chapel Hill: University of North Carolina Press.

Wootton, Graham. 1966. *Workers, Unions and the State*. London: Routledge & Kegan Paul.

Wortis, Joseph (ed.). 1977. *Mental Retardation and Developmental Disabilities*. New York: Brunner/Mazel.

Wrong, Dennis H. 1961. "The oversocialized conception of man." *American Socio-logical Review* 26: 183–93.
Zahra, Shaker A. 1984. "What supervisors think about QCs." *Supervisory Management* 29 (August): 27–33.

Index

About the Editors and Contributors

LISA K. ARMOUR is a graduate of the College of St. Francis in Joliet, Illinois, and is currently completing a graduate degree in the program in Public Administration of the Department of Political Science at Northern Illinois University.

ROBERT A. DAHL is Sterling Professor of Political Science Emeritus at Yale University. His most recent publications include *A Preface to Economic Democracy* and *Dilemmas of Pluralist Democracy*.

KATHI VALLONE FRIEDMAN is a political sociologist specializing in the connection between the individual and society, as that connection is formed by social values and the laws that enforce them. She has authored a series of items on the welfare state, taught Sociology at Tulane University, served as a consultant to various firms, and worked for several years on Capitol Hill. She currently lives in Washington, D.C. where she is writing *Beyond the Welfare State: Institution-Building for the Twenty-first Century*. Friedman did her graduate work at the University of North Carolina, Chapel Hill.

IRA GLASSER is executive director of the American Civil Liberties Union. His latest book, *Doing Good*, was a landmark volume on the limits of benevolence in the modern world. He appears frequently on television and writes for newspapers and magazines on civil liberties issues.

RONALD M. GLASSMAN is Associate Professor of Sociology at William Paterson College of the State University of New Jersey. He is also convener of the North American Max Weber Colloquium and has served as chairman of the Section on Comparative Historical Sociology of the American Sociological Association. His books include *The Political History of Latin America, Democracy and Despotism in Primitive Society,* and the essay collections *Charisma, History, and Social Structure* (with William H. Swatos, Jr.; Greenwood Press, 1986), *A Weber-Marx Dialogue* (with Robert J. Antonio), *Max Weber's Political Sociology* (with Vatro Murvar; Greenwood Press, 1984), and *Conflict and Control* (with Arthur Vidich). He is currently working on a new monograph, *The New Middle Class and Democracy.*

MARK GREEN has been a candidate for the United States Senate and Congress in New York state and runs the Democracy Project (a "think tank" and policy-oriented organization). His books include *Winning Back America* and *Who Runs Congress?*

ROBERT JACKALL is Associate Professor of Sociology and Chairman of the Department of Anthropology and Sociology at Williams College. In addition to many essays on work, workers, and bureaucracy, he is the author of *Workers in a Labyrinth: Jobs and Survival in a Bank Bureaucracy,* the co-editor (with Henry M. Levin) of *Worker Cooperatives in America,* and the author of *Moral Mazes: Bureaucracy and Managerial Work* (forthcoming).

WILLIAM M. JONES received his doctorate from Duke University and teaches political science at Virginia Wesleyan College, Norfolk.

ERNEST KILKER is a member of the social science faculty of the College of Basic Studies at Boston University. He is the author of several articles, including "Max Weber and the Possibilities for Democracy," in the anthology *Max Weber's Political Sociology* (Greenwood Press, 1984).

WOLFGANG J. MOMMSEN is the author of many books and articles on Max Weber, the most well known of which to English-speaking audiences are *The Age of Bureaucracy* and *Max Weber and German Politics.* Mommsen is also co-director of a project to reorganize, republish, and retranslate the entire corpus of Weber's work.

RALPH NADER is best known for his consumer advocacy against giant corporations. He is co-author of dozens of books and hundreds of articles and is in great demand as a public speaker. In addition to *Taming the Giant Corporation,* from which the selection in this volume is taken, his work includes *Whistle Blowing, The Lemon Book, Verdicts on Lawyers,* and the multivolume *Ralph Nader Congress Project.*

KENNETH O'REILLY is a historian on the history and philosophy faculty of the University of Alaska, Anchorage. He has written widely on the FBI in both scholarly and popular periodicals. His book, *Hoover and the Un-Americans: The FBI, HUAC, and the Red Menace*, was published in 1983, and he is soon to issue a sequel, *Racial Matters: The FBI and the Struggle for Black Equality*.

PAUL L. ROSEN teaches political science at Carleton University, Ottawa, Canada. He has lectured on sociology at New York University and was Visiting Professor of Political Science and Canadian Studies at the Hebrew University of Jerusalem. He has written on the dialectics and interplay of politics, social science, law and psychoanalysis, and is the author of *The Supreme Court and Social Science*.

DONALD C. ROWAT is a Professor of Political Science at Carleton University, Ottawa, Canada, and has gained a reputation as a leading expert on the ombudsman, laws on access to official documents, and local government. He is author of *The Ombudsman Plan: The Worldwide Spread of an Idea* and editor of *The Ombudsman: Citizen's Defender*. He is also author of *The Canadian Municipal System* and *Your Local Government*, and editor of *Basic Issues in Public Administration*, *The Government of Federal Capitals*, *Administrative Secrecy in Developed Countries*, *International Handbook on Local Government Reorganization* (Greenwood Press, 1980), and *Public Administration in the Western World* (forthcoming).

WOLFGANG SCHLUCHTER is one of the foremost contemporary interpreters of Max Weber. He has written dozens of books and articles on Weber's work including *Aspekte Burokratischer Herrschaft*, from which the chapter in this volume is taken, and *Wertfreiheit und Verantwortungsethik*. Two volumes of his essays translated into English have recently appeared: *The Rise of Western Rationalism* and, with Günter Roth, *Max Weber's Vision of History*.

JOEL SELIGMAN has written many essays and several books including *The High Citadel*.

WILLIAM H. SWATOS, JR., is a member of the faculty of the Department of Sociology at Northern Illinois University. His major areas of interest are the sociology of religion and classical sociological theory. He is a member of the Board of Directors of the Religious Research Association and serves as book review editor of *Sociological Analysis*, the journal of the Association for the Sociology of Religion. He is the author of numerous articles in scholarly journals and several monographs as well as a new essay collection, *Religious Sociology: Interfaces and Boundaries* (Greenwood Press, 1984).